1750

ART AND LOGIC IN HEGEL'S PHILOSOPHY

The Hegel Society of America wishes to thank the following for their financial support in the preparation of this volume for publication:

Errol Harris
    Northwestern University

Howard Kainz
    Marquette University

Hans-Martin Sass
    Bochum University
    Bochum, Germany

Larry Stepelevich
    Villanova University

ART AND LOGIC
IN
HEGEL'S PHILOSOPHY

edited by

WARREN E. STEINKRAUS
State University of New York at Oswego

and

KENNETH I. SCHMITZ
Trinity College, University of Toronto

NEW JERSEY: HUMANITIES PRESS
SUSSEX: HARVESTER PRESS

First published in 1980 in the United States of America by Humanities
Press Inc., and in England by Harvester Press Ltd.

These are the papers delivered at the 1974 meeting of The Hegel Society at
Georgetown University

Library of Congress Cataloging in Publication Data

Hegel Society of America.
   Art and logic in Hegel's philosophy.

   Bibliography: p.
   Includes index.
   1. Hegel, Georg Wilhelm Friedrich, 1770-1831—
Aesthetics—Congresses. 2. Hegel, Georg Wilhelm
Friedrich, 1770-1831—Logic—Congresses. I. Steinkraus,
Warren E. II. Schmitz, Kenneth L. III. O'Malley,
Joseph J. IV. Title.
B2949.A4H44 1978   193   77-25081
ISBN 0-391-00542-1

Harvester Press Ltd.
England ISBN 0 85527 317 8

CONTENTS

Preface

Each previous volume in this series has centered upon a single theme in Hegel's philosophy. All have been based upon papers presented at biennial meetings of the Hegel Society of America. The first conference was held at Wofford College and dealt with Hegel and the Philosophy of Religion. The second conference, at Boston University in 1970, treated of Hegel and the Philosophy of Science. The third at Notre Dame in 1972, focused on Hegel and the History of Philosophy. The fifth, held at Villanova University in 1976, centered upon Hegel's Social and Political Philosophy. This volume incorporates papers presented at the 1974 meeting of the Society, which was held at Georgetown University. The present volume makes available scholarly work on two of the most creative parts of Hegel's philosophy, his Aesthetics and his Logic.

The double theme does not suggest that the topics are minor in character or of insufficient scope to warrant a conference each for itself. Rather, quite the opposite is true. There is so much work being done on these topics today that it is difficult for scholars to keep in touch with the vigorous interest in them. For that reason a conference with a double theme was proposed in order to bring to light some of the work being done in each area. Indeed, Hegel may be said to be one of our contemporaries, as Raya Dunayevskaya remarks in her essay when she calls attention to the new editions, new translations and re-issues of Hegel's works as well as the frequent conferences and plethora of articles on Hegel that are occurring with such frequency.

Many persons are involved in a joint endeavor of this kind and the editors are grateful to the contributors for their cooperation and patience. At the time of the Georgetown conference, Sir Malcolm Knox was bringing to completion his magnificent translation of Hegel's *Lectures on Aesthetics*. He made the journey over from Scotland to present the keynote address at the conference. That address is the first essay in our volume. After his translation was published in 1975, the contributors to the Aesthetics section re-worked their papers to take into account new insights offered by Sir Malcolm's work. Most of them revised their papers to provide citations to this new authoritative translation. The editors are indeed appreciative.

Moreover, special gratitude is due to Professor Rüdiger Bubner of J. W. Goethe University in Frankfurt, Germany. Though unable to attend the Georgetown conference, he prepared an essay especially for this volume at the editors' request. Editor of the Reclam edition of *Hegel's Vorlesungen über die Ästhetik* (1971) and known for his scholarly work on Kant as well as others, Professor Bubner places Hegel's aesthetic theory in broad historical perspective in his very skillful and instructive essay.

Readers will recognize at once other contributors to the volume. Professor John Findlay's comment on the coherence of the dialectic is fresh and illuminating and makes a strong end-piece to the book. Newton P. Stallknecht and Robert Perkins provide substantial comments. Murray Greene, already known for his book *Hegel on the Soul* (1972) offers a careful essay on "Hegel's Concept of Logical Life" which was initially a symposium paper at the Georgetown conference. When presented, it elicited suggestive comments from Henry Harris, George Kline and Rolf Ahlers. Their essays are printed here following Professor Greene's. Ms. Raya Dunayevskaya, now at work on a book about Rosa Luxemburg, has had an abiding interest in Hegel and her vigorous lecture at the conference appears in this volume as the third essay in the Logic section. George Di-Giovanni, Merold Westphal, John Burbidge and Clark Butler are currently very active in Hegel studies and we include important papers by them in this volume. Newer work in the area of Hegel's aesthetic is represented here by the scholarly work of Gary Shapiro, Michael Mitias, and Curtis Carter. Michael MacDonald served as one of the commentators. Joseph Flay has graciously provided us with selected, relevant excerpts from his extensive bibliography of Hegel and we are grateful to him for his careful work.

The editors wish to thank Professor Louis Dupré, of Yale University, who was president of the Society during its Georgetown meetings. He participated creatively in the planning and realization of the 1974 conference. Thanks are due also to Wilfrid ver Eecke who diligently took care of the many details involved in local arrangements. And John Findlay merits our thanks for assisting the program chairmen.

This volume would not have been brought to fruition without the untiring efforts of Joseph O'Malley of Marquette University. He assisted in completing important practical arrangements with the publisher. We are glad to note that he has been appointed general co-ordinating editor for future volumes. Special thanks are due also to Frederick Weiss, first editor of the *Owl of Minerva*, the Society's newsletter. It was his initiative that led us to Mr. Simon Silverman of the Humanities Press whom we wish especially to acknowledge for his encouragement, assistance and patience. We are grateful too to Lillian, Donald, and Jonathan Schmitz for their willing help in proof reading.

The responsibility for the volume is a joint one, shared by the co-editors. Warren Steinkraus gave special attention to the section on Aesthetics and prepared the Index, and Kenneth L. Schmitz focused on the essays in Logic and did some of the preliminary editing.

Warren E. Steinkraus
State University of New York at Oswego

Kenneth L. Schmitz
Trinity College, University of Toronto

September 1978

KEY TO ABBREVIATIONS

to the works of Hegel most frequently cited

EL or *Enzyklopädie der philosophischen Wissenschaften (1830)* [Part
END I:Logic] (edd. Fr. Nicolin and O. Pöggeler), Felix Meiner,
Hamburg, 1959.

ELW *The Logic of Hegel* (trans. Wallace), Oxford 1874

EN *Enzyklopädie der philosophischen Wissenschaften* (1830) [Part
II:Nature] (edd. Fr. Nicolin and O. Pöggeler), Felix Meiner,
Hamburg, 1959.

HA *Hegel's Aesthetics: Lectures on Fine Art,* (trans. T. M. Knox),
Oxford, London 1975.

JS *Hegel's Science of Logic,* (trans. W. H. Johnston and L. G.
Struthers), 2 vols., Humanities Press, New York (1929),

Phän. *Phänomenologie des Geistes,* (ed. Joh. Hoffmeister), Felix
Meiner, Hamburg,

PhM *The Phenomenology of Mind,* (trans. J. B. Baillie). Macmillan,
New York 1931.

PNM *Hegel's Philosophy of Nature,* (trans. A. V. Miller), Clarendon,
Oxford, 1970.

SL *Hegel's Science of Logic,* (trans. A. V. Miller), Humanities,
New York, 1969.

W *Sämtliche Werke,* Jubiläumsausgabe in XX Bänden, (ed. H.
Glockner), Stuttgart, 1927-30.

WL *Wissenschaft der Logik,* (ed. G. Lasson), 2 vols. Felix Meiner,
Hamburg, 1934.[2]

A. The Aesthetics of Hegel

I

The Puzzle of Hegel's Aesthetics
by
SIR T. M. KNOX

Plato was clearly a lover of beauty and he was a master of style. Yet at the end of his Republic, he banishes Homer from his state along with all "representative" art, although in some passages indeed the qualification "representative" is omitted. Art, in short, may be pleasant, but it is deceptive; it appeals to emotion and not the intellect, and poetry and philosophy are irreconcilable.

Now Hegel surely had Plato's discussion of art before his mind when he was lecturing on aesthetics and it may well seem that his attitude to art becomes even more negative than Plato's. He says quite specifically that art for us is a thing of the past (11),[1] that it reached its zenith in Greece, that life contemporary with him was inimical to art, and that art's vocation to reveal truth had been discharged by religion and philosophy. This seems plain enough, but while at the end of his lectures Hegel says that in comedy art finds its dissolution altogether (1236), he also ends his general Introduction (90) with the remark that the wide Pantheon of art is rising but that to complete it will take thousands of years. "We may well hope that art will always rise higher and come to perfection." (103)

If we take pronouncements like these and others literally and out of their context, then their inconsistency is glaring and it can hardly be explained away by remembering that we are dealing with the text of lectures delivered in different years and that Hegel changed his views from time to time. Nevertheless, there may be some significance in the fact that in 1817, when the first edition of the *Encyclopedia of the Philosophical Sciences* was published, the inconsistency to which I have referred is no more than implicit. There, as in the earlier *Phenomenology,* there is no section devoted explicitly to art; instead there is one on the "Religion of Art", in which there is one reference to "beauty", and this "Religion" is then superseded by "Revealed Religion".

Having read the lectures on Aesthetics seven times in the course of translating them, I have come to the conclusion that there is only one way of solving the puzzle presented by the inconsistency to which I have referred and finding in Hegel a view of art which indeed is unacceptable in part but which is at least exempt from the charge that he regards art as dead and useless. My proposed solution depends on taking into account all that Hegel does *say* and attempting to discern what he really *means*. Some things which are *prima facie* inconsistent or contradictory may not be so in the last resort.

For Hegel, art has a vocation of its own, not one given to it or forced upon it from the outside (152). In other words, its vocation is not utility (55), not to be something useful whether in the interests of morality, or as an amusement, or as a decoration. It shares with religion and philosophy the vocation of revealing the truth (7), and though it reveals it in a sensuous form it is essentially an intellectual activity, whether on the part of the productive artist or of the spectator or the listener or reader. Nature as a temporal and spatial series of finite events and things cannot provide any adequate revelation of the spirit or the truth, and the *necessity* for the beauty of art arises from this deficiency of nature. (152) Artistic beauty is called upon to display in an external fashion both life and spiritual animation, and thus to lift the truth out of a purely natural environment.

It follows from this, however, that for us (i.e. for Hegel) art, as a vehicle of truth, is no longer simply to be enjoyed for its own sake. (11) It can be, indeed has to be, *judged*, in the sense that we can distinguish between the meaning of a work of art and its shape, or between its content and its form; and we can and do consider the adequacy or appropriateness of one of these to the other. At one time, Hegel thinks, the meaning was so perfectly embodied in the shape that truth had then reached a stage at which it could be adequate to itself in the sensuously perceived object. This happened, in his view, in Greece. There, at the point which truth had reached, or at the extent to which the spirit had reached consciousness of itself, art fulfilled its "highest vocation" because meaning and shape coincided. (301) The spirit had risen to a certain level of self-consciousness, and this was the stage which truth had reached. And that level and that stage were embodied without remainder in the shape of the work of art, and this is apparently why Hegel said that art had reached its "zenith" in Greece.

Symbolic art was superseded by the glory of classical art where meaning and shape coincided; in the plastic figures of Greek statuary, and even of great men and dramatic characters, objective and subjective coalesced. It was as if art and religion were one. Greek religion, however influenced from Egypt and the East, however molded by Homer and Hesiod, *needed* temples and statuary as the very embodiment of the Divine. The gods were worshipped *in* the statues, and the Greeks bowed the knee to the statues for that reason.

This coalescence, however, was only temporary, because in Greece the subjective had not developed into its full rights. So far indeed the world-spirit had travelled, but it moves on: its self-revelation is as gradual as its own self-knowledge. By the end of the fifth century B.C., religion was losing its sway in Greece. Socrates did pay tribute to a dying orthodoxy by sacrificing a cock to Aesculapius, but Aristophanes was shortly to ridicule the gods of Olympus, and Plato sounded their death-knell.

As Hegel put it, "the hinge of the world was turning."[2] Aristotle had foreshadowed something higher than the religion of Greece, and some of the Jewish prophets had already preceded him. The advent of Christianity by superseding Greek religion brought to an end what Hegel had earlier called the "religion of art", and along with it the perfection of Greek art. Now Hegel might have said that a new art was the harbinger of a religious change, but he did not and perhaps could not. What he called "romantic art", which has nothing to do with what we call the romantic art of the nineteenth century but which was essentially medieval art, had its content or subject-matter given to it from outside, whereas in Greek art the content or meaning was, as it were, formed by art itself *pari passu* with the shape produced. Greek religion did not precede Greek art, or so Hegel believed, but the Christian religion did precede and provide content or subject-matter for art to illustrate, and this is what "romantic" art did.

The most important thing about this, Hegel thought, so far as art was concerned, was that the subjective consciousness, including conscience, was at last given its due by Christianity. It was because of the lack of explicit subjectivity in the Greek outlook, and therefore in Greek art, that Hegel could say that art "reached its peak" in Italian painting from the thirteenth to the sixteenth century. (Although we had already been told that the "zenith" was in Greece).

Once again, however, the hinge of the world was turning. With the coming of the Reformation, romantic art which had been centered in Roman Catholicism, began slowly to crumble. To images and pictures of the Madonna and the saints, the Protestant knee could bow no longer. The religion presented to feeling and imagination in these pictures and images had been so revised or reformed that it was now available to the intellect in the Symbolical Books and in philosophy. It was because the "highest vocation" of art could not now be fulfilled by art itself that art had become, in Hegel's words, *etwas vergangenes,* a thing of the past. Religious truth, as expounded in Protestantism, and the self-consciousness of the Spirit as finally achieved in philosophy had resulted in art's being "no longer a fulfillment of our highest spiritual needs". And these words have led some to say that for Hegel art is "useless", — but it might still fulfill *a* spiritual need even if not the highest one; and who but a Philistine is to deny this? Did Hegel?

No. But if I am to defend this answer, I must state at greater length the case against it, and in the course of doing so I will try to deal with what is a minor but not unrelated puzzle, namely: If art is perfect in Greece, why does Hegel so often mention Shakespeare and give him such high praise?

Hegel's laudatory account of Greek art is expressed firmly and repeatedly. (301, 427) In Greece "art has reached its own essential nature". The Greeks "produced art in its supreme vitality". (436) "The perfection of art reached its peak (in Greece) precisely because the spiritual was completely drawn through its external appearance. . . . Nothing can be or become more beautiful". (517) The statement is emphatic but Hegel does say *more* beautiful, not *as* beautiful; and he goes on to say that there is something "higher" than this beauty of Greek art.

What Hegel has in mind here is simply that Christianity is a higher and truer religion than Greek religion. (435ff) Greek religion is the "religion of art" but the content of this religion and of Greek art is defective because it does not pass beyond the classical ideal. (508) It lacks the moment of the negative: it remains sensuous; sense has not died and then become resurrected as spirit. Consequently, romantic art is the most concrete form of art and a "higher form" of art than the Greek. (79)

Nevertheless classical art is "the true manifestation of art" (317) because it achieves the complete coincidence of content and form which symbolic art only *seeks*. In Greece, art has developed to maturity and at that stage art must of necessity produce its representations in the form of man's external appearance. (434) Hence the supremacy of Greek sculpture.

In passages like these we can see that the perfection which Hegel ascribes to Greek art is derived from his contrasting Greek art, its measure and restraint, with the formless, boundless, colossal productions of Indian and Egyptian art. The Greeks achieved beauty, and it is beauty which was missing in earlier art. Romantic art finds room for the ugly as well, and this makes it more concrete than Greek art, and it is a higher form because it is more subjective and brings painting and music to perfection.

At this point doubts about Hegel's whole theory of art and his attitude to it begin to arise. If art is truly manifested in Greece, then music and painting are inferior arts and Shakespeare is outclassed by the Greek dramatists. If there is something defective in Greek art, we are told, the defect is just art itself and the restrictedness of the sphere of art. (79) The "proper essence of art" is the identity of meaning and shape. (576) But if the meaning is known, independently of art, in religion and finally in philosophy, art seems to be required no longer. (535) This criticism Hegel tries to meet in a short paragraph.

The religious material, he says, which is the content of romantic art, *needs* art because in Christianity the Divine coalesces with an individual actually perceived and therefore entwined with the finitude of nature; the events in the life of Jesus Christ have passed away, his sufferings, death, Resurrection and Ascension belong to history, but all these events are repeated and perpetually renewed in art alone.

This must be one of the weakest arguments which Hegel ever used, even if only because it seems to be contradicting his view of art as something not useful but valuable in itself. Art cannot repeat or renew historical events; it cannot bring the past to life. It can provide only statues or pictures of persons or events, or poems about them, or set words about them to music. But in that case art has a purpose: it is useful in reminding us of the past, or picturing some of it for our imagination. But no one has argued more powerfully than Hegel against the view that the essence of art is utility. By trying to save the necessity for art by arguing in this way, Hegel is entering a blind alley. He is led into it by his own fundamental error about art itself.

His distinction between meaning and shape, content and form, may be allowed; but his belief that the meaning or content can be discerned and expounded is a fatal flaw in his philosophy of art. Art means what it says. But what it says is the work of art itself and this cannot be translated. Hegel's distance from a true understanding of art comes out once when he says that a poem can be translated into another language *without loss,* or even into prose. He does say repeatedly that genuine poetry does not arise from the poet's apprehension of some philosophical idea and then decorating it with fine language; but if this be so, there is no reason to suppose that the poem can be translated into prose. He thinks that some of Schiller's poems are too philosophical, and he never suggests that the merit of Homer is to remind the Greeks of the Trojan war and its aftermath or to renew it in their experience.

But it is in his treatment of music that his theory becomes most glaringly inadequate.

Hegel certainly loved pictures and he studied them with care wherever he went. His remarks about them are regarded as very "sensitive" by one who can speak with authority on this subject (Sir Ernest Gombrich);[3] and yet Hegel might well have agreed with a remark much used by advertisers in England when I was young, namely "every picture tells a story", and he would certainly have repudiated with scorn the "abstract" art of our own day. But if it was clear to Hegel what a picture was a picture *of*, he was in a difficulty when it came to music. So long as there were words, he could understand it; the music meant what the words said or could even impart a new and profounder meaning to the words themselves. Consequently he was at home with opera, which he adored. The libretto did not need to be very good: indeed I suspect that, for him, the worse it was the better, for he thought Schiller's poems quite unsuitable for musical setting. Presumably they were too good; music could add nothing to them or do anything to interpret them. Those who love Schubert's songs may well gasp at this judgment.

It is when Hegel writes about instrumental music that his misunderstanding becomes almost comical. The amateur, he thinks, can appreciate music and realize what it is about provided that it is an accompaniment to words. But if there are no words, what is it about? Bach's *St. Matthew Passion* or Handel's *Messiah* are intelligible because we know the words, but what are we to make of a string quartet or a symphony? These, Hegel suggests, are for the expert and the professional only, because, unlike the amateur, the expert can follow the modulations and what might be called the mathematical background of the thing. Hegel does say that Mozart was a master of instrumentation and the context might suggest that he has the symphonies in mind, but I doubt it. I think he is still doting on *The Magic Flute* or *Don Giovanni.* It follows

that instrumental music may be ingenious, but it is apparently meaningless; at any rate Hegel cannot find a meaning and therefore pays it
only lip service. It does not occur to him that it means what it says, but
can express the meaning only in its sounds, notes, and melodies. He says
that the amateur does hunt for a meaning and tries to associate his mood
as a listener with the landscape or emotion which may have aroused the
mood in which the composer had composed. And it is true enough that
many people have indeed made attempts like these, i.e. to make the
music say something definite about moonlight and so on, i.e. to make
music *imitative*: but here again we encounter Hegel's violent and justified repudiation of the view that art is imitation or that the imitation
of nature is its business.

The puzzle of Hegel's theory of art is thus two-fold: First, despite the
repeated eulogy of Shakespeare, art is said to attain its zenith in Greece.
Homer and Sophocles seem to have reached the height of art, and yet
Raphael, Dutch painting, Mozart's operas, Goethe's and Schiller's
poetry seem to be in the first class too, let alone Shakespeare.

Secondly, with comedy art is said to "annul itself". (529) Thus in the
work of artists since the seventeenth century (excluding some operas and
the work of Goethe and Schiller) art has come to an end. What it
proclaimed in the sensuous beauty of religious and national life is a thing
of the past; what painters and the builders of Gothic cathedrals expressed in their own media was the Roman Catholic religion, and the
adornment given by some even to the Protestant faith (and did Hegel
include Shakespeare amongst these?), have all become unnecessary.
What art portrayed in a sensuous form is now our intellectual possession, either in the creeds, or in the teachings of modern philosophy. And
yet, to repeat, the completion of the wide Pantheon of art will take
thousands of years. (90)

Here is the fundamental puzzle. — The other is whether Hegel really
put Greek drama above Shakespeare.

Having propounded puzzles, I must advance tentative answers. I take
the lesser puzzle first. Hegel regarded the *Antigone* of Sophocles as the
finest dramatic portrayal of a conflict between the duty of private or
family life and the political order. This *kind* of conflict he did not find in
Shakespeare. Since it is of no use to compare things which are not *in pari
materia,* Greek tragedy and Shakespearean cannot be compared; each is
excellent in its own kind. It is futile, to take an example from a sphere

where I am more at home, to compare the excellence of Bach's Toccata and Fugue in D Minor with the first Piano Concerto of Brahms.

Nevertheless I think that Hegel did regard the Homeric epics as unsurpassed by later epics, Greek sculpture as not surpassed by any of its successors; in short, he may have preferred masterpieces of what he called the classical form of art to those works of the romantic form of art which could be regarded as similar *in basic belief and character*. He compared many romantic poems with those of the eighteenth century to the disadvantage of the latter. He compared like with like. But he could not compare classical art with romantic art because the latter was higher and more concrete. Sophocles and Shakespeare cannot be put in the same class. So much for the lesser of my puzzles. I now turn to the other, which I described as fundamental.

Hegel saw that a great deal of seventeenth and eighteenth century art was poor, as romantic art, in comparison with its predecessors. And despite Goethe and Schiller, Mozart, Gluck, and Rossini, he had no taste for contemporary or recent art and so thought that art was a thing of the past. Well, I too, a lover of nineteenth century music (for I am not versed in painting, though modern painting seems to me to be similar in execution, and inspiration, to modern music) can only regard the successors of the great nineteenth century masters in a way which might make me say now that "music is dead". No one is going to convince me that Bartok or Schoenberg, or Stockhausen, etc., are anything but far beneath Schumann, or Brahms, or Liszt. As Hegel might have said, "Music is a thing of the past". Nevertheless, although I do regard the music of the last fifty years or so as decadent, doomed eventually (and, I hope, shortly) to oblivion, I would not say of it that *music* was dead, no matter how ephemeral some composers may be.

It is easy to take some of Hegel's (or his editor's) words out of their context and say that he thought that art had come to an end in his day, and we need not be surprised to find Croce saying (*Aesthetic,* Eng. tr. 2nd edn., pp. 302-3) that the "Aesthetic of Hegel is thus a funeral oration: he passes in review the successive forms of art . . . and lays the whole in its grave. . . . Art [for metaphysical idealism is] absolutely useless".[4] But if this verdict of Croce's were true, it would be very hard to explain what Hegel meant when he said that art would continue its task for thousands of years and that we would hope that it might come to perfection. I am bold enough to say that here Croce, for whose work I have a profound respect, was mistaken. He has not considered all of Hegel's statements and therefore has not set himself to solve the puzzle which they present.

This I have ventured to set myself to do, and whether my answer is correct or not, its importance, if any, is that it is at the same time virtually an answer to those who have maintained that Hegel regarded his philosophy as final, so that philosophy had finished its task and come to an end with his *Encyclopaedia of the Philosophical Sciences*.

Hegel insists, as we have seen, that art is an intellectual activity, charged like religion and philosophy with the task of revealing the truth, although it veils the truth in a sensuous form, unlike philosophy which declares its message in plain prose, in intellectual terms, for *thinking,* not for *feeling*. But this must be a *continuing* task.

Thus when Hegel says that art transcends itself, or annuls itself, and so on, it is the dissolution of *romantic* art which he has in view, and this is said once quite specifically. (608) It is true that earlier (529) he says that we now require higher forms for the apprehension of truth than art is in a position to supply, but his point, I think, is that the thematic material of *romantic* art, though richer than that of Greek art, has been apprehended explicitly in religion and philosophy, and that in comedy and humour it is *romantic* art that has come to an end. But art does still fulfill *a* spiritual need.

I place my reliance, not only on a general reading of Hegel, but on a passage of the *Aesthetics* in the section on "poetic diction". (1007) Here Hegel says that poetry must put us on different ground from that of ordinary and everyday life, from our religious ideas and actions, from our scientific and philosophical thinking. Now, despite what Professor Sir Karl Popper thinks, Hegel was no fool. He knew that "ordinary everyday life" had changed and was changing. The world-spirit did not stand still. Hegel saw the beginnings even of street-lighting in some places, for example, and he had travelled enough to find that what had been ordinary in one place had already been superseded in another. His own writings on religion showed how the art adapted to Roman Catholicism had altered after the Reformation, and he was so dissatisfied with his contemporary Lutheranism that he foresaw the coming of Modernism and therefore, on his own principles, of a new art to adumbrate or illustrate it. His dissatisfaction with the science of his day is clear enough to any reader of the second section of his *Encyclopaedia* and some parts of the *Science of Logic*. His philosophy of history ends with the emphatic words *bis hieher* has consciousness come. Consequently whatever his philosophy had done to *begreifen* the course of the world, and whatever the Spirit had revealed of itself, *up to that time,* the Spirit still lived and its further revelation would come first in art, and then in religion and science, and philosophy's task to *begreifen* this new world would be unceasing.

Hegel's own life had not been particularly happy; fame he did not enjoy until near the end of his life, and even then he had official vexations enough. His survey of contemporary life did not encourage hope. The owl of Minerva spread its wings only with the falling of the dusk. An age of the world had grown old and the prospect of what a new age was to be like filled him with gloom. And today as we survey what looks all too like the collapse of European civilization, in Great Britain we may be gloomy too.

A great deal of art had come to a dead end shortly before Hegel's time. It was to burgeon forth anew later in his own century; Modernism was to appear in the Christian religion; in science Darwin lay ahead, to say nothing of his epigoni; the course of history did not stop nor did attempts to understand it; and philosophy, following Hegel, as he followed Plato or Aristotle or Spinoza, flourished as well. But in the last fifty years or so, thanks to some extent it may be to wars, art has turned its back on beauty, theology has relapsed into the cul-de-sac of a dead orthodoxy, and philosophy has deserted its vocation and sunk from considering the great problems of human life and destiny into exploring the meanings of words and playing language-games.

Placed as he was in the culture of his time, Hegel may well have had his moments of despair. It is easy to have the same today. But art and religion and philosophy, whatever may be said of too many of their contemporary practitioners, are not dead. *Nil desperandum,* or, as Galileo is reported to have said, *eppur si muove*.

NOTES

1. Parenthesized numbers throughout this essay are citations to pages in Professor Knox's new translation of Hegel's *Lectures on Aesthetics*. (Oxford: 1975). [eds.]
2. In his Preface to the *Philosophy of Right*.
3. In a letter to the author.
4. Benedetto Croce, *Aesthetic* (tr. D. Ainslie) (New York: Noonday Press, 1953) pp. 302-303.

COMMENT
NEWTON P. STALLKNECHT

I readily accept Sir Malcolm's conclusion concerning the status of the arts in Hegel's thought. What little I have to say by way of comment does no more than supplement what he has made clear to us. Let me begin by pointing out in passing that Hegel's "owl of Minerva" possessed an intelligence essentially epimethean in capacity, yet astute enough to recognize his own limitations. Thus Hegel refrained from outlining the history of the future as, for instance, Oswald Spengler was to attempt a century later. Thus, although he surmised, rightly enough, that the arts of the century that was to follow him were to be very different from those with which he was familiar, he made no effort to anticipate their direction. He recognized that what he chose to call "romantic" art had in modern times come, so to speak, to challenge itself and to express this self-criticism in comedy and satire. Thus he found that the "subjective" post-classical tradition emerging from Christian thought and feeling had completed its contribution and outlived the period in which it could celebrate, as a spokesman of human destiny, a synoptic vision comparable in contemporary effectiveness to that of Greek tragedy or Dante's *Divine Comedy*. In this respect, modern artists, including the poets, must, in Hegel's view, yield to the philosophers. The latter, as heirs of the maturing wisdom of the ages, may interpret recorded history as a dialectical progression of conflicting attitudes and institutions moving gradually toward an inclusive resolution in which the human individual may find true freedom, i.e., fulfillment as a responsible and self-disciplined member of a social organism. Such a comprehensive theory of what we might call "normative history" lies beyond the reach of the artist, whose dependence upon a sensuous medium keeps him from mastering the movement of a dialectic that is open only to rational reflection.

This position did not, however, require Hegel to insist upon any forthcoming dissolution of the arts. After all, Hegel had challenged the methods of the mathematician even more firmly than he had those of the artist. He had argued that the terse abstractions of the former quite fail to capture the movement that underlies the development of human consciousness. But certainly Hegel had no intention of suggesting that in the intellectual life of a maturely organized society mathematical reasoning and calculation would cease to have a place, although, to be sure, they would be clearly distinguished from philosophy both in method and subject matter.

The same might be said of the arts. Surely the last paragraph of Hegel's introduction to the *Philosophy of Fine Art* would seem to indicate a belief that the arts will continue, as the ages pass, toward a clearer recognition and realization of the Idea of beauty, although, it is hoped, they will not attempt to displace the more inclusive thoughtfulness of the philosopher, who in his turn will not attempt to predict the course open to the arts.

Here we may, profiting by hindsight extending over a century and a half, offer an historical comment that Hegel, if he were living today, would surely have to take under advisement. We may call attention to an attitude that was in Hegel's time beginning to make itself felt and was to grow increasingly widespread throughout the course of the 19th century. Its first prominent exponent was Schopenhauer, although he drew largely upon both Kant and Plato in systematizing his thought. Subsequent ways of thinking came in time to appear sharply in contrast with the tradition of Marx and his followers whose left wing Hegelianism tends to subordinate art to what they consider the wholesome development of a social consciousness.

From the new point of view the enjoyment of the beautiful is recognized as an end in itself and as such constituting a profound satisfaction in the life of the individual. As a secondary but important consideration one may notice that such satisfaction offers the individual refreshment through release from the tedium of daily routines on the one hand and on the other the bewildering and frustrating complexity and the destructive contingencies of human affairs. Thus art is seen to offer a realization of value that history, whatever the optimism of the philosopher who interprets it, seems forever to postpone. So interpreted, the contemplation of beauty in whatever form appears as a sabbath of the human spirit and, as Santayana would put it, one of the things that "make a long life better than a short one."

Such enjoyment may be thought of as a personally disinterested admiration that is not far removed from thankfulness and often inspires in us a lively impulse to communicate our delight to other people. The sense of value so engendered is not self-centered. It does not further our practical interests or satisfy our intellectual curiosity. Nor is it to be confused with a fanciful identification of our lives with the achievement of others as in the enjoyment of escape fiction. Genuine aesthetic satisfaction transcends rather than satisfies the uneasiness of our pedestrian or normal consciousness.

It is, after all, the quality of aesthetic awareness rather than the nature of its object, whose actual existence need not concern us, that we find most profoundly satisfying. This quality, as Kant would describe it, is apparent in moments of consciousness where understanding and sensibility support each other harmoniously, as for instance in poetry where sound and paraphraseable meaning unite in concert with one another. Kant found in such happy awareness a sense of heightened vitality, or "furtherance of life" (*Gefühl der Beförderung des Lebens*) also a source of congenial fellowship among those who share the enjoyment of the same values.

Schopenhauer went further, finding in aesthetic enjoyment a brief respite from the anxiety, envy, frustration and boredom that characterize so much of our insecure and competitive consciousness, with which Schopenhauer was by disposition all too well acquainted. As he put it, in a moment of aesthetic disinterestedness the "wheel of Ixion stands still." Being something of a Platonist, Schopenhauer found a paramount beauty in imagistic evocation of those forms, such as the human body, that nature seems to pursue but forever fails fully to realize. Again he describes a less exalted mode of contemplation that may also free the human spirit from its gnawing anxieties. This appears as the detailed recovery through imagination of incidents of our own past, if only these are distant enough to stand outside the sphere of our present narrow concerns. Disinterested recollection holds for us a charm comparable to the enjoyment of the arts. Here Schopenhauer anticipated the theme of Marcel Proust's great novel.

In one way or another, many 19th and 20th century thinkers have in discussing the arts emphasized the freedom from anxiety and ennui, from insecurity and commonplace routine, that our modern life cannot otherwise wholly escape. Besides Proust, we may think of Walter Pater, Mallarmé, and Santayana in his later writings as giving expression to this attitude each in his own way. And there are many others, especially Benedetto Croce and his followers who insist upon an absolute distinction between aesthetic intuition or expression and all other modes of normative consciousness such as the economic, the moral, and the logical, firmly resisting the temptation to unite these in a quasi-Hegelian synthesis. After all, the arts contribute to our well-being something besides an imaginative anticipation of a philosophical system. The artist need not help us to understand our world or to justify the ways of God or of history — indeed Hegel felt that the artist can no longer do so — but he can offer us moments of heightened consciousness whose value we feel no need to question.

In conclusion, we may remark that in our century much thinking about the arts has tended to center about one or the other of two poles. There is the position of the Marxians, who, owing not a little to Hegel, are inclined to value the arts primarily as they contribute to a social consciousness. In opposition there appears a line of thought that seems less Hegelian in aspect, a movement or group of related movements that we have just now mentioned. Here the arts possess what we might call a substantial value of their own and need no apologist to honor their achievement as he interprets their contribution to other forms of value.

Some may wonder: if Hegel were alive today would he find it necessary to attempt a reconciliation of these conflicting evaluations? Certainly many thoughtful people are hardly satisfied with either alternative; and their sincere uncertainty in this matter stands as a challenge to the philosopher. But a more interesting question arises. Has not Hegel already committed himself to an answer? Had he lived on to follow the development of the arts throughout the 19th century and in our own period, would he not have recognized their increasing autonomy as springing from a healthy recognition of their predicament as he had himself described it in his own later writings? If the modern artist is likely to be unsuccessful in anticipating the philosopher and serving as a spokesman of human destiny, may he not be wise in devoting himself more modestly and effectively to a realization of the beautiful as it lies open to human experience and thus to refrain from trespassing on the domain of the philosopher, the political leader, or the religious teacher?

Perhaps we should leave open the question whether Hegelian thought is logically committed to this position, remarking only that today an epimethean owl of Minerva might find himself quite content with such a conclusion.

II
Hegel's Aesthetics: Yesterday and Today
by
RÜDIGER BUBNER

At the dawn of the nineteenth century, the German poet, Jean Paul, expressed a complaint which surely can no longer be ours. "Our time is swarming with aestheticians as with nothing else." In our own time, no longer so crowded with aestheticians, we have come to look ever more longingly to a period when the theory of arts flourished. Aesthetics was one of the main intellectual occupations of the late eighteenth century, even becoming a popular subject among artists themselves, especially writers and painters. Jean Paul, who began his *Vorschule der Ästhetik* with this complaint against the aesthetical "inflation" was only one such. And, more significantly, philosophy began to take the problems of art seriously. Of course, beauty, its production and its understanding, had always stimulated philosophical thought. In the first place, there was the classical theory of art and its revival in the Renaissance. During the following centuries, France had developed a tradition of combining artistic creation with reflection upon it. The English brought the analysis of artistic appreciation into the foreground.[1]

However, it was not until Kant that the problem of art was considered a philosophical problem of the *first* order. It is no exaggeration, I think, to say that the intellectual movement originated by Kant's transcendental philosophy was the first one to realize the importance of aesthetics for philosophical thinking. Although the topics dealt with by Kant are well known,[2] he widened the analysis by bringing them into a systematic perspective. The full range and complexity of the problems hidden in such a seemingly innocent sentence as "This is beautiful" become apparent only within the transcendental framework of Kant's third *Critique*. This work opened a new path of philosophical inquiry into the principles of art, along which path Kant's followers and critics, especially Schiller and Schelling, continued. All this contributed to the controversial and often overheated atmosphere referred to by Jean Paul above.

Historians of philosophy are agreed that the culminating point of idealistic aesthetics is represented by Hegel's philosophy of art. It is within his encyclopaedic system of dialectics that the most exhaustive exploration of this fascinating realm takes place and art is assigned its final status, adjacent to that of philosophy, as the reflection of Thought in a sense medium. A more mature speculation upon the principles of beauty and a more fruitful use of contemporary scientific and historical knowledge are to be found in Hegel's *Lectures* than in the efforts of any of his predecessors.

It was, thus, with good reason that during the century and four decades since the publication of the *Lectures*, Hegel's Aesthetics was considered as a paradigm for what philosophy could and could not or should and should not do with art. Aesthetic discussion, at least in Europe, has until now been related in one way or another to the accomplishments of dialectical philosophy. New theories still tend to be measured against the speculative system and a polemic against Hegel is still the means by which genuine insights are given a clearer profile. Hegel seems to have determined once and for all what philosophical aesthetics is about. In this function he invites imitation as well as opposition. So his heritage emerges as both a challenge and a burden.[3]

I

This situation needs to be taken into account in trying to understand what Hegel's Aesthetics meant and may still mean. The role of dialectical theory for our own comprehension of art can be appreciated only if we are conscious of the role it played in the last century. It is my conviction that no question about Hegel's aesthetics today can be seriously raised without regard to Hegel's aesthetics yesterday. It was the *classical ideal of beauty* as convincingly articulated in Hegel's Aesthetics which provided the most controversial point of discussion for his followers. And it is surely no coincidence that it is the loss of this ideal which we perceive as the most prominent feature of the radical change in the arts marking aesthetic modernity.

Indeed, Hegel's whole theory of art can be seen as an effort to establish a purely rational foundation for this ideal and to defend it against the competing alternatives already at hand in his own epoch. The unquestioned dominance of the classical ideal is by no means detached from contemporary concerns, but contains an implicit criticism of destructive romantic forms. Better known nowadays is Hegel's provocative thesis stating the *definite end* of any interesting development in art. This thesis is but a logical consequence of the superiority which the ideal of classical art has for Hegel. The high tide of art production has gone with antiquity. Romantic art already represents a decadence. The more an intellectual force of reflection enters the production of art (thereby becoming a constitutive part of the works themselves), the less the art can be considered an autonomous form of absolute spirit. A reflective element starts to overwhelm the work of art. This is the expression of the essential process of transition from art to philosophy through history. The loss of independent value suffered by all the arts in modern times represents a gain of power for pure philosophical understanding. The last important step leading from the aesthetic realm of art to the philosophical realm of speculative reason was made in Hegel's time and, as Hegel himself does not hesitate to affirm, by Hegelian philosophy.

The accomplishment of thought corresponds to the decadence of romantic art exemplified in Hegel's contemporaries. The witty and complicated novels of Jean Paul, overloaded by theory and reflection, serve as an example. Hegel showed himself very critical of the purely aesthetic qualities of such works of transition. Historically and philosophically speaking they demonstrate artistic decay. Both the verdict declaring the end of art in modern times and the praise of antiquity were based mainly on philosophical reasons.[4]

This sharp criticism of contemporary artists together with the corresponding preference for the classical ideal, had already become a crucial issue of discussion during Hegel's lifetime and became yet more so among pupils and opponents in the following generation. The position taken with regard to the classical ideal of beauty favored by the master was to be, for decades to come, the true touchstone for partisanship pro and contra Hegel. It showed also what value a theoretician was prepared to attribute to the autonomous development of modern art.

To my knowledge, Christian Hermann Weisse was the first to make this point. Adhering in general to an orthodox Hegelianism, he nevertheless had a mind of his own. In the year 1830, one year before the master died and five years before the *Lectures on Aesthetics* were posthumously edited by Hotho out of compiled manuscripts and student notes, Weisse published a *System der Ästhetik*.[5] In this book he

follows mainly the course of argument Hegel must have taken in the
Lectures at Berlin University and with which Weisse was obviously
familiar. At a decisive stage, however, Weisse disagrees fundamentally
with Hegel, but in order not to charge Hegel with error, he attributes
Hegel's position to an anonymous group of students. The disagreement
concerns the appreciation of modern art. For the contemporary period,
Weisse conceives of a "modern ideal" of perfect harmony between art
and reflection. This, on the one hand, contradicts the romantic
postulate of a "New Mythology" such as Schelling and Friedrich
Schlegel had hoped for, but it is at odds, too, with Hegel's harsh verdict
on modernity.

> Hegel's pupils, in particular, affirm their master's philosophical
> position, one which is the necessary result of the historical process of
> philosophy, as an absolute, and, defending him against all direct and
> indirect attacks, not so much in brave and skillful combat, as with their
> eyes closed and their lances held out in front of them, are now the ones
> who have taken on the Herculean labor of proving to the Day of Art,
> freely and brilliantly dispensing in all directions its radiant dawning
> beams, to its very face, that it is not Day at all, but Night.[6]

It is, however, not quite accurate to say that all of Hegel's pupils
stubbornly repeated his statement of the end of art. The young Karl
Rosenkranz, who later in the century proved one of the most loyal
defenders of Hegel against the wave of common criticism, tried in his
early days to combine the diagnosis that art has come to its final stage
with romantic prophecies. The future form of art production still to be
brought to fruition, is, according to Rosenkranz, the genre of the novel.
Rosenkranz gives some pointers towards the novel construed as the
universal apotheosis of what art should be.[7]

Though Weisse gave the most convincing picture of a modern ideal of
art to overcome traditional forms by the integration of the power of
thought into the work, there remained another way of leaving classical
models behind. The step back from the classical ideal of beauty in
Hegel's sense was taken quite unanimously by the following generation.
These aestheticians are mainly concerned with its opposite. Negative
phenomena of the anti-beautiful play a prominent role in post-Hegelian
aesthetics. The comical, the sublime, the ugly, seemed to attract all the
philosophical interest at that time.

Years before his political collaboration with Karl Marx, the young

Arnold Ruge started his career as a philosophical journalist with a *Neue Vorschule zur Ästhetik* (1837). This book recalls Jean Paul's unorthodox essay and foreshadows Ruge's later commitment to the struggle for human emancipation. The "new propaedeutics" concentrate on the comical as a kind of concrete effect art can have on the individual. The comical, says Ruge, can only be understood on the basis of the relationship of the living subject to its given situation. Laughter is seen as a way of liberation from circumstances. Reacting to the comical by laughing is an aesthetic way for the individual to free himself from the objective conditions which surround him in his life.

To be sure, by the time that Ruge was forced into exile in Paris, (after his political writings had gotten him into trouble in Saxony), he was no longer of the opinion that laughter and aesthetic responses were enough to set human beings free. This much can be seen in the *Deutsch-Französische Jahrbücher* which he published with Karl Marx.

More scholarly work was done on these diverse aesthetical phenomena by Friedrich Theodor Vischer, Kuno Fischer, and Karl Rosenkranz. Vischer of Tübingen won considerable attention with his early study *Über das Erhabene und das Komische* (1837). In his later years, he set out a philosophical system of aesthetics following Hegel's model.[8] This huge work turned out to be the only serious imitation of the encyclopaedic undertaking of the master. In addition, Vischer's public reputation was due to many literary essays and witty articles which attracted readers far beyond academic circles—an unusual achievement for a German professor from a small provincial town around the middle of the nineteenth century! Kuno Fischer, whose fame as an historian of modern philosophy was based upon a series of voluminous works written in later life, participated, in his earlier days, in the discussion of aesthetics. His *Diotima, die Idee des Schönen* (1849) does not confine itself, as the title might suggest, to the subject of beauty in the traditional manner, but has some interesting things to say about the comical and the ugly. Often quoted, though not completely original, is Karl Rosenkranz's book *Philosophie des Hässlichen* (1853), which constructs the ugly as the opposite of the beautiful, —out of logical necessity. He thereby proposes rather to amend Hegel's theory of art than to criticize it. Basically, Rosenkranz's contribution aims to prove the legitimacy of Hegel's approach by extending it to a neglected realm of aesthetic phenomena. In claiming that Rosenkranz was not original, I not only have Fischer's booklet in mind, for Weisse's programme of a *System der Schönheit* had already included ugliness as a countervailing element which no comprehensive theory of beauty can do without.

Let us return from the right-wing Hegelians to the leftist critics of Hegel. We mentioned Ruge's quasi-political application of an aesthetic experience. In a rather well-known passage in the Parisian Manuscripts of 1844, Marx stated that beauty is a special character of human production:

> Animals construct only in accordance with the standards and needs of the species to which they belong, while man knows how to produce in accordance with the standards of every species, and knows how to apply the appropriate standard to the object: thus man constructs also in accordance with the laws of beauty.[9]

The ideal of beauty which supposedly distinguishes the results of human labour with regard to the products of nature or animal activity, reproduces the classical norm of harmony. It is not the grotesque, the bizarre, the comical, which lifts one out of the common rut. Nor is it laughter which promotes emancipation. Rather, the work of any human hand is marked by features of beauty, such that the structure of the object formed reflects the universality and all-embracing organization of the forming subject. The underlying assumption takes beauty as a sign of harmony and the beautiful as a measure of objective production in unalienated human nature. The full richness of our nature manifests itself through the aesthetic appearance of everything we have formed.

The classical ideal of beauty displays its critical implications insofar as it allows a diagnosis of alienation. All production lacking the essential feature of beauty makes perceptible what a given situation lacks of our true nature. It would be hardly unfair to say that among Marxists of this century only Herbert Marcuse has realized the emancipatory potential of art. His vision of a future society is one that is aesthetically marked. Free life must be beautiful, for it gives room to the entirety of human talents. The negative power of art vis-à-vis the reality of one-dimensional social life is due to the inherent beauty and harmony of artificial production.[10]

Another remark about the function of art makes very clear that Marx himself was a classicist as far as aesthetic problems go. In connection with the controversy about so-called "materialistic aesthetics," the concluding paragraphs from the unfinished and unpublished Introduction to the *Grundrisse der Kritik der politischen Ökonomie* (1857) are always cited.[11] Short as this textual basis may seem, it is the only reliable evidence for the systematic place left open to art within the framework of a *Critique of Political Economy*. Marx asks himself why, in the age of capitalism with growing industrialization and the power of the press, a work of art as far away as Homer's epic should still be appreciated for its aesthetic value. How does it happen that an artistic production which as a piece of literature belongs to an outdated genre and which as a historical document reflects the totally different society of archaic Greece can still be understood and enjoyed? This is so, says Marx, because art production does not stand in an immediate and fixed relationship to the economic conditions of production as does the ideological sphere in general. Art is more than a mirror reflecting the given base. In the case of art, the relationship between base and superstructure is not simply parallel, but unequal, as Marx puts it. This sounds astonishingly quite idealistic compared with the radical plea for materialism which Marx is never tired of repeating. In the published Introduction to *Zur Kritik der politischen Ökonomie,* for example, which dates from the same time, the view of art is deliberately much more simplified.[12]

In the text from the *Grundrisse*, two rather sketchy arguments are brought forward, both originating from idealistic philosophy. The one claims a special status for art because artificial production is not directly rooted in the realm of material conditions, but mediated with this realm through mythology. The imaginative world of Greek myth provides art with its authentic material. Schelling and the Romantics had first developed this notion. Mythology is shared by the collective human mind, but is not a purely intellectual product; it still contains unreflected raw material from social reality. The ambiguity of anonymously half-formed material invites the artist to complete the process of formation. Mythology was the basis of classical art and was supposed to become the basis of the new universal art anticipated by the Romantics. Hegel adopted the notion of mythology as a special material for art-production and Marx, too, seems to have inherited it.

The other argument we find in the Introduction to *Grundrisse* has even more Hegelian flavor. Marx explains the lasting importance of classical works of art as an act of recognition. Just as a man may recognize his own youth in an adolescent and thus bring his own evolution to mind, so too, we can recognize ourselves in an early stage of history when we appreciate aesthetically classical literature or sculpture. The idea of a unity of historical development as a whole governs this concept of recognition which is obviously borrowed from Hegelian idealism — if not from the Aesthetics, then at any rate from the *Phenomenology of Mind*.

This passage cited from Marx is most important, because it shows the dilemma of any "materialistic" aesthetics. While subsequent Marxist discussion has closed its eyes to the idealistic implications, in fact it may be said that all overtly materialistic aestheticians have fallen back upon a covert Hegelianism. In view of the fact that non-Marxist theory of art in our century has also taken its stand in relation to Hegel, we come to the surprising conclusion that both discussions revolve in smaller or wider circles around a center where we find the dialectical philosophy.

II

I have now come to the point where I leave post-Hegelian aesthetics and turn to our own situation. The variety of attitudes toward Hegel, imitative and critical, which we have seen in the nineteenth century gives us the necessary background for a better understanding of the panorama of aesthetics nowadays. It seems useful to start with Marxist positions since they are directly related to the materialistic point of view born out of a sharp criticism of Hegel. After considering the positions of Marxism, where a reference to Hegel does not come as a surprise, it will turn out to be easier than one might expect to uncover Hegelian ideas in most of the alternative views which philosophers who do not belong to the Marxist tradition have taken with regard to art.

The first name to be mentioned in any discussion of Marxist aesthetics in the twentieth century is that of Georg Lukács. His merits remain undisputed in spite of politically motivated polemics from within and without the Communist movement. He was more intelligent than the official party-theoreticians and more cultured than those of his political friends who despised bourgeois culture without ever having acquired it. The young Georg von Lukács made his name with a collection of refined essays on the arts at the beginning of the century *(Die Seele und die Formen)*[13]. He planned to build an academic career upon a philosophy of art written before and during the first World War. It owed most of its philosophical apparatus to the Neo-Kantianism of the so-called "Southwest German school". During his years in Heidelberg, Lukács had the opportunity to become acquainted with the revival of Kantian ideas especially through his contacts with E. Lask and M. Weber, both of whom thought highly of his work. It was not until after Lukács' death that the *Heidelberger Philosophie der Kunst* (1912-1914) received its first publication.[14] In the following years the Hegelian influence grew constantly. The famous *Theorie des Romans*[15], cleverly applies some of Hegel's insights into the structure of the novel on recent epic writing, especially that of Dostoijevsky. The article "Die Subjekt-Objekt-Beziehung in der Ästhetik" appeared in *Logos* in 1917-18,[16] and declares right at the start that it takes Hegel's phenomenological method as its paradigm.

After his conversion to Marxism and his political career in Hungary following the first World War, the theoretical activities of Lukács were mainly dedicated to the problems of revolution and its intellectual prerequisites. The masterpiece, *Geschichte und Klassenbewusstsein* (1923)[17], which tries to reanimate Marxist orthodoxy by a recourse to Hegel's concept of reflection, continues to inspire the theoretical debate on revolution to the present day. His forced retirement or exile in Moscow was necessary to bring Lukács back to aesthetic studies. There he wrote many of his lengthy essays and books on European literature, especially that of the nineteenth century. The concept of *realism* gives the basic orientation. In the thirties it stirred a fervent controversy among the exiled Marxist theoreticians in which Bertholt Brecht and others took part.[18] The leading figure opposing Lukács was Ernst Bloch whose affinities to the artistic movement of Expressionism led him to object in principle to the dominance of traditional realism.[19] The central question is: Does the well-structured and thoroughly organized harmony of realistic fiction reflect the truth about the world as it is, or do we have to resort to the extreme and unbalanced means of expressionist provocation in order to dig out the truth about reality.

What is at stake here turns out to be the old controversy between the classical and anti-classical avant garde-ideal of art, and their relation to truth. The old controversy of Hegelian times reappears under the Marxist heading of an adequate image of economic reality and society. What is present, too, is the burden of truth laid upon art by Hegelian aesthetics. Art is not considered as something in its own right, but has to be an appearance of truth, and it is worthless if it does not meet this philosophical demand. The Marxist debate about realism depends for its aesthetic principles on Hegel's conception. It adds, however, its own definition of truth. Truth is no longer the essential domain of philosophy (i.e. Hegel's dialectics), of which art is only a vague, sensuous appearance, such that it automatically becomes outdated when philosophy is fully worked out. Truth in the Marxist sense means the revelation of the concrete structure of capitalist society analyzed by the *Critique of Political Economy*.

This definition of truth may be more concrete, but it leads to a problem analogous to Hegel's thesis of the end of art. If the truth about the historical reality of capitalism cannot be found except by an economic theory which is able critically to penetrate the ruling ideology, what else is possible? What is the use of art, if not as the illustration of a truth already established by theory? Art then becomes an instrument of propaganda. Moreover, if truth is the concern of theory and art nevertheless remains bound to just this theoretical truth, then what are the standards by which to judge art if not those of an adequate or inadequate transposition. In other words: which art represents the truth without distortion and which does not? Who defines the borderline separating correct promulgation of the truth through propaganda from the use of the same instrument in support of a false ideology? I am not dealing here with the bitter experience in recent history of the persecution of the arts in the name of truth. It is, nevertheless, essential to consider the *theoretical paradox* of an aesthetics based upon a preconceived theory of the truth as needing artistic representation. Max Raphael, a long forgotten Marxist aesthetician, was aware of the ambivalent role art has to fulfill between truth and ideology and wrote an insightful essay *Zur Kunsttheorie des dialektischen Materialismus*.[20]

Lukács, however, as well as defending the classical ideal on a high theoretical level with his notion of realism, could play the political trump card of orthodoxy. In his later years, his theoretical statements, too, showed the burden of this orthodoxy. The Introduction to an edition of Hegel's *Lectures on Aesthetics,* written in 1952, is, for a man of his capacities, very poor and worse than narrow-minded even if one takes into account the complicated historical situation in which it appeared. The huge systematic work on aesthetics[21] to which Lukács devoted his last years but was unable to finish, is verbose and often repetitious. It neither proposes a substantial new idea, nor does it succeed in formulating the old concept of realism more convincingly. The Hegelian heritage is present on most of the pages, but now the author seems to build his view completely on a trivialized version of dialectics.

More interesting than the commonplaces of the later Lukács is another contribution to a theory of art grounded on a speculative neo-Marxism. The philosophically most profound contemporary work on aesthetics in this direction is that of Theodor W. Adorno. To my mind the only book of our time deserving at least a moderate comparison with Hegel's *Lectures* in its level of philosophical reflection, and for the richness of concrete detail which it contains, is Adorno's *Ästhetische Theorie.*[22] This volume was prepared for publication, but had to be edited from the manuscript to its present form after the author's untimely death. It should be considered as the last word of Adorno's philosophy in general and at the same time as a *'summa'* of a lifelong interaction of reflective thought and intimate connoisseurship in different arts. I hope this eulogy singling out Adorno does not seem exaggerated, but if one becomes aware of the primitive standard of the official Marxist publications on aesthetic questions and the poverty of current philosophy dealing with art, it will be plausible.

Adorno constantly declared his indebtedness to his friend Walter Benjamin. In spite of commonly held views, Benjamin is neither a dialectician *ab ovo*, nor a genuine Marxist, even though his language may initially remind one of rhetorical figures known from dialectical writers. In fact, quite late in his philosophical career, after having written two important books, he was informed of a striking parallel in his ideas with Hegel's aesthetics. He replied by declaring that he had never read it and found Hegel's philosophy as a whole hard to understand. The documents can be found among his letters,[23] where one finds also all the ambiguity of his theoretical partisanship for

Marxism. His friend Adorno thought it necessary to point out the flaws of Marxist theory in Benjamin's celebrated article "Das Kunstwerk im Zeitalter seiner technischen Reproduzierbarkeit," (1936). Much ink has been spilled over the adequate understanding of Benjamin and the alleged repression of original Marxist elements by Adorno. Apart from political factions, it seems evident to me that the Marxism of Benjamin is an epihenomenon of his original theory, generated under the dominating influence of Brecht out of political and moral motives. The only text by Benjamin that could be considered as an authentic contribution to aesthetics from a Marxist point of view is his politically-minded speech on "The Author as Producer" given before anti-fascist intellectuals in Paris in 1934.[24]

Benjamin's original standpoint could best be described as a kind of cabalistic theory. Art is the symbol of a deeply hidden truth: the more one tries to grasp it, the more it withdraws. Strangely enough, the hope of revealing the final mystery one day is best preserved by strictly abstaining from every effort at plain understanding. Benjamin interpreted his hermetic insights and utopian perspectives first in terms of the romantic theory of Friedrich Schlegel which projects a coming convergence of the work of art and its critical reflection. (Cf. *Der Begriff der Kunstkritik in der deutschen Romantik,* 1920) Later he reassessed his theory by means of a Neoplatonic speculation (*Der Ursprung des deutschen Trauerspiels,* 1928, Introduction). Marxist dialectics was only another way of making the eschatological idea of a hidden truth to be uncovered as a final act more acceptable to the modern mind.

Adorno coined the term "Dialectic of Enlightenment" for the same experience, namely, that the process of Enlightenment does not necessarily further the grasping of the final truth. In the last analysis, the growing rationality of the modern age, instead of bringing more light into the prevailing darkness, has helped to make the actual world darker. During his American exile in the forties, Adorno and his mentor Max Horkheimer condensed their observations on contemporary fascism and the Stalinist degeneration of Marxism into an essay published in 1947, under the title *Dialektik der Aufklärung.* The pessimism vis-à-vis any historical progress of rationality combined with the Marxist distrust of all pure theory worked together to make philosophy as a whole appear unreliable. Adorno's way out of a radical skepticism is aesthetics. Theory of art is not only one philosophical discipline among others, it tends increasingly to coincide with philosophy. That theory which cannot simply "state" *the* truth, because its understanding is absorbed in aesthetic experience, offers the best chance *to* truth. In a situation in which ideology is universal and unbroken the philosophical claim to truth can only be made by giving up the immediate expectation of mastering reality by theory.

The old Hegelian standard of aesthetics, namely the philosophical concept of truth, is maintained while the Hegelian thesis about the end of art is abolished. Not only does art in fact survive the apotheosis of the dialectical system, it has become the last refuge of philosophy's own claim to truth against the universal menace of ideology. Philosophy now takes the form of 'aesthetic theory'. The unreliability of unfixed aesthetic phenomena is the only thing left to be relied on. The pivotal concept for such a change of roles is *"Schein"*, in the Hegelian sense. *"Schein"* means phenomenon, the appearance of something else, but it can also take the meaning of an autonomy of appearance which can no longer be identified as the phenomenon of something else, because there is nothing behind the appearance and different from it. Hegel called art the sensuous appearance (*sinnliches Scheinen*) of truth.[25] Adorno holds that there is no truth stated by philosophy and separated from its appearance in art. Rather, in the age of ideology, art is the only way for truth to make itself present.

I am not going to discuss the thesis of the *universal rule of ideology*. It contains a radicalization of Marx's statement concerning the ideological character of all philosophical theory isolated from economic conditions. However, this is, if anything, a theoretical statement and thus claims to be truth. *The Critique of Political Economy* is supposed to say what really is the case, but it is constantly dissimulated by the existing theories about reality. It is the fundamental dilemma of Marx's own theory, that in criticizing other forms of political economy, it establishes a new political economy or, in other words, it cannot help theorizing via negation of theory. Adorno's strong thesis that all theory has to give up the status of traditional theory, if it wants to fulfill the task of theory, draws the last conclusion. As astonishing as it may sound, the transition of philosophy into aesthetics answers a problem raised by the construction of Marx's theory. One could hardly have foreseen that Hegel's philosophy of art would serve as a maieutic for Adorno's Marxism.

In the theory of art there exist striking affinities between neo-Marxism and thinkers of quite a different school. *Hermeneutical philosophy*, too, distrusts the traditional type of theory, of which Hegel's system is the last example. It would be nothing but hubris to compete with the *Encyclopedia of Philosophical Sciences*, and it would be bad philosophy to imitate it. Instead, pure thought has to acknowledge its limits and the philosopher's main virtue now becomes modesty with regard to his own capacities of understanding. Philosophy can learn from aesthetic experience that conceptual thinking is not everything. Art reveals a truth of its own that has to be taken seriously by those who "want truth to be their special subject". Aesthetic experience can teach us how far-reaching the realm of truth is and how small the field covered by concepts and reflection is. There is much more to be understood than philosophical thinking in the traditional sense was able to control. Hermeneutic *'Verstehen'* suggests a wider and richer way of grasping truth.

Again, art is viewed with a quasi-Hegelian bias. Truth is its essence, therefore it comes closest to philosophy. The un-Hegelian switch in hermeneutic aesthetics consists in the change of supremacy. No longer is art a domain to be finally encompassed by philosophy. Art becomes the best school-master for philosophy, defining its task and preparing its solution. Hans-Georg Gadamer has expounded this point of view in his foundation of a philosophical hermeneutics, *Wahrheit und Methode* (1960).[26] It cannot be overlooked that apart from Hegel's influence on the formation of the philosophy of art, Heidegger's ontology was the main source for Gadamer. Martin Heidegger's famous article "Vom Wesen des Kunstwerks" (1950), turns to art as pointing the way to philosophy's task. The work of art has its essence in a sort of incorporation of the truth *(Ins-Werk-setzen der Wahrheit)*. Heidegger, to be sure, had no Hegelian concept in mind. Art is not considered as a preliminary and transitory form of truth whose perfection is to be found in philosophy. Throughout the different phases of his philosophizing, Heidegger chose Hegel as his main antipode. The self-consciousness of a philosophy which took itself to be the sublime perfection of all and every truth in the world seemed to imply for Heidegger the danger of making itself immune against original, unforeseeable and unrecoverable experiences. Art offers such an experience, the revelatory quality of which is likely to be destroyed if one tries to extract its substance and translate it into philosophical formulae. The appeal to art is a means to bring the awe of truth back to a philosophy which has become too conscious of itself.

Over against the latent anti-Hegelianism in Heidegger which like all opposition meant a kind of molding influence by the opponent in question, Gadamer developed Heidegger's suggestions in his Kunstwerk-paper on much more Hegelian lines. Art that is a paradigm of understanding becomes *ipso facto* a genuine object of philosophy. The hermeneutic effort of understanding covers both areas, aesthetics and thought. When Gadamer criticizes Kant's restriction of his analysis to the aesthetic reaction of the subject and supports the legitimacy of the search for knowledge and truth in art, he is in line with Hegel's arguments.

Let me mention, in this context, the interest which Hegel's philosophy in general and his aesthetics in particular has raised in recent French discussions. In the structuralist circles which at the beginning declared a radical epistemological break with existentialist dialectics à la Sartre or Merleau-Ponty, the name of Hegel has become prominent again. Perhaps in some cases, however, he is little more than a welcome new ingredient to the esoteric sauce of contemporary structuralism. A good example of the renewed reputation of Hegel is a more serious essay on Hegel's semiology by J. Derrida.[27]

Among those who are less interested in any absolute philosophical claim than in understanding *concrete phenomena of modern art,* a widespread argument has started from Hegel's provocative thesis on the end of art. After a century and a half of accelerated artistic evolution, of mostly adventurous but never regressive exploration into unknown land, one feels that Hegel's thesis is outdated, to say the least. Certainly, Hegel never doubted that actual art production would go on after the writing of his philosophy, so that the trivial argument of continued art production makes no real point. More fruitful is the question whether Hegel's judgment has anything to say about the structure of that art which was to come after the culmination of reflection. Hegel stated that the reflective power had infiltrated works of art, that it was about to explode their inner coherence, and that the autonomous process of reflection had by then superseded the truth present in art. What does this external diagnosis mean for the internal structure of the works?

In the last fifteen years or so, a lot of speculation has been centered around this question. As far as I can see, the most distinguished contribution comes from the pen of Dieter Henrich.[28] He stands the accepted view on its head and thinks he can find evidence in the text for an anticipation by Hegel of the art of the future. Although this interpretation sounds fascinating, it is, I am afraid, mistaken. Henrich mainly refers to a marginal note about 'objective humour' that can be found on the last pages of the *Lectures* on the romantic form of art. It seems as if this category, if one may call it that, has been added later to the corpus of the lectures that Hegel gave several times in the 1820's. As a matter of fact, in Hegel's published work the term 'objective humour' appears first in the Hamann-Review of 1828. It is conceived of as contrary to 'subjective humour' which represents the degenerated form of romantic dissolution and which Hegel finds in Jean Paul's novels. Objective humour can be exemplified by the poetry of Goethe's later years (*West-östlicher Divan*).[29] The term means a reconciliation with the objective content which the forms of romantic subjectivity had all too freely disposed of. Objective humour, therefore, creates a new balance between omnipotent reflection and the manifold of possible contents and historical forms at the latecomer's disposal.

It is impossible to neglect the fact that textually this is nothing more than one marginal note to which only a few lines out of hundreds of pages in three volumes are devoted. Besides the philological contingency of the term, its philosophical use has to be considered. Objective humour is the name for an art without a future, an irrelevant form which has lost all force or tension and can go on forever. The artist unrestrictedly playing around with content and historical figures is unable to create anything original; there is no historical hindrance to his continuing, but there is no philosophical value in it. The category of 'objective humour' is thus in complete harmony with the general verdict, and only helps to cover phenomena contemporary with Hegel. It seems far-fetched to read into such a simple category a full-fledged prophecy comparable, say, to the hopes so emphatically expressed by the old-Hegelian Weisse. He who looks in the corpus of Hegel's *Aesthetics* for analytical means to penetrate the structure of modern art, would do better to keep to the section dealing with the structure of romantic art. Here one finds more support in understanding the partiality, the lost unity and the integrated reflective element which for Henrich are typical of modernity.

It may not be out of place to add a more personal remark to a rather lengthy survey of the influence of Hegel's aesthetics. Every philosophy of art has to be written with actual art productions in view, otherwise it becomes empty speculation for speculation's sake. Aesthetics nowadays must be aware of contemporary art. The concepts we form must be applicable to the phenomena we see. Taking this postulate seriously, I have to doubt the relevance of Hegelian dialectics. The pillar of his aesthetics is the concept of truth. It is only because art shows some sort of truth that it becomes an apt subject for aesthetics understood as the philosophical science of art. Being a subject of aesthetics, therefore, means for Hegel being translatable into authentic philosophical ideas. However, the affinity of art and philosophy marked by the concept of truth seems to be the firmest barrier against an unprejudiced understanding of modern art. We saw how many different senses the respectable philosophical term "truth" can have. It can mean the pure idea dealt with in speculative logic as well as the socio-economic reality in the Marxist theory. It can mean a final convergence of life and reason in the vision of cabalistic eschatology as well as the deepest roots of traditional ontology which Heidegger wants to excavate. It can mean that which philosophy has not yet understood, is asked to understand or can only help to understand. The highly reputed concept of truth has unduly dominated the appreciation of art works. Aesthetics, thereby, falls prey to a philosophical heteronomy.

If one wants to do justice to the actual phenomena, one has to abstain from a priori idealizations through concepts. The approach which remains then available is through the original *aesthetic experience*. This clearly is the only reliable basis for analysis of the art with which we are now faced, an art which seems to have deliberately left behind all that 'art' used to be. Now, an aesthetic theory which systematically chose aesthetic experience as its starting point and took every pain to investigate what is logically involved in that experience, was worked out by Kant. I have elsewhere tried to show why it is Kant and not Hegel, who is the author to be more fruitfully exploited in the perspective of modern art.[30]

In fact, Hegel is the harshest critic of Kant's methodical restriction, thinking that the time was ripe to overcome the purely formal analysis of artistic judgment and to make art an authentic philosophical subject. This is one of the reasons why Hegel is generally supposed to be much more akin to the spirit of modernity. There is no denying that the setting of Kant's *Critique of Judgment* is stamped by the eighteenth century. To reread his aesthetics with the latest expressions of art in view cannot mean to attempt to identify some secret anticipation of aesthetic things to come. Kant's strength rather is a methodological one. He sharpened instruments of analysis which Hegel thought useless but which still can do a good job. So it turns out that a philosophical inquiry of modern art must take its path between two classical positions instead of following one. But to develop this point would be to begin another and more complicated story.

NOTES

1. For the whole tradition, see P.O. Kristeller "The Modern System of the Arts" *in Renaissance Thought* (New York: 1965).
2. See for example, Hume's essay "Of the Standard of Taste" (1757).
3. Cf. the comprehensive *Bibliographie zur Ästhetik Hegels, 1830-1965,* compiled by W. Henckmann, *Hegel-Studien,* 5, 1969.
4. A. Hofstadter sympathetically defends the Hegelian claim on truth in art in his "On Artistic Knowledge: A Study in Hegel's Philosophy of Art", *in*, F. Weiss, ed., *Beyond Epistemology: New Studies in the Philosophy of Hegel* (The Hague: Nijhoff, 1974).
5. Weisse, *System der Ästhetik als Wissenschaft von der Idee der Schönheit* (1830. Reprinted, Hildesheim, 1966.)
6. *Ibid.,* 304.
7. K. Rosenkranz, *Ästhetische und Poetische Mitteilungen*, (Magdeburg, 1827). E. g. page 10.
8. See his *Ästhetik oder Wissenschaft des Schönen* in several volumes beginning in 1846.
9. K. Marx, *Frühe Schriften*, I, (Lieber, ed.), 1962, p. 568. (Translated by Bottomore, London: 1963.)
10. Herbert Marcuse, *Counterrevolution and Revolt* (Boston, 1972) Chapter 3.
11. English translation by Nicolaus, (London: 1973).
12. English edition by Dobb, (Moscow: 1971).
13. Published in Berlin in 1911. (English translation, London: 1973.)
14. G.Lukács, *Werke,* Vol. 16, (Neuwied: Luchterhand Verlag, 1974).
15. First published in 1916. (English translation, *The Theory of the Novel,* London: 1971.)
16. Actually, it was part of a longer manuscript now available as *Heidelberger Ästhetik, Werke,* Vol. 17. (1974.)
17. English translation (London 1971).
18. Cf. the documents in F. Raddatz (ed.), *Marxisms und Literatur*, II, (Hamburg: 1969). Translations in Block et al, *Aesthetics and Politics* (London: 1977).
19. There has been a renaissance of this controversy in the 1950's. The arguments were more or less the same. Theodor Adorno in "Erpreßte Versöhnung" (from *Noten zur Literatur*, II,

Frankfurt: 1961) is now the opponent of Lukács (*Wider den missverstandenen Realismus*, Hamburg: 1958).

20. In Beck, ed., *Philosophische Hefte*, III, 3 and 4, 1932. Cf. *Theorie des geistigen Schaffens auf marxistischer Grundlage* (1934. Reprint, Frankfurt: Fischer, 1974).

21. *Die Eigenart des Ästhetischen, Werke*, Vol. 11-12 (Neuwied: 1963). See also *Über die Besonderheit als Kategorie der Ästhetik*. (First published in *Deutsche Zeitschrift für Philosophie*, 1956. Neuwied: 1967).

22. *Werke*, Vol. 7 (Frankfurt: 1970).

23. *Briefe* (G. Scholem & T. Adorno, eds.) Frankfurt: 1966. Cf. also G. Scholem, *W. Benjamin—Geschichte einer Freundschaft* (Frankfurt: 1975).

24. W. Benjamin, *Der Autor als Produzent; in Versuche über Brecht* (Frankfurt: 1966).

25. G. Gray, ed., *Hegel on Art, Religion, Philosophy* (New York: Harper, 1970), p. 30.

26. Abridged English translation: *Truth and Method* (New York: Scribners, 1975).

27. "Le puits et la pyramide" *in* J. D. Marges, *Introduction à la sémiologie de Hegel* (Paris: 1972).

28. "Kunst und Kunstphilosophie der Gegenwart, Überlegungen mit Rücksicht auf Hegel" *in* W. Iser (ed.) *Poetik und Hermeneutik*, II (Munich: Fink, 1966).

29. One may also think of *Faust II*, Goethe's last work which came out shortly after Hegel's death. (Cf. my essay "Hegel und Goethe", *Euphorion-Beiheft*, Heidelberg: Winter 1978)

30. R. Bubner, *"Über einige Bedingungen gegenwartiger Ästhetik"* in *Neue Hefte für Philosophie*, Vol. 5 (Göttingen: 1973).

III

Hegel On The Meanings Of Poetry*
by
GARY SHAPIRO

Since Socrates' attack on poetry, philosophers and critics have been faced with the problem of reconciling two convictions which seem equally pressing. While poetry (or imaginative literature) is and has been valued as a source of insight and knowledge, it also seems clear that poetic meaning is of a rather different sort than that found in science, ordinary language or (to introduce the classical contrast) prose. Philosophical theories of poetry, then, take one of two forms: either they deny one of these two beliefs, implying perhaps that poetry has only nonsensical or literal meaning, or else they provide a cognitive analysis of poetry which differentiates its meaning from that of prose. Hegel took the second alternative, maintaining both that poetry "has been and still is the most universal and widespread teacher of the human race" and that the logic or meaning of poetry is radically unprosaic. (HA, 972) Poetry's cognitive value, like that of philosophy, religion and the other forms of art, can be expressed most generally by saying that it is a form of absolute spirit in which knowledge is thorough self-knowledge; the mode or form of this knowledge is reason or dialectic as opposed to the rigid categories of the understanding. These formulas by themselves are not illuminating, being in Hegel's terms mere abstract universals; they take on concrete meaning only when we see them functioning in their capacity of actually explaining

* This paper was originally published in the journal *Philosophy and Rhetoric* (Vol. 8, No. 2, 1975) after it had been initially presented at the Georgetown Hegel Conference. The author is grateful to that journal for permission to reprint it in this volume. This version differs only in its use of quoted material from the recent Knox translation of *Hegel's Aesthethics: Lectures on Fine Art* (London: Oxford Univ. Press, 1975). Parenthesized numbers throughout this article are citations to that translation, hereafter HA.
Work on this paper was supported by Kansas University General Research Grant 3414-5038. I am grateful for that support and for helpful comments on an earlier version of this paper made by Albert Hofstadter, Rex Martin, and the reader for *Philosophy and Rhetoric*.

the essential forms, aspects, expressions and historical varieties of poetry.

What is interesting about Hegel's analysis of poetry, then, is his attempt to show that it is not only a form of knowledge, but a form which is quite distinct from that of prosaic thought. Both features follow from the claim that the content of poetic knowledge is dialectical, as is the content of all art, religion and philosophy for Hegel; all are concerned with comprehending the contradictions, movements, and resolutions of spirit (*Geist*) which is the fullest expression of dialectical activity. Hegel's conception of poetry could be approached simply within the context of his own system by following his exposition of the idea, means of expression, and realized varieties of poetry, or regressing further, by examining poetry's place among the arts or by considering the general notion of dialectic or spirit. While all of these aspects of Hegel's thought need to be understood in order to comprehend his theory of poetry, it may clarify things to see how his analysis handles a difficulty which has been encountered in the philosophical and critical analysis of poetic meaning. After suggesting the force of Hegel's analysis in this way I will examine it in some detail; and since the theory offers a cognitive defense of poetry by assimilating poetic to philosophical meaning, it will be necessary to raise some questions about the relationship of philosophy and poetry which pose difficulties for Hegel's account.

I

One might begin by questioning one or both of the claims mentioned earlier: that poetry is a form of knowledge and that it is to be clearly distinguished from a conventional or literalistic type of knowledge (traditionally called prose). Yet a denial of either runs against the firm convictions of most of those who have taken poetry at all seriously. A philosopher might very well hold a theory, like the positivist criterion of meaning, which had the consequence that poetry was either meaningless or had merely emotive meaning. But the conflict of such a theory with both common and uncommon sense concerning poetry would itself be a good reason for doubting it. It is, of course, conceivable that we might be led to give up either or both of these claims by some very convincing philosophical system or theory. In the absence of such a theory, however, what is needed is to understand what is already believed, following Anselm's example in regard to the existence of God.

There is a popular cognitive conception of poetry which sees the need for a non-prosaic analysis of poetic meaning. The conception is not only popular among critics and aestheticians, but can make some claim to being the dominant poetics of our time. It is general enough to be found among literary critics, analytic philosophers and existentialists who are otherwise of markedly diverse persuasions. Since it is an approach which Hegel was aware of and consciously rejected it offers us a point of access to his own thought about poetry. The conception I have in mind will be called the theory of implicit meaning. (This follows a suggestion by Monroe Beardsley, although the theory itself is a set of claims which cannot as a whole be attributed with ease to any specific person, although many share them in large part.[1]) The theory begins with the realization that poetry is meaningful rather than nonsensical although its deviation from science, semantically and syntactically correct language (or, pejoratively, "stenolanguage" or *"Gerede"* — idle chatter) is clearly seen. Poetic meaning is said to be implicit because it is suggested, referred to, or symbolized rather than being actually present in the literary work. Moreover the meanings in question are intrinsically and not accidentally implicit; they are not literal meanings which could be directly stated, for which poetic expressions would in that case simply be a code, but they remain implicit because of some special characteristic. The nature of this characteristic is variously understood in theories of metaphorical, symbolical, mythical and imagistic meaning. The central point of the theory from which these competing versions derive, however, is the insistence that the meaning in question is not and cannot be fully presented in the poem. In a theory of poetic ambiguity like William Empson's, for example, poetic significance is understood as the ability to suggest a wealth of possible meanings which are interrelated in a complex fashion. Such ambiguity cannot be explicit because it involves a continuum of possibilities which no actual linguistic structure can include or contain, and so it can only be evoked. When questions of poetic value arise it is natural that such theories find the higher forms of poetry to be those which not only maximize the element of implicit or suggested meaning but show an awareness of the tension between what is (or can be) actually said and what is evoked or symbolized. It is in this perspective that we can make some sense of Heidegger's puzzling claim that "in the familiar appearances, the poet calls the alien as that to which the invisible imparts itself in order to remain what it is — unknown."[2] Although those who are given to close analyses of the nature of metaphor or symbol might protest rather vigorously at being associated with apocalyptic utterances of this sort, the common element in the many theories of implicit meaning is precisely the insistence on a tension between the limited actuality of the poem and the indefinite possibility of the poetic meaning.

From Hegel's point of view, the difficulty with such a theory is not so much in working out the details of the analysis of implicit meaning, but with the assumption that such meaning is paradigmatically poetic. There is indeed a variety of poetry which can properly be called symbolical and the metaphor is a conscious comparison of an indefinite sort; yet these are the absolutely minimal forms of poetry and its language rather than its exemplars. The fact of poetic tension and symbolism derives on Hegel's account from the general conditions of art: it seeks to express a spiritual content within a sensuous form. Simply as art, poetry, whose imaginative medium is the finest attenuation of the sensory forms of the other arts, will exhibit a symbolical aspect. Symbolical poetry proper, however, is that which does not go beyond this sense of disparity or opposition.[3] In certain forms of religious poetry, for example, God is conceived as utterly sublime and unknowable and yet a wealth of specific things and properties of the world are mentioned simply in order to emphasize the contrast of the finite and the infinite. Metaphorical language is a conscious development of the same tendency to make meaning merely symbolical or implicit, although it generally reflects a more conscious artistry than the poetry of the sublime. A metaphor has both primary and secondary subjects which are juxtaposed in such a way as to create a novel spectrum of possible meanings which could not be expressed by a literal comparison. Such forms however testify to their own incompleteness, for they point to a fulfilled meaning which, by hypothesis, can never be made present. The symbolical or metaphorical poet, like the religious man of the unhappy consciousness, is acutely aware of the opposition between what he actually does and says and what he wants

to mean and enjoy; and while he may succeed in showing the limits of
the former he is prevented by his own methods from making the latter
manifest. The symbolic poet may also appear in the form of the oracle
whose utterances are deliberately vague and open to endless interpretation.

At this point it may seem as if Hegel's objections to the theory of
implicit meaning hold only for those varieties of it which agree with
him that poetry is intentional. Suppose, however, that one regards
such things as metaphors and symbols as simply part of the texture or
surface of a poem which can be recognized and understood without any
reference to the poet's intentions. Still, insofar as one holds that these
aspects of poetry are to be analyzed as implicit meanings, Hegel's
criticism applies equally; for it is not the meaning which is supposed
to be manifest here but simply the reference to it.

Hegel's own conception of poetry is based not on the minimal
characteristics of the art but on its realization in those works of the
imagination whose meaning is luminous and compelling. Along with
the advocates of implicit meaning he realizes that poetry is not propositional or prosaic. For Hegel, however, the poetic alternative to the
prose of the understanding is not an indefinite meaning or an ineffable
experience, but the speculative comprehension of the dialectical nature
of spirit. The tension which the theory of implicit meaning detects
between the actual and the possible in a poem is a kind of image of this
dialectic of spirit but one that turns out to be ultimately inadequate in
the same way that symbolism generally fails to fulfill its promise. It is
true that the symbolical or metaphorical tension itself must be exhibited or presented, rather than merely described, and to this extent
it is radically other than what can be communicated through prosaic
propositions. Yet there is a tendency to equate the non-propositional
with the ineffable or the non-conceptual in this account which Hegel
strongly resists. As in philosophy, the propositional form is inadequate
in poetry not because its content is available only through an esoteric
intuition of some sort, but on account of the spiritual content being
itself dialectical. Hegel's arguments against romantic intuitionism in
philosophy (as in the "Preface" to the *Phenomenology of Spirit*) find a
parallel in his characterization of symbolic poetry as an indefinite
groping toward an indefinite content.

II

The theory of implicit meaning requires us to suppose that poems have purposes or intentions, although some of its proponents are skeptical in various degrees about the possibility of discerning any such purposes which are not immanent and manifest in the text of the poem. Hegel's conception of poetry's dialectical meaning also depends upon noticing this purposive feature; but Hegel differs from the theory of implicit meaning in his claim that in the paradigmatic cases of poetry such purposes are actually fulfilled in the poem. As in his analyses of other phenomena of spirit, like history and religion, Hegel's interest is to show just *how* the purpose of the activity in question is fulfilled. Since the subject-matter (spirit) is dialectical, the study of the purpose and its realization will exhibit the tensions and contradictions which are appropriate to that particular form of activity. It is not that Hegel applies a "dialectical method" to a subject-matter in order to deduce its necessary characteristics; it is the subject-matter itself which has a dialectical character. In his *Encyclopedia* he emphasizes that dialectic is primarily a feature of the world:

> It is customary to treat Dialectic as an adventitious art, which for very wantonness introduces confusion and a mere semblance of contradiction into definite notions . . . But in its true and proper character, Dialectic is the very nature and essence of everything predicated by the mere understanding . . . by Dialectic is meant the indwelling tendency outwards by which the one-sidedness and limitation of the predicates of understanding is seen in its true light, and shown to be the negation of them.[4]

So far there may not appear to be any decisive difference between Hegel's conception and that of the theory of implicit meaning. For the latter insists, as does Hegel, on the *limited* character of the images, figures, and symbols actually presented in a poem, contrasting it with the many possible meanings which are implicitly referred to. Poetry of the symbolic type, which is paradigmatic for the theory of implicit meaning, could be viewed as a way of demonstrating the mere finitude of that which is finite. Now Hegel himself describes symbolic poetry in just this way. The difference between the two perspectives has to do with Hegel's analysis of *how* dialectical meanings are realized in poetry. Typically, Hegel analyzes spiritual activities in terms of three aspects:

the general idea or purpose, abstractly considered; the medium or means in which or by which the purpose is carried out; and the concrete or realized end of the activity. In understanding history as the development of freedom, for example, we must inquire into the general idea of freedom (rational conscious self-determination), the means by which freedom is actualized in the world (the passions and interests of human beings), and the end or realization of freedom (concrete ethical life having its goal in the state). The corresponding aspects of poetry are the idea of a comprehension of the dialectical nature of spirit, the medium and means of poetic expression, and the actual poetic genres (the epic, lyric, and drama).

The purpose or idea of poetry sets it apart from prose both because its object is explicitly taken to be spirit and because it comprehends this object through a dialectical transformation of the categories of the understanding. In this respect, poetry is simply one form of art which, along with religion and philosophy, are the three modes of spirit's knowledge of itself. A more definite notion of the idea of poetry in particular and of its medium emerges when poetry is located within the general context of art. According to Hegel, art is spirit's knowledge of itself in a sensuous form. Philosophy and religion are also modes of spiritual self-knowledge; while religion can dispense with sensuous representations (although it employs figures and myths), philosophy reaches its goal through the medium of thought itself without limitation by either sense or story. The various arts can be understood in terms of the relation in each between sensuous form and spiritual content: there is a progressive liberation from material and sensuous constraints in the series which begins with architecture and sculpture and passes through painting (the art of color) and music (the art of tone) to poetry which employs language simply as an external sign of the imaginative life of spirit. In contrast to all other arts "it expresses directly for spirit's apprehension the spirit itself with all its imaginative and artistic conceptions but without setting these out visibly and bodily for contemplation from the outside." (HA, 961) Poetry is an art in the process of dissolution, for its external and objective aspect is, paradoxically, "the inner imagination and intuition itself" (*das innere Vorstellen und Anschauen selbst*). (HA, 964) Hegel conceives of the imagination as thought in a concrete form or aspect: it is not the images of Plato's painters or the faculty of recalling or reproducing such images which is at stake here, but a creative power of thought which nevertheless retains some of the specificity and particularity of the sensuous world. The distinction is close to that which English critics, especially of the romantic period, have drawn between fancy and imagination, or the primary and secondary imagination. (HA,281) The poetic comprehension of the hero differs from the philosophical because it imagines him as Achilles or Oedipus, a man of a particular nationality, character, and individuality rather than analyzing in what heroism of this or that type consists. Poetry and speculative thought are alike in considering the hero dialectically, but it is only poetry which is constrained to do so imaginatively. Hegel's conception of poetry can be briefly characterized as imaginative dialectic, if we remember that imagination is not reducible to static images. It is a striking fact, for both Plato and Hegel, that poetry not only employs or conjures up such images but that they are often unnatural and even internally inconsistent or incongruously connected with one another from a naturalistic point of view; while Plato takes this as evidence for assimilating poetry to mere opinion and illusion, Hegel detects a power and structure in the play of images which is fundamentally analogous to the dialectical structure which philosophy finds in things generally. It is worth noting that it is imagination, not language, which is the medium of poetry. Language is simply a sign of the imaginative idea.

Accordingly Hegel claims that a great poem is in principle translatable not only from one language to another, but from verse to prose. (HA,964) Although many modern critics might dispute this, it seems to be empirically confirmed in addition to following from Hegel's views. Certainly it is less strange to suggest that a poem can be translated than to claim that a building or a painting could be translated into a different material medium or colors. Paradigmatic works of the literary imagination—Homer, Sophocles, Cervantes, Shakespeare—are translated and read in translation incessantly. Those aspects which seem to escape translation are either specific associations of the original language which have no equivalent in the translator's, or the effects of tone, metre, and rhythm. Yet to some extent these are not difficulties in principle, but only in practice; explanations or metaphors may elucidate a strange meaning where there is no single literal equivalent and foreign metres may be approximated by a skilled poet. Where the claim of untranslatability is most plausible—in respect to a short lyric poem—it is usually because we are concerned with a work which lies somewhere on the boundary of poetry and music.

As imaginative dialectic, poetry does what philosophy does but in a more immediate form. In the following contrast which Hegel draws between the comprehension of the dialectic of things in pure thought and in poetry, there are grounds for doubting that he takes philosophy to be capable of doing poetry's job better than poetry does:

> Thinking, however, results in thoughts alone; it evaporates the form of reality into the form of the pure Concept, and even if it grasps and apprehends real things in their particular character and real existence, it nevertheless lifts even this particular sphere into the element of the universal and ideal wherein alone thinking is at home with itself. Consequently, contrasted with the world of appearance, a new realm arises which is indeed the truth of reality, but this is a truth which is not made *manifest* again in the real world itself as its formative power and as its own soul. Thinking is only a reconciliation between reality and truth within thinking itself. But poetic creation and formation is a reconciliation in the form of a *real* phenomenon itself, even if the form be presented only spiritually. (HA, 976)

The realization of this imaginative dialectic occurs in the actual poems which carry out this program of overcoming the fixed oppositions of the understanding. The sequence of these forms is not so much chronological as logical; they form a series in which the purpose of poetry is actualized more and more fully. That is, they show a progressive overcoming of the usual categories of the understanding, in particular cause and effect and subject and object.

The epic is appropriately the simplest form of major poetry because its approach resembles the impersonal, spectatorial attitude of history. The epic poet seems to simply describe a world in his song as the naive historian or chronicler narrates a series of events. So far the usual distinction of subject and object is observed, but an analysis of the world and action of the epic discloses a different conception. The hero's career itself can be understood neither as a direct effect of the social world from which it arises nor, alternatively, as the cause of that world. Using the categories of the understanding we might view society as composed of independent units, externally related either by voluntary acts or contingent circumstances, or as a cultural unit whose holistic properties determine the characteristics of its members. The epic offers (at least in imagination) an alternative to these one-sided views. The hero emerges out of his world, and to that extent he is an expression of it; yet at the same time he is a distinctive individual with a remarkable character who undertakes unusual actions. Achilles is not simply a paradigm of what the Greek warrior should be, but in his demand for honor from Zeus and his consuming wrath his individuality transcends its origins. The world of the epic, in order to make such figures and actions possible, must itself be a poetic world. Socially, it is one in which loose relations of allegiance based mainly on personal quality and achievement have not yet been superseded by law and order. It is even poetic in its attitude toward objects of daily use; a division has not yet been made between the fine and the useful arts, so that a door, a tripod or a knife are as worthy of description as the battles of the heroes. Here Hegel uses "poetic" in his own systematic sense: it is a world which is not yet ruled by the prosaic categories of the understanding but is imaginatively conceived. The epic poet is a kind of primitive phenomenologist who observes the dialectical patterns of the heroic world. (HA, 1040-1110)

The lyric poem is an individual, subjective expression which lacks the compass of the epic; yet its imaginative structure is a variation on the same theme. The lyric attitude is that of a reflective mind which has withdrawn from a highly regularized external world, and now assimilates that world through the power of its own expression. The lyric itself involves a clash between this individual expression and the subject-matter (whose variety is infinite) which is to be assimilated. Here again the division is not a fixed one:

> It is mainly the pressure of this opposition which necessitates the swing and boldness of language and images, the apparent absence of rule in the structure and course of the poem, the digressions, gaps, sudden transitions, etc.; and the loftiness of the poet's genius is preserved by the mastery displayed in his continual ability to resolve this discord by perfect art and to produce a whole completely united in itself, which, by being *his* work, raises him above the greatness of his subject-matter.[5]

The burden of the lyric is the clash between "the compelling force of the subject-matter" and "the independent freedom of the poet"; since it occurs in the imagination it requires a feeling of shock or randomness in the texture of the poem itself. Not only does Hegel make no effort to deduce or justify the specific nature of this clash, it is a consequence of his theory that such characteristics are necessarily contingent. Hegel's theory is deductive here not in its attempt to determine concrete details but only in its insistence that it is part of the idea of the poem that there be striking features of it which present themselves as random, indeterminate or chaotic.

The drama is not only dialectical in its structure but represents a dialectical combination of the epic and the lyric. While it presents characters before us in their objectivity, like the epic, these characters have the self-expressive power of the lyric poet. The dialectical relationship between the individual and his world is roughly similar to that in the epic; but in this context the "world" is nothing but similarly situated individuals. In the drama subjective spirit arises out of a world, becomes individual, determinate, and constitutive of the world. In this process it can be said with equal justification that the subjective becomes objective and the objective becomes subjective. The dramatic careers of the various characters are what they are only through conflict, collision, and resolution; the appearance of self-subsistency is pushed to the extreme by the dramatic mode of presentation but dissolved or mediated in another perspective by the dramatic action. Insofar as a resolution or reconciliation is offered in the drama, it cannot have its source in the individual characters, but to accomplish this the drama itself "must display to us the vital working of a necessity, which, itself self-reposing, resolves every conflict and contradiction."[6] In dramatic poetry the metaphor finds one of its true artistic functions, for in modern drama (and Hegel is thinking of Shakespeare in particular here) the richly metaphorical speech of the characters does not point to an indefinite meaning but, as an action of their own, shows an ability to transcend and dissolve the objective situation, even at the height of danger or despair. Metaphor is poetic just to the extent that it is *aufgehoben*.

If we make a distinction between form and content in poetry, metaphoric tension or implicit meaning arises out of the formal contradiction which poetry exhibits between its imaginative medium and spirit, while the content of poetry has to do with spirit's contradictions with itself. The converse of Shakespearean drama, in which metaphorical form is transmuted into spiritual content, is that type of modern poetry in which the poet takes the poetic activity itself as a subject for metaphorical or symbolic exploration. As in Hölderlin's poetry, which Heidegger so admires, spiritual content becomes the vehicle of implicit meaning. Of course, poetry which is conscious of itself as poetry illustrates Hegel's own categories of analysis as well as providing a parallel to his conception of philosophy as the conscious knowledge of its own history. However, by inverting the relationship between form and content, romantic symbolism finds its appropriate theme in the prophetic anticipation of an unknown god, falling back into another variation of the unhappy consciousness.

By insisting on the dialectical nature of poetic meaning Hegel makes a cognitive defense of poetry which allies it with philosophy. The analogy between the two is not their shared deviation from tautology or empirical verifiability, as the positivists suggested, but their possession of a common object and mode of thought, each of which is highly articulated. One way of approaching this structure, which presents another contrast with the theory of implicit meaning, is to attend to Hegel's conception of organic unity. The first image in the *Phenomenology of Spirit* is that of the growing plant whose fruit is not the refutation but the truth of the stem and blossom; in his lectures on the fine arts Hegel insists that poetry also aims at organic unity. What must be noted here is that the notion of organic unity is not a mere metaphor for Hegel in either of these contexts, but is drawn from his analysis of life. As analyzed in the *Phenomenology,* for example, life is the entire process by which particular living forms attain independent status, contribute through reproduction or sustenance to the herd or tribe and then by their death reveal their partiality and testify to the strength of the whole. Organic unity, then, is not simple interrelation or harmony, but involves a conceptualizable dialectic of the one and the many which includes negativity, opposition, and contradiction. While critics and aestheticians sometimes interpret organic unity as if it were a seamless whole which could tolerate no contradiction, it is part of Hegel's conception that distinction, separation, and contingency are necessary aspects of a genuine organic unity. In this respect his approach is more responsive to poetic experience than is the dogmatic assertion that every poetic part must be necessary and make a difference to the whole. In each of the major genres of poetry it is even necessary that the poem contain contingent elements; the epic, for example, must generate a sense of facticity and inexhaustibility by focusing on a multitude of details which might very well have been otherwise. The theorists of implicit meaning often treat organic unity as an ideal by which critical evaluations are to be guided. Insofar as they have in mind the notion of the seamless whole, they falsify that aspect of poetic experience which corresponds to the disunities, death, and struggle which Hegel recognizes in his idea of life; and one wonders, in any case, how such a whole could be based on the irreducible tension involved in implicit meaning without appealing to something like Hegel's notion of infinity or totality.

For Hegel, poetry and philosophy are different modes in which consciousness recreates for itself the dialectical pattern which it finds in life (remembering that life has a specific meaning here). The point of the reference to the notion of life is not to endorse a vague conception of poetry as vivid or emotional, but to stress the fact that the way in which poetry does what the abstract understanding cannot do is by presenting the conceptualizable and the determinate—although in an imaginative form. Poetry does not simply reduplicate the tensions and resolutions of life, however; the poem is not simply a quasi-organic object, as it is in Kant's aesthetics. Poetry is the consciousness of life and its unity is not that of an abstract universal but of human action. Aristotle also had something like this in mind in defining poetry as the imitation of human life; for human life is a determinate subject-matter in which universal principles are true only for the most part, thus setting up certain irreducible contradictions between the ideal as such and its instantiation. If Hegel extends this Aristotelian thought he does so because of a metaphysical analysis which sees the dialectical relations of human life as paradigms rather than anomalies. His defense of poetry meets Socrates' critique by attempting to show that poetic knowledge is self-knowledge.

III

The problem with analogies is that they cut in more directions than is usually anticipated. As Hume observed, we attribute some form of rational design to the world only at the price of picturing the world's creator as a craftsman (or guild) of rather uncertain abilities. Since

Hegel defends the cognitive value of poetry by emphasizing its ties to philosophy, it can very well be asked whether he views philosophy itself as a form of poetry or if his own philosophy is simply an esoteric poem of some sort. Hostile critics have suggested that philosophy of the Hegelian type is *merely* poetry, meaning, apparently, that it is (at best) a lyrical expression of an individual perspective with no more general validity than a sonnet by Wordsworth or a *Howl* by Ginsberg. More sympathetic readers have suggested that the *Phenomenology of Spirit* in particular is an epic, drama, or *Bildungsroman* of the world-spirit, and that it offers insights into the history of human thought which are as profound and partial as those that we get from Shakespeare or Goethe.

Hegel himself clearly rejects such a view because of the distinction which he makes between the imaginative and the thinking comprehension of spirit's dialectic. All of the poetic genres are tied to the immediate and specific because they present dialectical ideas only in imaginative form. Neither the Hegelian system nor any of the particular works within it has the specific emotional unity of the reflective individual which characterizes the lyric. The breadth of the subject-matters, the changes of perspective, and the aim at a universality which transcends such limited perspectives as the lyric offers, suggests that the affinity might be rather with one of the more objective literary genres, the epic or drama.

Hegel does indeed consider the question whether the history of the world, as an action of spirit, could be the subject of an epic. Since many have credited Hegel with composing just such a work, it is worth quoting his rejection of this possibility:

> From this point of view the supreme action of the spirit may be world-history itself, and we might propose to work up this universal deed on the battlefield of the universal spirit into the absolute epic; the hero of such an epic would be the spirit of man, or humanity, which educates and lifts out of a dullness of consciousness into world-history; but precisely because of its universality this material could not be sufficiently individualized for art. For, in the first place, such an epic would lack from the start a fixed and specific background and world-situation in relation alike to locality and to morals, customs, etc. The one foundation that could be presupposed would be the universal world-spirit itself which cannot be visualized as a specific situation and which has the entire earth as its locality (HA, 1064).

In general, Hegel continues, an epic of the world-spirit presents two possibilities: the absolute idea which governs history could be personified, embodied in a specific human form, or presented only as the necessity underlying the actions of specific nations and world-historical figures. The first alternative is not feasible "owing to the infinity of this subject-matter, the vessel of art, always limited in size to contain specific individuality alone, would burst," while the second would collapse into "a series of particular figures appearing and disappearing in a purely external succession" because the world-spirit, unable to appear as an individual agent, would be relegated to a shadowy role behind the scenes. (HA, 1065)

Hegel's objection to an epic of the world-spirit is equally applicable to a dramatic version of the same story because here, too, the specific characters could not embody a universal content. Yet there does seem to be a strong dramatic strain in Hegel's philosophy, although commentators have disagreed as to whether it is essentially tragic or comic.[7] Usually the heart of this analogy is said to lie in the fact that drama raises up and examines an individual's career only to show his ultimate destruction simply because of his own finitude. In Hegel's view of comedy, in particular, the figure is one which falsely claims a universal importance and whose dissolution leaves the audience with a sense of the infinite power of spirit as opposed to all that which is finite. Now while this pattern is recognizable both in drama and in Hegel's philosophy itself, it manifests itself differently in the two modes of discourse. For the protagonists of drama are finite individuals, imaginatively conceived, while the actors in Hegel's philosophical "comedy" are the *ideas* of individuality as well as all the major attitudes which spirit can assume in a collective fashion. Comedy is the imaginative version of what is thought universally in dialectical philosophy. The very analogies employed here come from Hegel's own philosophical analysis of the drama in which the forms of poetry themselves play a role analogous to (yet distinguishable from) Falstaff or Moliére's misanthrope.

Even if these poetic interpretations of Hegel's philosophy are inconsistent, both in principle and in detail, with his own conception of philosophy, they suggest a criticism of Hegel's system which could be expressed in another way. The point of adopting a poetic view of a philosopher's work may be either to disparage what bills itself as high metaphysics as mere poetry, whose meaning is alleged to be emotive only, or to salvage the cognitive value of a system whose universal and literal truth we feel impelled to deny. The first approach is one which begs the question as to the relationship between philosophy and poetry; it represents, from Hegel's point of view, the dichotomous thought of the understanding which is unable to comprehend dialectic, whether in imaginative or purely speculative form except by noticing the bare feelings which accompany them. The second approach is more charitable but inconsistent with Hegel's view of philosophy. For in this context the object of comparing a philosophical with a poetic work is to suggest that it is one perspective among several, a story told in one way which is to be complemented by stories with a different imaginative coloring. The cognitive significance and value of the story is preserved insofar as it is taken to suggest an actual pattern or order which does obtain, even if it also attempts to include material which is properly extraneous or makes an exaggerated claim to be the exclusive version of the truth.

Hegel does take up an attitude of this sort to his philosophical predecessors, but he holds it to be an inadequate description of his own standpoint of absolute knowledge. Even if the way to truth necessarily involves the sympathetic comprehension of error, truth is one and error is manifold. At the end of his *Encyclopedia* Hegel makes this claim explicitly in considering the relationship of art and philosophy: "Whereas the vision-method of Art . . . shivers the substantial content into many separate shapes . . . Philosophy not merely keeps them together to make a totality, but even unifies them into the simple spiritual vision, and in that raises them to self-conscious thought."[8] The basis of the contrast here is Hegel's logic of determinacy. Spirit, in its teleological drive towards self-knowledge, knows itself at first only vaguely and indeterminately. Symbolic art is the poorest of artistic phases just because it involves a juxtaposition of abstract material forms, like the Egyptian pyramids, with a spiritual content which is merely indicated rather than manifested; it is not only that spirit in this stage of art is indeterminate in its substance, but that its connection with its external embodiment is subject to the radical indeterminateness which infects all reference of the pointing or indexical variety. As we have seen, Hegel argues that it is the purpose of poetry to overcome such indeterminateness and that this purpose does realize itself, at least within certain limitations. Philosophical knowledge, which dispenses with the imaginative and figurative limitations of art and religion accomplishes the transition from the indeterminate to the determinate in the realm of thought in an apparently unrestricted fashion. The thoughts of Being and Nothing, with which Hegel begins his *Logic,* are as abstract and indeterminate as thoughts can be; an analysis of their deficiencies and contradictions eventually leads to the concrete and determinate Absolute Idea. Spirit exhibits a similar process, traced in the *Phenomenology,* in its development from undifferentiated subjective feeling to philosophical self-knowledge. In all such movements it is the dialectical contradictions of the subject-matter which produce negations which are themselves determinations. Hegel always derides the interest in the possible (the "merely possible") for its indifference to attained actuality, whether in art or political life.

The logic of determinacy which governs Hegel's thought is in most cases presupposed; it is simply the form of the transition from a purpose or intention which is apprehended and adopted vaguely to the concrete realization of that purpose or intention. In any such teleological activity possibilities seem abundant at the beginning but are gradually narrowed down as irreversible decisions are made and we acquire a more determinate knowledge of our own purpose which has itself become more determinate. In the last chapter of the *Science of Logic* Hegel discusses the process of determination more specifically. The absolute method, that is, his method of philosophical exposition, is said to be both analytic because it is attuned to the structure of things themselves and synthetic because it observes the subject-matter as tending to become other than itself. This analytic and synthetic moment of the judgment, "by which the universal of the beginning of its own accord determines itself as the *other of itself* is to be named the dialectical method."[9] The progress of the method is from the bare or empty universal beginning to the more determinate conclusion. Although the method reveals that even the beginning is not wholly or completely indeterminate (e.g. being, essence, and universality are determinately distinct forms of indeterminate beginnings) the movement which it traces is from the less to the more determinate, pursuing one determinate result on the basis of those already attained: "First of all, this advance is determined as beginning from simple determinatenesses, the succeeding ones becoming ever *richer and more con-*

crete."[10] Hegel seems to deny in the case of the determinate and indeterminate (as he does explictly in the case of the mediate and immediate) that there is anything at all which is solely one or the other. But the whole progress of his system requires that in all important or significant respects that which is always tends toward greater determinateness.

The theory of implicit meaning, although not elaborated with specific reference to Hegel, challenges this logic of determinacy insofar as it applies to poetry. It claims that ambiguity, metaphor and symbolism are the heart of poetry just because they are surrounded by a halo consisting of an indefinite variety of possible meanings and interpretations. At this point the theory converges with a similar critique, this time explicitly addressed to Hegel, which bears on his conception of philosophical meaning and communication. Much of Kierkegaard's attack on Hegel, repeated with variations by Sartre and Heidegger, is based on the claim that Hegel supposes an impossibly determinate relationship, amounting to identity, between himself and his readers. According to this critique, a discursive communication, whether poetical or philosophical must exhibit a certain amount of indeterminateness simply in order to engage its readers. Since the reader as an actually existing person lives by continually projecting possibilities of action and understanding, communication is defeated by the assumption that he can coincide with the author in a determinate "we" which excludes further possibilities of interpretation. Such a completely determinate communication would mean the end of the reader's existence. What is required for philosophical communication, then, is an analogue of Socratic dialectic or Platonic dialogue which preserves the reader's possibilities and allows him to generate "fresh words" in his own soul. The existentialist critique of Hegel aims at demonstrating that in neglecting the Socratic problem of the written word he did not take a sufficiently dialectical attitude toward his own dialectic. Taking this line of criticism together with the previous one, they converge in the claim that the distinction between determinate and indeterminate meaning does not lead to an adequate account of the difference between poetic and philosophical discourse.

To the extent that Hegel is committed to a logic of determinateness, he sees the metaphorical character of poetry as a necessary defect and the philosophical appeal to possibility as a failure to achieve wisdom

which shrouds itself in a mystery. The scorn which Hegel addresses to
the appeal to the merely possible in the moral life has its counterpart
here in his theory of discourse. In both areas it answers to a common
and substantial intuitive preference for the articulate and developed as
opposed to the incomplete and fragmentary. Nevertheless, the contrast
between the concretely actual and the vaguely possible seems undialec-
tical in its dualism. It appears to rest on the assumption that the
determinate (or actual) and the indeterminate (or possible) are in-
versely related. Yet this seems to be one of those principles of the
understanding which Hegel was so skillful at dissolving by an appeal
to experience and dialectic. One who has a determinate situation in life
and actual talents or skills certainly has more genuine possibilities of
action than the man who refrains from any definite undertaking so as
to remain free for all possibilities. In general, the actual must arise out
of some set of possibilities, but once actual, it offers a new set of
possibilities.[11] The principle is operative in both poetic and
philosophical discourse. It is the complex and highly structured work,
whether Shakespeare's plays or Hegel's *Phenomenology*, which is typically the ground of many interpretations. Here there is an observable
reciprocity of the possible and the actual, for interpretation is a development of possibilities ingredient in the actual structure of a work.
There is something puzzling about Hegel's failure to discern the
dialectical relationship of the actual and the possible; if he had, the
result might have been a recognition of the pluralism inherent in
philosophical as well as poetic discourse. The germ of truth in the
poetic interpretations of Hegel's philosophy, then, is the reintroduc-
tion of indeterminateness into a system which seeks to exclude it by
comprehending it. Either in regard to poetry or philosophy, however,
the alternative to the priority of the actual need not be the priority of
the possible, as the theorists of implicit meaning and the existentialists
have supposed. To return to the question of poetic meaning, it should
be possible to account both for the dialectic of spirit which Hegel
recognizes in great poetry as well as those holistic patterns of metaphor
and image to which modern criticism has drawn our attention. Fire in
the *Iliad*, sight and blindness in *Oedipus,* or the storms in Shakespeare's
plays tend to be neglected in Hegel's account of these poems just
because of his unidirectional logic of determinateness. If modern critics have tended to give brilliant but one-sided account of such

metaphors which omit the dialectic of spirit, Hegel sees the dialectic but omits the implicit dimension of the poem. What is needed is an analysis of poetic meaning which does some justice to the relations of the actual and the possible or of spiritual meaning and metaphorical tension.

NOTES

1. For Beardsley's version of the theory see his *Aesthetics* (New York: Harcourt Brace & World, 1958), 114ff. Others who subscribe to the theory in one form or another are Philip Wheelwright and Max Black in their theories of metaphor, William Empson in his study of ambiguity, and Martin Heidegger in his conception of the poetic image (cited below).
2. Martin Heidegger, ". . . Poetically man dwells" in *Poetry, Language, Thought* (tr, A. Hofstadter)(New York: Harper & Row, 1971), 225.
3. Hegel discusses several forms of symbolic poetry in his *Lectures*. See especially pp. 378-420.
4. *Encyclopedia* §81, Wallace translation.
5. P. 1142. For Hegel's analysis of the lyric see 1111-1157.
6. *Ibid.*, 1163. For the drama see 1158-1237.
7. Josiah Royce suggests an analogy of the *Phenomenology* with *Faust* in his *Lectures on Modern Idealism* (Lecture VIII), (New Haven: Yale Univ. Press, 1919). Walter Kaufmann disagrees in detail but offers his own version of the analogy in his *Hegel: A Reinterpretation* (New York: Doubleday, 1965) 115ff. Jacob Loewenberg argues that the *Phenomenology* and Hegel's system as a whole can best be construed as a comedy in his Introduction to *Hegel: Selections* (New York: Scribners', 1929).
8. *Encyclopedia* §572, Wallace-Miller translation.
9. A. V. Miller, tr., *Hegel's Science of Logic* (New York: Humanities Press, 1969), 831.
10. *Ibid.*, 840.
11. Justus Buchler defends an interesting version of such a theory of possibility and actuality, but without specific reference to Hegel in his *Metaphysics of Natural Complexes* (New York: Columbia Univ. Press, 1966).

COMMENT

ROBERT L. PERKINS

At the very beginning of modern philosophy, poetry was put in its place by Descartes. Though he admitted that "poetry has enchanted delicacy and sweetness" it is "rather a gift of nature rather than a fruit of study." He admits that style, color and expression belong to poetry, but he denies any truth claim whatsoever to poetry.[12] The last stand of such a view was in A. J. Ayer's *Language, Truth and Logic*. The practitioners of poetry responded in numerous ways to this charge, but the response seems always to be a defensive statement, i.e., fighting over the issues marked out in scientific philosophy. This was all too apparent in the New Criticism. Allen Tate's essay "Literature as Knowledge" is an attempt to formulate an argument to prove that the knowledge-claims of literature are superior to those of science, industrialism (and economics) and technology.[13] The whole discipline of letters has been undercut as an order of society, and Tate and the other representatives of the New Criticism attempted to restore the literary order of culture. Of course, neither Tate nor the other pundits of the New Criticism were able to restore the literary order, whatever that is, and so the literary enterprise is required to show its credentials. Some feel that it is without credentials, unnecessary and unwarranted. Professor Walter Darring of the University of South Alabama vividly demonstrated the alienation of poetry and modern industrial society when he ran a satirical advertisement in the local press in which he offered to write a laudatory sonnet or ode for the reasonable fee of $10.00. The obvious irony he intended was reduplicated *(sic)* when (with an irony worthy of Kierkegaard) the only person to pay Professor Darring $10.00 for a sonnet was a professor of literary criticism. Though in no sympathy with the position, Hannah Arendt apprehended that the case against poetry was but a particular application of the attack on ordinary human meanings. She wrote:

> If we would follow the advice so frequently urged upon us, to adjust our cultural attitudes to the present status of scientific achievement, we would in all earnest adopt a way of life in which speech is no longer meaningful, for the sciences have been forced to adopt a 'language' of mathematical symbols which, though it was originally meant only as an abbreviation for spoken statement (meaning written as well), now contains statements that can in no way be translated back into speech.[14]

In this controversy Hegel is on the side of the poets and is as opposed as Tate to the reduction of all meaning to a narrow, abstract and positivistic order. For Hegel, what

55

is pictured by the arts is the truth. There is a "cognitive" claim in the arts and Professor Shapiro, Hegel, the New Criticism, and others, all appear to be in agreement on the matter.

However, there is another direction of recent criticism which appears to empty entirely poetry of meaning. What I refer to is the effort to show, as Mr. MacLeish stated in his poem "Ars Poetica" that "A poem should not mean, but be." The situation in recent criticism was such that the critics attempted to study and understand literature purely and simply as literature, and they were indeed all too successful in this effort. If one separates literature from every other form of discourse and meaning, it is entirely possible that literature is then reduced to silence. The effort in literary circles to discuss literature simply as literature resulted in the conclusion that if criticism is only a secondary literature about a primary literature which has little or no relevance to other worlds and realms of discourse and meaning, then both literature and criticism are a harmless indoor sport of otherwise relatively normal human beings. Poetry and criticism then is an activity of a closed society of elitists. This view is reinforced by the attitudes toward language held by some of the architects of recent criticism. For instance, Professor Blackmur argues:

> Words, and their intimate arrangements, must be the ultimate as well as the immediate source of every effect in the written or spoken arts. Words bring meaning to birth and themselves contained the meaning as an imminent possibility before the pangs of junction. To the individual artist the use of words is an adventure in discovery; the imagination is heuristic among the words it manipulates. The reality you labour desperately or luckily to put into your words . . . you will actually have found there, deeply ready and innately formed to give an objective being and specific idiom to what you knew and did not know that you knew.[15]

This strong emphasis upon the power of poetic language and the medium of the genre suggests that again poetry is separated and uninfluenced by, and has no influence upon, the meaning of the ordinary world in which poetry occurs. Such a view is reminiscent of the more obvious relegation of the ordinary world to boredom and stupidity by the earlier romantics.[16] But be all that as it may, we can now envision somewhat the impasse of modern criticism because one line of development argues that poetry does have a meaning, indeed, a meaning superior to any of the other meanings of our time, and on the other hand, another element of criticism attempts to demonstrate that literary canons and judgments are irrelevant to anything else, or uninfluenced by anything else. On this score Hegel would be opposed to the self-centeredness and supposed autonomy of the literary tradition. Thus Shapiro is on the main track when he attacks the problem of the logic of poetry in Hegel's aesthetic. There are, however, certain difficulties. His effort to interpret Hegel's view of the cognitive value of poetry by contrasting it with what he calls the implicit theory of meaning is suggestive but puzzling. His contrast leads him to some extravagant claims for poetry in Hegel's view of knowledge. Shapiro has indeed grasped the dialectical nature of the arts generally, and poetry in particular, but he confuses the place of poetry in the total system of philosophic truth.

One must question the meaning of the claim of the proponents of implicit meaning (hereafter, the proponents) that "The meaning in question is not and cannot be fully represented in the poem." Moreover, "the meanings in question are intrinsically and not accidentally implicit. . . ." The meaning "cannot be explicit because it involves a continuum of possibilities which no actual linguistic structure can include or contain, and so it can only be evoked." One wonders whether this is indeed the case, i.e., whether the proponents would claim that *"no* actual linguistic structure" is capable of setting forth the putative meaning. If so, they also mean that not only is poetry condemned to ambiguity, but so is every other form of linguistic structure that attempts to state the same meaning. This may lead one to conclude that we should let esoteric poets and some queer philosophers worry about these obscure meanings, but that sensible men should say only what can be said clearly and let the remainder be unsaid. Thus my first point is that Professor Shapiro has compelled us to examine again whether poetry is a cognitive discipline. For these proponents, if there is a cognitive meaning, it is only an evoked, suggested cognitivity, not an explicit or inferred one. An aesthetic theory that set out to defend the cognitive rights of poetry could lead to its dismissal as a cognitive medium. We will leave unexamined the question, "What is an evoked cognitivity"?

There is a further implication of Professor Shapiro's interpretation of the theory of implicit meaning. If *"no* actual linguistic structure" can include and contain a certain set of meanings, either the theory of implicit meaning or Professor Shapiro (or perhaps both) condemn Hegel's philosophy to incompleteness. If that universal statement stands, then Hegel's claim to philosophical completeness, ("The truth is the whole") is patently false, i.e., some forms of meaning have escaped his system. This inference is no doubt an easy one for the proponents and Shapiro, but it is a difficult one for Hegel and Hegelians.

I would like to expand a little a facet of Hegel's aesthetics that Professor Shapiro mentioned that indicates that Hegel was quite aware of the implicit nature of at least some poetry. I refer to Hegel's brief treatment of metaphor and simile.[17] Such figures Hegel approves because they cause us to re-feel or re-evaluate our experience. A metaphor assigns a meaning to things which they do not have before the metaphor is used. By constant use metaphors may become hackneyed; they may become assimilated into the ordinary language and so lose their poetic effectiveness. These observations are not too subtle, but they do indicate that Hegel was aware of the implicit nature of some poetry. At least to this point, Hegel and the proponents of the implicit theory of poetic meaning are in agreement.

There is another note that could be struck to show that Hegel and the proponents are in agreement. Hegel cautions the poet that words may designate more than one thing. *Aufheben* is a good example. Then too, every person has his own set of images for the expressions he uses. Such variations, which are sometimes local or regional, must be known to the poet. (The use of the word "Yankee" in Boston, Atlanta or Rio would serve as a not very poetic example.) According to Hegel, poets have attempted to control the elusiveness of words by means of sentence structure, versification and rhythm.[18]

These two facts show that Hegel was aware of the implicit view of some poetry and that this awareness penetrates into his own aesthetics. But there is another way to approach the problem of the implicit meaning of art in Hegel. *Let me suggest that Hegel's own aesthetics is an aesthetics of the implicit meaning of art.*

Art for Hegel has as its purpose the disclosure of truth. The vital question is, does it disclose truth as knowledge? "No" must be the answer.[19] Let me explain.

The purpose of all art is to represent spirit in some sensible form.[20] Shapiro has certainly grasped this. The making of an art object is the act of the spirit and it is an externalization of spirit itself. The art object for Hegel has as its content the externalization of spirit itself. The art object for Hegel has as its content the externalization of spirit (formal cause) at the hands of spirit (efficient cause) in some medium (material cause) in order that the spirit can be intuited and felt in its sensible appearances (final cause). The sensible showing of the idea is the beautiful. (W, XII, 160; XIII, 144, 149) In the fine arts the sensible form and the ideal content coalesce and ideal beauty results. This absolute correspondence between the ideal content and the sensuous form occurs only in classical art where art reaches its highest perfection. (W, XII, 117) The work of art has, according to Hegel, the truth as its object although this truth appears only through the intuition and for the feelings. (W, XII, 89, 123) These sayings of Hegel are explicitly contrasted with sayings that indicate that truth itself is conceptual and that the absolute idea has its foundation and meaning in concepts. (W, XII, 135) The highest truths can be attained only through the resolution of the greatest contradictions and contrasts. (W, XII, 146, 88f) Finally, we must affirm with Hegel, that truth can be comprehended, i.e., cognized only by philosophy. (W, XII, 146) It is not possible for art, even poetry, to *know* spirit, for art can perceive it only in sensuous form, and "absolute truth achieves its *appearance* as the beautiful."[21] The appearance is of course essential to the essence, for truth could not be, if it did not appear. (W, XII, 28) Yet sensibility which is the domain of art in absolute spirit, is not knowledge of the absolute as such; it is only the appearance of the absolute, not knowledge of the absolute.[22] Thus the claim to explicit or literal cognitivity in poetry is rejected by Hegel.

Each of the above sentences is a translation of a sentence from the *Lectures* and each goes counter to Shapiro's claim that "Poetry's cognitive value, like that of philosophy, religion, and the extra forms of art, can be expressed most generally by saying that it is a form of absolute spirit in which knowledge is through self-knowledge: the mode or form of this knowledge is reason or dialectic as opposed to the rigid categories of the understanding." In poetry, there is no knowledge in any literal sense for Hegel; there is an appearance or show. The dialectic of poetry is imaginative as Shapiro argues; it is not rational in the sense that philosophy is a rational dialectic. The rationality of the dialectic of poetry is not known to poetry; it is known, i.e., explicit only to philosophy. Yet as the above paraphrases show, poetry's claim is not, and in Hegel's logic of poetry cannot, be as high as knowledge. It is rather only an appearance, a show. Thus Shapiro's claim that poetry is a mode of knowledge of the absolute is incorrect. Shapiro's emphasis upon the implicit theory of poetic meaning is indeed suggestive, but it spreads over all of the arts as discussed in Hegel's aesthetics. The view of the implicit nature of poetry and the arts which I am asserting is entirely different from that of Shapiro and the proponents, for it makes sense of the structure of absolute knowledge in Hegel's philosophy.

There is another aspect of Shapiro's paper which raises more questions than it answers. Beginning on the first page and running throughout there is a sustained critique of the understanding. Shapiro suggests in the quotation already referred to that (1) "poetry . . . is a form of absolute spirit in which knowledge is through self-knowledge; the mode or form of this knowledge is reason or dialectic as opposed to the rigid categories of the understanding." (2) Later he adds, "For Hegel, however, the poetic alternative to the prose of the understanding is not an indefinite meaning or an ineffable experience, but the speculative comprehension of the dialectical nature of spirit." (3) More pointedly he asserts, "The purpose of the idea of poetry sets it apart from prose both because its object is explicitly taken to be spirit and because it comprehends this object through a dialectical transformation of the categories of the understanding." (4) The most striking claim is that "The realization of this imaginative dialectic occurs in actual poems which carry out this program of overcoming the fixed oppositions of the understanding." The notion of the understanding running through these quotations is quite different from that which we find in Hegel. In all four quotations we find poetry contrasted with the understanding.

For Hegel the understanding and the sensible elements of experience, among which must be named the arts, stand in contrast to the speculative idea. In the *Lectures on the Philosophy of Religion* Hegel writes that the speculative idea of God is *"dem Sinnlichen entgegengesetzt, auch dem Verstande: sie ist daher ein Geheimnis für die sinnlich Betrachtungsweise und auch für den Verstand."* (W, XVI, 233) At least in this one place Hegel couples the sensibilities, the perceptible *(die Sinnliche),* of which one instance is the arts, with the understanding and declared that for both the speculative idea of God is a secret. For Hegel, both the perceptible in the arts and the categories of the understanding are excluded from the speculative idea. In this text, the arts in general and poetry in particular do not have an advantage on the understanding, but Shapiro is incorrect to think they ever have such an advantage in Hegel's philosophy.

In the second quotation just adduced Shapiro says that the "poetic alternative to

the prose of the understanding . . . is the speculative comprehension of the dialectical nature of spirit." To be sure, the alternative to the understanding is dialectic, but
the adjective "poetic" throws the whole thing off. Poetry just does not have the
capacity to overturn a category of the understanding in Hegel's philosophy. To be
sure, poetry and the understanding are two different categories in Hegel, even
antithetical ones, but poetry whose dialectic is of the intuitive has no power over the
understanding which is explicit knowledge of the particular. Hegel criticizes Kant's
"*intuitiver Verstand*" in his *Aesthetics,* but this is only a sidelight of his notion of the
understanding in his total philosophy. (W, XII, 91) There are brief references in each
of the volumes of the *Aesthetics* to the understanding, but nowhere does Hegel
suggest that there is a poetic alternative to it.[23]

Regarding the third quotation, it is not necessary in this context to summarize
Hegel's arguments to show his whole notion of the understanding as knowledge and
that the only instrument of knowledge which can overcome its limitations is rational
dialectic. However, it must be noted here, that Shapiro moved from the dialectical
nature of art, which he clearly understands, to suggest that because art is dialectical,
it can overcome the understanding. It is not art that overcomes the understanding,
though the understanding is frequently the antagonist in art (as in music criticism).
It is not religion that overcomes, though the understanding is frequently the antagonist in religion (as in deism). It is the speculative idea through dialectic that
overcomes the understanding. The understanding is overcome only when philosophy
emerges from the limited perspectives of art and religion.

Regarding the fourth quotation, Shapiro claims that the poet has a program and a
very philosophic program at that, to overcome "the fixed oppositions of the understanding." An examination of the context, however, shows that Shapiro is all too
modest. Hegel is also very critical of man's ordinary consciousness. The context also
shows that Hegel claims that speculative thought, not poetry, effaces the defects of
the understanding and ordinary consciousness. In all the texts Shapiro refers to,
understanding actually means common sense or ordinary healthy platitudinous
understanding of the world, not the philosophical categories of the understanding.

If one wishes to maintain a cognitive theory of literature as Shapiro does and
claims Hegel does, the question that must arise is how is poetry cognitive? Some
poetry, such as the greatest allegory, Dante's *Divine Comedy,* is obviously *not* cognitive in any literal sense of cognitivity but only implicitly cognitive in a loose possible
sense of cognitivity. Wallace Steven's "The Emperor of Ice Cream" is cognitive, if
Shapiro still wishes to insist on his thesis only in a non-sensical, evocative and
probably meaningless sense of "cognitivity." If I may assume that a cognitive statement is true or false, how is a plot of a novel cognitive? How can a character in a
novel be cognitive? Anyone who seriously sets forth a cognitive claim to literature
generally or poetry in particular has assumed a heavy burden of proof. Shapiro may
be willing to assume such a burden, but I think Hegel refused it and his refusal is
inherent in the nature of his system.

Turning to the third and last section of the paper, Shapiro attempts to assimilate what he takes to be the existential critique of Hegel to the implicit theory of meaning. The difficulty is first of all in what Shapiro takes to be the commonality of Kierkegaard, Sartre and Heidegger. Shapiro claims first of all that these three claim that "Hegel supposes an impossibly determinate relationship, amounting to identity, between himself and his readers." Perhaps the major note that will hold these three together in a common front against Hegel is their concern for the individual and the dialectics of communication. It is the latter which concerns Shapiro, and I agree with most of what he says. However, his claim that "According to this critique, a discursive communication, whether poetical or philosophical, must exhibit a certain amount of indeterminatives simply in order to engage its readers" seems to be a misapplied emphasis or at least, in the context of Shapiro's excellent analysis of possibility, a very unfortunate sentence. The indeterminateness in the writings of Kierkegaard is there not merely "to engage the reader" or to sell books, but because its presence testifies to the truth of the human situation. Existence is indeterminate and a literature or philosophy that would show or explicate the truth about existing must have possibility as a major category.

NOTES

12. Descartes, *Discourse on Method*, (tr. L. J. Lafleur)(New York: Liberal Arts Press, 1950), 4-6.
13. Allen Tate, *Collected Essays* (Denver: Alan Swallow, 1959), 16-48.
14. Hannah Arendt, *The Human Condition* (Chicago: Univ. of Chicago Press, 1958) 3-4. This and the above references were called to my attention by Prof. Lloyd A. Dendinger of the University of South Alabama. See also Lewis P. Simpson, "The Southern Writer and the Great Literary Succession," (*The Georgia Review,* XXIV, 410-412).
15. Nathan A. Scott, ed., *The New Orpheus* (New York: Sheed & Ward, 1964). Cited on page 148. This aesthetic appears to be an attempt to make a virtue of the necessities to which the philosophic tradition from Descartes to Ayer reduced poetry.
16. Robert L. Perkins, "Hegel and Kierkegaard: Two Critics of Romantic Irony" (*Review of National Literatures,* I, 232-254).
17. See Jack Kaminsky, *Hegel on Art* (New York: State Univ. of New York Press, 1962) 137ff.
18. Hegel, *The Philosophy of Fine Art,* (tr. F.P.B. Osmaston) (London: G. Bell & Sons, Ltd., 1920) Vol. IV, 72. *Werke,* XIV, 291 Glockner edition. Parenthesized numbers in the text hereafter are citations to volume and page of that German edition.
19. To all appearances, this opinion flies in the face of all received opinion on the subject. See also Albert Hofstadter, "On Artistic Knowledge: A Study in Hegel's Philosophy of Art," *in* F. G. Weiss's *Beyond Epistemology* (The Hague: M. Nijhoff, 1974) 58ff.
20. For an excellent and extended treatment of these themes, see Albert Hofstadter, "Art: Death and Transfiguration," (*Review of National Literatures,* Vol. I, 149-164; especially, 153).
21. *Werke,* XIII, 149. Italics added.

22. *Werke*, XIII, 17; XII, 20, 22, 110f. In art the spirit appears not as an actual concept, but only as an appearance or representation *(Darstellung)*.

23. During the oral discussion of the reply, Professor Shapiro read some passages from Osmaston's translation to support his arguments against the understanding. My disagreement with him is summarized simply by saying that an "imaginative grasp of the truth, a form of knowledge" (Osmaston translation Vol. IV, p. 22) is not a good translation for *"Sie ist das ursprüngliche Vorstellen des Wahren, ein Wissen, welches das Allgemeine noch nicht von seiner lebendigen Existenz im Einzelnen trennt . . ."* (*Werke*, XIV, 239). There is no "grasp" of the truth in the German text, and neither a thoughtful knowledge in any literal Hegelian sense as the rest of the sentence in German shows. The first sentence on page 24 of the Osmaston edition is a mistranslation of the second sentence on p. 241 (*Werke*, XIV). This in no way refers to "the limited categories of science or the Understanding." What is said in Osmaston's translation against the understanding and science is actually against "gewöhnliche Bewusstseyn" not the rational category of the understanding.

REJOINDER
GARY SHAPIRO

I'm grateful to Professor Perkins for pointing out at least one possible ambiguity in my paper and for sharpening the question about the relation of poetry to knowledge and dialectic. Let me deal with the ambiguity first. I meant to say that the theory of implicit meaning holds that the meaning of a *successful poem* "cannot be explicit because it involves a continuum of possibilities which no actual linguistic structure can include or contain." Neither I, Hegel, nor the theorists of implicit meaning endorse this as applicable to all discourse; the implicit theorists endorse it with respect to certain *good* poems, and as I suggest at the end of the paper, I am in partial agreement with them; Hegel endorses it with respect to metaphorical or symbolical poetry but (at the very least) sees that serious qualifications must be made in the principle when it is applied to great poetry. Therefore, although I confess to harboring some lingering doubts about Hegel's claim to "philosophical completeness," they are not arrived at as an "inference" from this principle, as Perkins suggests.

The searching questions which cannot be clarified so quickly are:

1. Does poetry, on Hegel's view, transcend the understanding?
2. Does Hegel himself have an implicit theory of artistic and/or poetic meaning?
3. Is poetry, on Hegel's view, a form of knowledge?
4. Is the cognitive theory of poetry plausible and defensible?

I shall examine these in sequence.

The first three questions raise significant issues about the meaning of Hegel's system. Perkins quotes Hegel's (or Hotho's?) text at several points to support his interpretation. Yet as I shall attempt to show in what follows, he has confused what Hegel says about art in general with the Hegelian analysis of poetry in particular. This is to mistake concrete universals for abstract ones.

1. In the section of his *Aesthetics* devoted to poetry, Hegel clearly draws the contrast between poetry and prose by associating the former with speculative reason and the latter with *both* scientific understanding and the understanding of everyday common sense. "The prosaic mind, which poetry must shun" is said to have two forms: (1) which "treats the vast field of actuality in accordance with the restricted theory of the *Understanding* and its categories, such as cause and effect, means and end, i.e., in general with relations in the field of externality and finitude"; (2) "ordinary thinking" which is "content to take what is and happens as just the bare individual thing or event, i.e., as something accidental and meaningless." (HA,

974f). Moreover, the kind of poetry in which Hegel is specifically interested at this point, which is both the culmination and dissolution of all preceding art-forms, is not merely distinct from prose, but self-consciously aims at such distinction. For, as Hegel says, an "essential distinction" is to be made between primitive poetry which precedes the clear articulation of prose and a poetry which, being subsequent to prose, "knows the sphere from which it must liberate itself in order to stand on the free ground of art and therefore it develops in conscious distinction from prose." (HA, 974 and 976) Hegel does not stop with this general claim. He analyzes each of the major poetic genres in terms of the way in which it *does* transcend the categories of the understanding; the development in the treatment of subject and object or cause and effect in the progression from ancient epic to modern drama is precisely what gives Hegel's account of poetry a rational structure. As Perkins points out, Hegel does sometimes associate sensuousness with the understanding. But in poetry sensuousness has been attenuated into the imagination, and its sounds are mere signs of imaginative ideas. Poetry is dialectic in imaginative form. Even the non-poetic arts are not rigidly bound to sensory immediacy as such; Hegel claims at several points that they are all essentially imaginative.

2. Perkins claims that Hegel himself has an implicit theory of poetic meaning. His argument rests on Hegel's recognition of the importance of metaphor and the limitations of sensory experience in articulately rendering the Absolute. As I see it, Hegel treats metaphors, similes, sublime and oracular poetry as deficient and very minimal forms of the art. Such forms have a place in great poetry only when they are subordinated to a dialectical movement, as in the use of metaphors by dramatic characters to exhibit their own freedom and self-conscious artistry. Hegel might very well endorse the criticism made by some Marxists, that the reversion to myth and symbol in modern art and poetry (and aesthetic theories based on such modernism) are flights from the articulate comprehension offered by more realistic literature.[24] The metaphorical by itself is simply not paradigmatic for understanding poetry as such in Hegel's view.

The sensuous limitations of art do play a very important role both for establishing the boundaries between art and philosophy and in clarifying the rather special place of poetry within Hegel's system of the arts. Perkins cites Hegel's strictures on sensuousness from the standpoint of philosophy and emphasizes that Hegel sees art as the presentation of truth within a sensuous form. Yet to conclude from these premises that poetry must share in the restrictions of art in general appears to be a confusion. Art, for Hegel, is a concrete and not an abstract universal; it specifies itself through a process of development and articulation. To understand the place of poetry for Hegel we must recall his general strategy in the *Aesthetics* (to which he often calls attention): he *first* explains the general conception of art, *second* shows how this idea unfolds into the symbolic, classical, and romantic types, and *third* explains the fulfillment or actualization of the idea of art in the particular art-forms as manifest in the history of art. (E.g. HA, 613f) How is poetry actualized? It is clearly not sensory, material or external in any simple sense. As Hegel says, its "proper external object" is "the *inner* imagination and intuition itself . . . *spiritual* forms take the place of perceptibility." (HA, 964) This is why Hegel makes the rather startling claim that poetry is translatable and that our comprehension of it does not depend on whether we hear it or read it. Poetry is also described as keeping a "mean between the abstract universality of thought and the sensuously concrete corporeal objects" of the visual arts. (HA, 965) Therefore poetry's peculiar mode of sensory expression makes it a uniquely unrestricted and universal art; (HA, 966f) it is the point at which art, turning inward, begins to dissolve into religion and philosophy. (HA, 968) The *way* in which poetry is sensuous is not the way in which art as such is sensuous; when Hegel speaks of the latter he often has in mind the middle terms of art—sculpture, painting, and music. Architecture and poetry represent extremes in their dependence on or freedom from sense. So the sensory restriction does not condemn poetry to having a merely implicit meaning.

3. The same considerations suggest that poetry's claims to knowledge cannot be dismissed simply on the grounds of its alleged sensory form. Perkins, by attempting to draw a sharp contrast between sensible form or appearance and knowledge as such seems to be reading the arch-rationalist Hegel who figures, alternatively, as villain or hero in the works of Kierkegaard or the British neo-Hegelians, and not the Hegel of the *Aesthetics*. Poetry is not cut off from the Absolute because it deals with appearance; it is a knowledge of the Absolute insofar as it appears or manifests itself in sensuous form.

Perkins claims that poetry cannot be knowledge because it is not aware of its own rationality. Now for Hegel poetry is indeed not *fully* aware of its own rationality, but does exhibit a very large measure of self-knowledge. Hegel brings this out in his comments on cultured poetry's self-conscious opposition to prose, its attempts to include the other arts, and his unqualified praise of Shakespeare for making his characters into self-conscious artists. Moreover, Hegel's account of *Kunstreligion* in the *Phenomenology* shows how art self-consciously takes up within itself the struggle against merely implicit or "abstract" meaning, culminating in comedy in which the artist and the audience clearly recognize their identity within difference.

4. In asking *how* poetry can be cognitive, Perkins seems to be appealing to the prosaic conception of knowledge which Hegel denies is relevant to poetry. He seems to suggest that the paradigm of cognition is the "statement" (Hegel's "proposition") and then asks how characters or plots can measure up to statements, taken as cognitive models. What I take Hegel to be doing in his account of poetry is first rejecting the statement model, and second, through his analysis of the dialectical content of the genres, showing how plots, characters, etc. can exhibit dialectical knowledge. As Perkins says, the burden of working this out in detail is a large one and he and I seem to be in agreement that Hegel has not done the whole job, at least

in part because of his defective treatment of possibility and indeterminacy.

The temptation to give cognitive explications of the *Divine Comedy* and "The Emperor of Ice Cream" is great while my remaining space is brief. Hegel's own comments on the first have been recognized to be illuminating by Dante scholars.[25] The *Comedy* is richly Hegelian in its depiction of the attained unity of hero and narrator, object and subject. It prefigures Hegel's own voyage of discovery through *Erinnerung* in the *Phenomenology* as well as the modern novel of the artist who finds his own identity by dissolving his past into art (Proust is the paradigm). "The Emperor of Ice Cream" with its images of transient enjoyment and the physical details of death is a poem *about* appearances, but its involvement with appearances does not preclude cognitivity. This even takes the apparent form of a proposition—a form which in good Hegelian fashion is subverted by its content—"Let be be finale of seem." The emperor of ice-cream is the principle of melting or dissolution which pervades this world of appearances. However fanciful and sketchy this may be, it should indicate both the suggestiveness of Hegel's poetics and the work which needs to be done in order to achieve a dialectical criticism of poetry.

NOTES

24. See, for example, Willis H. Truitt, "Ideology, Expression, and Mediation in Marx, Raphael, and Lukács," *Philosophical Forum,* N.S. Vol. III, Nos. 3-4 (Spring-Summer 1972), 468-497.

25. See Daisy Fornacca Kouzel, "The Hegelian Influence in the Literary Criticism of Francesco De Sanctus" in *Review of National Literatures,* (Vol. I, No. 2, Fall, 1970) 214-231, and Erich Auerbach, *Mimesis* (Princeton: 1956), 191 and 194.

IV

Hegel On The Art Object
by
MICHAEL H. MITIAS

Hegel's view of art has been frequently characterized as 'intellectualistic'; that is, a work is *artistic* primarily because it expresses truth. Accordingly the aesthetic experience *par excellence* is cognitive in character. Croce, for example, argues that "in a greater degree than any of his predecessors Hegel emphasized the cognitive character of art."[1] Similarly Steinkraus in a recent essay writes: "though there is much in Hegel's *Lectures on Aesthetics* which is empirical, shows profound sensitivity, and gives specific insight, his main theory may be characterized as 'intellectualistic' for he views art primarily as a mode of cognition, even as a mode of truth."[2] However, the question which merits special attention is: in what sense is art in Hegel intellectualistic, cognitive, or expressive of truth? What sort of truth does art express? Hegel clearly asserts that the Idea manifests itself concretely in art, religion, and philosophy. (Enc. §556) Thus the content of the religious, artistic, and philosophical experience is the Idea. But does the Idea express itself in the same way in these three modes of human experience? To hold, with Croce, that it does is in effect to reduce the aesthetic experience to cognitive, conceptual experience. This is indeed what led Croce to view Hegel as an enemy of art: "art, being placed in the sphere of Absolute Spirit, in company with Religion and Philosophy, how will she be able to hold her own in such powerful and aggressive company, especially in that of philosophy, which in the Hegelian system stands at the summit of all spiritual evolution?"[3] He dismisses the possibility that art fulfills a function "other than the knowledge of the Absolute," and instead asserts: "the principles of Hegel's system are at bottom rationalistic and hostile to religion, and hostile no less to art."[4] Of course, if the content of the philosophical and aesthetic experience is identical, that is, if art aims at the knowledge of the absolute, art would no doubt be quite inferior and subordinate to philosophy. But, again, let us suppose that the aim of art is not exactly the *knowledge* of the absolute, does this fact make it necessarily inferior to philosophy?

In this paper I intend to show that art, for Hegel, is not inferior to philosophy. On the contrary, it occupies a respectable place in the realm of the Spirit. I shall argue that truth in philosophy and in art is not identical, and that the aesthetic experience is generically different from the philosophical experience. The tendency to interpret Hegel's theory of art as intellectualistic stems from an inadequate consideration of his penetrating analysis of the nature of art in general and the art object in particular. A treatment of these two concepts will shed considerable light on his conception of the distinctive features of art as a human activity and, consequently, on the relation of art to philosophy. I shall also argue that Hegel does not espouse an essentialist theory of art; that is, for him the content of the aesthetic experience, on the one hand, and the defining feature of the art work, on the other, is not an abstract quality or essence attached mysteriously to the art object. It is, rather, an Ideal content; and as such it is the capacity of the object to realize an experience of beauty. The analysis of this aspect of Hegel's theory of art will lend further credibility to the claim that the aesthetic experience is unique and not discursive or intellectualistic in character.

I. The End of Art

There are three views on the end or general nature of art which Hegel rejects.

(1) *Imitation of Nature as the End of Art.* Advocates of this theory hold that "imitation, as facility in copying natural forms just as they are, in a way that corresponds to them completely, is supposed to constitute the essential end and aim of art, and the success of this portrayal in correspondence with nature is supposed to afford complete satisfaction."[5] Thus an art work is good or beautiful insofar as it is a true copy of natural forms. Hegel advances four arguments against this view: (i) If the ultimate aim of the artist is to represent nature honestly his labor would be superfluous: he would not succeed in creating an exact copy of nature; and even if he does his product would be a deception and a poor rival to nature. (HA, 42ff) (ii) One may remark, as Aristotle did, that man derives pleasure from imitations. This may well be the case;

but, Hegel observes, it becomes a man better to derive enjoyment from things creatively made by man. Again, the pleasure derived from imitations is in many respects restricted and tends to be cold and unrewarding. Consider listening to a man who imitates the nightingale's song perfectly. As soon as we discover that it is a man who has been singing we get disappointed and consider it a trick, a deception rather than a work of art. (HA, 43ff) (iii) If imitation is the end of art we shall be in want of an objective criterion for evaluating the beauty of art objects. Indeed beauty as such would be neglected in the process of evaluation. What we would look for, instead, is whether or not a certain object correctly copies an aspect of nature or experience. (HA, 44ff) (iv) Even if we succeed in basing beauty on subjective taste, though this is a hopeless effort, still the theory of imitation does not help in explaining all the areas of art such as poetry, architecture, music, for which there are no parallels in nature at all. (HA, 45ff)[6]

(2) *Human Experience of the World as the End of Art.* This theory holds that the end of art is "to bring home to our sense, our feeling, and our inspiration everything which has a place in the human spirit." (HA, 46) It is expected that the work of art should not only move and delight our sense, mind and heart, but also reveal the ideal and actual nature of the world as a whole and provide an occasion to complete our partial experience of external existence. Hegel rejects this theory for two main reasons: (i) The art work is on this view deceptive, for the artist substitutes his creation for reality. The work becomes an occasion to experience some elements of the world imaginatively rather than actually. But the imaginative experience is a meager substitute for the direct experience of reality. (ii) As in the earlier theory, the art work and our enjoyment of it would be indifferent to beauty, for we would evaluate it primarily on the basis of its capacity to fulfill certain needed experiences in life. Thus from this standpoint it would be extremely difficult to determine what is the true end of art. But unclarity about such an end undermines the possibility of an objective standard in aesthetic evaluation. (HA, 46)

(3) *Mitigation of the Passions as the End of Art.* According to this theory, art is intended to educate the impulses and passions and "to adorn and bring before perception and feeling every possible material,

just as the thinking of ratiocination can work on every possible object and mode of action and equip them with reasons and justifications." (HA, 46) The art work externalizes certain emotions or feelings. It allows the percipient to experience imaginatively what he would otherwise experience in reality. This he does by reflecting upon the work. In this act he is able to see himself objectively. His abstract ego views the content of his savage passions as external; in this encounter it frees itself from them and, consequently, brings relief to the perceiver: "the man," Hegel asserts, "contemplates his impulses and inclinations, and while previously they carried him reflectionless away, he now sees them outside himself and already begins to be free from them because they confront him as something objective." (HA, 48f)

Now a work of art mitigates the passions by instruction and moral improvement. Its ultimate aim is, then, to teach, i.e., to impart a special kind of knowledge. But, Hegel objects, this theory does not only suffer from the same defects encountered in the earlier theory, it is also defective in at least two other respects. (i) If art is intended to teach then its content must be spiritual and universal. But if it is universal "and supposed to emerge and be explained directly and explicitly as an abstract proposition, prosaic reflection, or general doctrine, and not to be contained implicitly and only indirectly in the concrete form of a work of art, then by this separation the sensuous pictorial form, which is precisely what alone makes a work of art a work of art, becomes a useless appendage, a veil and a pure appearance, expressly pronounced to be a mere veil and a mere pure appearance." (HA, 51) Yet the art work is not an object for the understanding alone, but also for the senses and the imagination. Accordingly it should not bring before the imaginative vision a content in its universality as such, but rather this universality under the mode of individual concreteness and distinctive sensuous particularity. (HA, 51) (ii) Exclusive emphasis on the didactic or educative aspect of art minimizes its sensuous value: the other "side, pleasure, entertainment, and delight, is pronounced explicitly inessential, and ought to have its substance only in the utility of the doctrine on which it is attendant." (HA, 51) Again, we would necessarily be led to view the art work not as an end in itself but as a means to a higher or different end. Hegel admits that a work may have a moral, but this "depends on interpretation and on *who* draws the moral." (HA, 52)

(4) *Revelation of Truth as the End of Art.* The true end of art, Hegel maintains, is to reveal the truth "in the form of sensuous artistic configuration." (HA, 55) Accordingly an art work presents truth in a sensuous form. It should not, however, be viewed as a means, nor as a "useful tool for realizing this end which is independently valid on its own account outside the sphere of art." (HA, 55) It has its final end in itself. In what follows I shall elucidate this view in some detail.

II. Distinctive Characteristics of the Work of Art

The art object is, to begin with, an artifact creatively made by man. Hegel denies that it is the result merely of (1) mechanical activity or (2) inspiration. Advocates of the first position naively hold that in ordering his object the artist simply applies certain rules of artistic creation. Anyone who masters such rules and acquires skill in their execution would be an artist. According to the second view, the object is conceived as the product of inspiration or talent which nature bestows upon the artist. In the process of artistic production the artist does not follow set techniques or rules; he simply gives himself freely to his genius. The latter has its peculiar laws and content. Thus when the object is completed it would be difficult to explain how it was formed. But, Hegel argues, although no doubt the artist is a technician who knows the general rules by means of which he forms his work, and although he is a talented person with unique capacities, his genius is not merely given. What is given is the capacity for being a genius. This capacity "requires development by thought, reflection on the mode of its productivity, and practice and skill in producing." (HA, 27)[7] The distinctive feature of the creative process, however, is the ability of the artist to produce a form which embodies the 'Ideal' concretely and expressively.

Second, the art object is sensuous in character. It is a physical entity and the locus of perceptual experience. Indeed it is produced for man's sense. Thus since it is not immediately an object of thought some thinkers tended to believe that its purpose is to evoke in us a peculiar type of feeling, e.g., love, fear, exaltation, serenity, pleasure. A position like this would restrict aesthetics to the investigation of feelings, and of what feelings art should arouse.[8] But, Hegel insists, the analysis of beauty in general is the proper subject matter of aesthetics. The ultimate aim of the artist is to create a beautiful object. (HA, 33ff)

But, third, the art work is also addressed to the mind: "the spirit," Hegel maintains, "is meant to be affected by it and to find some satisfaction in it." (HA, 35) Yet the sensuous aspect has a right to existence only insofar as it exists for the mind, not *qua* sensuous object. This is exactly why the work cannot be viewed as a physical entity but as an artifact potential of a unique, aesthetic experience. Now what is the relationship between the sensuous aspect of the work and the mind? The relation between them is twofold. In the first place, the mind is not satisfied with the mere apprehension of the art work as external to itself by means of sight and hearing; it is, properly speaking, *craved,* desired by the mind. What is desired, however, is not the physical, natural aspects of it as such but certain modes or features which are not readily available to ordinary sense-perception. This is why (1) the cultivation of taste is a necessary condition for aesthetic appreciation; (2) it is easier to perceive and enjoy a natural rather than an art object. In the second place, the mind does not apprehend the work of art the way a scientist could apprehend it. The latter no doubt starts from the sensuous object in its concreteness and may study some distinctive aspects of it, but what he actually aims at is the universal, the notion, or the Ideal nature of the object. Artistic apprehension, on the other hand, recognizes the work of art as external, sensuous, and immediate determinateness; it "cherishes an interest in the object in its individual existence and does not struggle to change it into its universal thought and concept." (HA, 51) Thus the artistic mind seeks neither the sensuous nor the notional aspects of the work as such. It seeks a spiritual content, viz., beauty, which occupies a mean between what is perceived as sensuous and Ideal thought.

Finally, the art work imitates the Ideal, viz., Beauty. 'Ideal', however, should not be confused with 'Idea': "the Idea as the beauty of art is not the Idea as such, in the way that a metaphysical logic has to apprehend it as the Absolute, but the Idea as shaped forward into reality and as having advanced to immediate unity and correspondence with this reality." (HA, 73) The Idea as such may be true, and indeed may give rise to other types of experience; but as *the beautiful in art,* it is not abstract or conceptual; it is concrete and with determinate form. It is not an object of thought, but of immediate intuition. This is why "it is impossible for the Understanding to comprehend beauty." (HA, 111).

From what has been said so far it is clear that (1) the art work is an end in itself. If it is intended to reveal the nature of the Idea *qua* abstract thought, to educate morally, to inform us about human nature, etc., we would not anymore appreciate it for its beauty but inasmuch as it reveals cognitive truth. But we have already seen that Hegel rejects this way of viewing the art work. (2) The truth which the art work reveals presents itself to aesthetic perception as the beautiful. It is not an object for the senses or the understanding but for the imagination. Thus the content of aesthetic perception is not merely a feeling of pleasure or propositional knowledge, but a unique kind of imaginative satisfaction. (3) The aesthetic experience is immediate, intuitive, and as such it is poorest in concept. "Beauty," writes Hegel in the *Encyclopedia*, "is the immediate unity of nature and spirit in intuition *(Anschauung)*."[9] Thus the way the Idea expresses itself in art is quite different from the way it expresses itself in logic or nature, for example. This is why we should hold that, in Hegel, the aesthetic experience is uniquely different from the philosophical or religious experience. In these types of experience the Idea is certainly present but it is present differently in each case. Accordingly the truth which the art object reveals is not cognitive or conceptual, but artistic or Ideal.[10] Thus to argue, as Croce does, that Hegel is an enemy of art or that he subordinated art to philosophy, primarily because art does not express cognitive or discursive truth, is a mistake based on categorial confusion.[11] That Hegel, moreover, never intended to consider art an inferior objectification of the Idea may be seen in the following passage: "owing to this freedom and infinity, which are inherent in the Concept of beauty, as well as in the beautiful object and its subjective contemplation, the sphere of the beautiful is withdrawn from the relativity of finite affairs and raised into the absolute realm of the Idea and its truth." (HA, 115)

Finally, the art work is a human artifact. (HA, 25ff) In the process of artistic creation the artist does not add anything, ontologically speaking, to the sensuous medium. His sole contribution to the work is the *form* which he imposes on the material datum with which he is working. But though human and given to the senses, the art work is fundamentally spiritual, and this in two respects: (1) it is a product of imaginative creativeness; (2) it is an object of imaginative contemplation.[12]

> In art, these sensuous shapes and sounds present themselves, not
> simply for their own sake, and that for their immediate structure, but
> with the purpose of affording in that shape satisfaction to higher
> spiritual interests, seeing that they are powerful to call forth a re-
> sponse and echo in the mind from all the depths of consciousness. It is
> thus that, in art, the sensuous is spiritualized, the spiritual appears in
> sensuous shape.[13]

Accordingly in Hegel's aesthetic theory we cannot identify the
aesthetic object,[14] i.e., the content which is perceived by the critic or
the spectator and on which the judgment of aesthetic evaluation is
based, with the physical entity which we perceive with one or a
combination of five senses: "the work of art has no feeling in itself and is
not through and through enlivened, but, regarded as an external object,
is dead." (HA, 29) Nor can we identify it with an abstract or metaphysical entity or a universal type which the artist somehow incorporates in
the medium in the process of artistic creation (essentialism), as some
aestheticians tend to believe.[15]

But, as we have seen, the distinctive element of the fine work of art
is the Ideal *qua* beauty. This beauty is not an abstract essence or quality
mysteriously attached to the physical object. It is not, in short, given
as ready made but, rather, *uniquely formed* and enjoyed in the process of
aesthetic perception: "a work of art is such only because, originating
from the spirit, it now belongs to the territory of the spirit; it has
received the baptism of the spiritual and sets forth only what has been
formed in harmony with the spirit." (HA, 29, 2) In itself, then, the
physical object is not beautiful; it is a potential for an experience of
beauty.[16] It possesses such a potential by virtue of the form which the
artist imposes on the physical medium: "the perfect fusion of thought
and image in beauty is a concrete form of the aesthetic spirit."[17] As the
sensuous determination of the Idea, form is the objective ground of the
aesthetic experience and what safeguards the objective validity of the
aesthetic judgment.[18]

Thus since the art work is a completely human product, and since
the aesthetic, i.e., perceived, object is distinctively and creatively

formed in aesthetic perception, it would be extremely difficult to draw a comparative relationship of superiority or inferiority between the philosophical and the aesthetic experience. Each of these experiences plays a unique role in the life of the Spirit.

NOTES

1. B. Croce, *Aesthetic* (tr. D. Ainslie)(New York: Noonday Press, 1962), p. 301.
2. W. E. Steinkraus, "The Place of Art in Hegel's System," *Pakistan Philosophical Journal* (Vol. X, No. 2, Jan-June, 1972), p. 43. See also L. Rosenstein, "Metaphysical Foundations of the Theories of Tragedy in Hegel and Nietzsche," *Journal of Aesthetics and Art Criticism,* Vol. XXVIII, No. 4, 1972.
3. Croce, *op. cit.,* p. 301.
4. *Ibid.,* Cf. K. Gilbert and H. Kuhn, *A History of Aesthetics* (New York: Macmillan, 1939), pp. 436ff; L. Tolstoy, *What is Art?* (tr. A. Maude)(Oxford Univ. Press, 1938), p. 100.
5. G. W. F. Hegel, *Aesthetics* (tr. T. M. Knox)(Oxford: Clarendon Press, 1975), pp. 41-42. Parenthesized numbers after HA which follow in the text are citations to pages in this translation.
6. See also p. 115. The theory of imitation is also rejected in the *Encyclopedia,* §562.
7. In the *Encyclopedia* we read that the "genius is different from the artist in him who makes something according to rules and who has to accommodate himself according to the requirements of communication; this requires diligence, work and technical understanding." (G. Mueller's version of the 1817 *Encyclopedia* (New York: Philosophical Library, 1959) §460, p. 273.) See §560 of the regular edition.
8. For a criticism of this position, see pp. 32ff.
9. Mueller's version of the 1817 *Encyclopedia* §457. See also *Enc.* §557. In the *Phenomenology of Mind,* Hegel argues in some detail that sense-experience is immediate and devoid of conceptual content. See pp. 149-160 of the Baillie translation (New York: Macmillan, 1961).
10. For a detailed elucidation of this point, see pp. 110-115.
11. An interpretation similar to mine is found, though only in the form of a remark, in Bosanquet's *History of Aesthetics* (New York: Macmillan, 1904), p. 336. Steinkraus also rejects Croce's position but for different reasons. See Steinkraus, *op. cit.,* pp. 47ff.
12. This point is discussed by Hegel in detail. See p. 35f.
13. This passage is from Bosanquet's translation of the Introduction and is found in J. Glenn Gray (ed.), *Hegel on Art, Religion and Philosophy* (New York: Harper Torchbook, 1970), p. 67.
14. For a detailed treatment of this concept, see my essay "Another Look at the Ontological Status of the Aesthetic Object" (*Southwestern Journal of Philosophy,* III, No. 2 1972, pp. 29-49.

15. M. C. Beardsley, for example, views Hegel as an essentialist. See his *Aesthetics: Problems in the Philosophy of Criticism* (New York: Harcourt, Brace & World, 1958), p. 394. See also W. Charlton, *Aesthetics: An Introduction* (London: Hutchinson Univ. Library, 1970), pp. 82-83.

16. Cf. *Encyclopedia,* §557.

17. From Mueller's version, §460. See *Encyclopedia* §560.

18. See p. 43 of the Knox translation of Hegel's *Aesthetics*.

COMMENT

MICHAEL H. MACDONALD

Professor Mitias's chief concern in his paper is in what sense Hegel views art as "intellectualistic", cognitive, or expressive of truth. He has said correctly that "the content of the religious, artistic, and philosophical experience is the Idea." Furthermore he has seen that to maintain with Croce that the Idea expresses itself in the same way in art, philosophy, and religion would be "in effect to reduce the aesthetic experience to cognitive, conceptual experience."

I agree with Professor Mitias's argument "that truth in philosophy and in art is not identical, and that the aesthetic experience is generically different from the philosophical experience." Yet Croce is not entirely wrong in his evaluation when he wonders how art, in company with religion and philosophy, will "be able to hold her own in such powerful and aggressive company," particularly when one considers the power of philosophy, "which in the Hegelian system stands at the summit of all spiritual evolution."[19] While Hegel is certainly not an "enemy of art", a case can be made that Hegel indeed subordinated art to philosophy "primarily because art does not express cognitive or discursive truth," as Mitias himself has concluded.

Let us recall that historically transcendental idealism begins with the unity of subject and object in the philosophy of Fichte. Schelling's twist was that he believed he discovered the supreme objectification in a work of art. Hegel agrees with Schelling that art has metaphysical significance, yet in his polemics against Schelling, he disagrees with the view that art is the supreme form in which the Idea is apprehended. Hegel says, for example, that the "supreme mode of the Idea is really its own element; thought, the Idea apprehended, is therefore higher than the work of art."[20] Ernst Behler, in a recent article in *Hegel-Studien,* summarizes Hegel's views poignantly:

> For Hegel art and imagination cannot be "the supreme [form]" since we are dealing here only in the form of "sensuous intuition", which does not correspond to the Spirit, which does not truly express the Spirit.[21]

Hegel in the introduction to his *Lectures on Aesthetics* distinguishes at the outset between the beauty of nature and the beauty of art and contends that the beauty exemplified in art is superior to that found in nature. The reason for this judgment is that the beauty in art is one begotten of the mind, and mind and its creations are viewed as greater in significance than the isolated phenomena of nature. The beauty of human art, hand and mind is not subordinate to the beauty of nature. Hegel emphasizes the role of man's spirit and mind in the work of art. The work of art is plainly of higher worth than the natural beauty of nature, for nature has not been submitted to this spiritual baptism. Art is a more perfect and complete expression of the spiritual, which is the true essence of reality. Whether or not you regret Hegel's under-estimation of natural beauty as a manifestation of the Idea, it is clear that to Hegel's way of thinking, natural beauty is inferior to artistic beauty.

Hegel subsequently stresses that the greatest art, or genuine art, joins the ranks of religion and philosophy and expresses the "divine meanings of things, the deepest interests of mankind, and the most universal truths of the spirit."[22] What Hegel means here can best be understood by approaching it from the various ways man can have knowledge of the Absolute, the Totality, i.e., reality taken as a whole. According to Hegel, this Absolute can be apprehended in three ways: (1) under the sensuous form of beauty as manifested in nature, or more adequately, as we have mentioned, in the work of art; (2) in the form of figurative or pictorial thought as expressed in the sphere of religion; and (3) in purely conceptual language in the field of philosophy.[23] Art, religion and philosophy are therefore all concerned with the same content, each expressing this content in a form consistent with its own essence.

Art's distinctive attribute is its ability to represent even the most profound ideas in sensuous form, thereby bringing them closer to the world of nature and the human sphere of feeling. Pure thought reaches into a supra-sensuous world but at the same time often strikes one as somewhat alien and beyond. The world of art is a reconciliation between that which is external and sensuous on the one hand, and the world of pure thought on the other. Art's content is therefore spiritual whereas its form is sensuous. Its task is, then, to represent the spiritual in sensuous form, not in the form of thought or pure spirituality.

Hegel, as is well known, distinguishes between three types of art: the symbolic, the classical, and the romantic. This distinction is based upon how the spiritual content is unified with the external matter. In the symbolic the two elements are incongruous: the physical form is so definite that the art is stylized. In classical art the spiritual idea and the sensuous form are in perfect accord. In romantic art the unity achieved in classical art is destroyed. However, we are dealing in romantic art with an art which is more lofty in its aim. This elevation of Spirit to its own substance is that which makes up the fundamental principle of romantic art. Here Spirit finds true contentment in the infinite wealth of its own inner sphere. Of course romantic art, like symbolic and classical, must of necessity make use of an external mode (e.g. concrete character in the novel), for otherwise we would not be dealing with art but with philosophy. But the accent has gone from the external (symbolic) to the internal (romantic). It is my opinion that in terms of an analysis of art *per se*, Hegel's preference was for the classical, but when one considers art's ultimately highest function of expressing the Absolute, Hegel's heart lay with romantic art.

Romantic art is for all practical purposes the art of Christendom. Here no sensuous embodiment is adequate to the spiritual content. Christianity declares that the true essence of God is Spirit, in contrast to the Greek belief in the gods as the unity of the human and divine natures. This Greek conception permits a representation in a visible and sensuous form. Christianity raises the unity of the human and divine "out of this immediate into a self-conscious unity" and therefore,

> The genuine medium for the reality of this content is no longer the sensuous and immediate existence of what is spiritual, that is, the physical body of man, but the *self-aware* inner life of *soul itself*. Now it is Christianity — for the reason that it presents to mind God as Spirit, and not as the particular individual spirit, but as absolute in spirit and in truth — which steps back from the sensuousness of imagination into the inward life of reason, and makes *this* inward life of reason rather than *bodily* form the medium and determinate existence of its content.[24]

Christianity in the opinion of the mature Hegel better expressed reality than did the earlier myths of the Greeks.

Turning our attention to the particular arts, Hegel finds that they belong to one of the already mentioned general types of art. In architecture, the emphasis is on the material as mass, subject to certain mechanical laws. The relation to the spiritual world is remote, therefore architecture is essentially symbolic. In sculpture the spiritual aspect only hinted at in architecture is beautifully unified with sensuous form, with neither predominating over the other. It is the best example of the classical element. Spirituality in a concrete form is best represented through the arts of painting, music and poetry.

By the use of the plane surface painting is neither confined to three dimensions, as sculpture, nor the heavy voluminous mass, as is architecture. Music, on a higher level than painting, penetrates still deeper into the inner nature of the ideal world. Space is negated and the musical tones are able to express a manifold of feelings and passions. Just as sculpture forms the central point between the symbolic and romantic art forms, so music stands in the center of the romantic arts, and is thus the transitional point between the abstract spatial sensuousness of painting and the abstract spirituality of poetry.

Poetry is, then, the most spiritual form of romantic art. It is most eminently qualified to master such a material. Its content is chiefly directed to the life of soul and mind as occupied with the aims and events within its own sphere. Hegel emphasizes that even though poetic expression is obviously embodied in words, the words themselves represent abstract ideas, and the real significance of poetic speech is not to be discovered in the word *per se* and in the manner in which they are associated in elaborate phraseology (i.e., rhythm, rhyme, etc.). The significance of the word lies in the conception, the idea which is being expressed. The word indicates thoughts and ideas. Poetry frees itself from a dependence upon external sensuous matter, even though it simultaneously oversteps the boundaries of its own realm and passes into the "prose of thought."[25]

While I often find Hegel in his lectures genuinely trying "to do justice to his data"[26], I do not really think that Hegel found symbolic, classical and romantic art of equal significance, nor do I think that Hegel pretended that architecture was as great an art form as poetry, though he indeed had some positive things to say about it. Whether the greatest art is considered to be the unity of matter and spirit (in which case classical art is supreme) or its ability to express the action, movement, conflict of Spirit (where the romantic is deemed greater), still we are dealing with an evaluation of forms. We can also make some evaluative statements concerning the relationship of art, philosophy, and religion.

Whatever some critics maintain that Hegel ought to have said, it is my view that Hegel looked on art, religion and philosophy as permanent activities or moments of the Absolute as expressed by the human spirit. But I am further forced to conclude that Hegel considered philosophy the highest of these moments. Hegel undoubtedly exalted art, but he exalted religion and philosophy even more.

Perhaps the most correct conclusion would be to say that the aim of philosophy is the *knowledge* of the absolute, an aim which Hegel undoubtedly believed was superior to the aim of art, which is to express the Idea in sensuous form. Yet Hegel himself muddies the water somewhat by his high regard for romantic art, which begins to free itself from a dependence upon the material world, thereby simultaneously breaking the boundaries of its own sphere. Thus the divisions between art, religion, and philosophy are neither as rigid nor as clear as it might appear.

Professor Mitias' objective was to demonstrate "that art, for Hegel, is not inferior to philosophy. On the contrary, it occupies a respectable place in the realm of the Spirit." I conclude at this point that to show that art is not, in Hegel's view, inferior to philosophy is quite a separate problem (and a more difficult one, I might add) from saying that art occupies a respectable place in the realm of Spirit. My contention would be that art should be considered inferior to philosophy in light of Hegel's total system, even though no one should dispute that art occupies a respectable place in the realm of the Spirit.

NOTES

19. B. Croce, *Aesthetic*, (tr. D. Ainslie)(New York: Noonday Press, 1962), p. 301.

20. G. W. F. Hegel, *Lectures on the History of Philosophy*, (tr. by E. S. Haldane and F. H. Simson) (New York: Humanities Press, 1955), Vol. III, p. 542.

21. Ernst Behler, "Die Geschichte des Bewusstseins. Zur Vorgeschichte eines Hegelschen Themas," in *Hegel-Studien*, Vol. VII (1972), p. 187. The translation is mine.

22. Hegel's *Introduction to the Philosophy of Art* (tr. J. Loewenberg) in J. Loewenberg (ed.), *Hegel Selections* (New York: Scribners', 1929), p. 314.
23. G. W. F. Hegel, *The Philosophy of Fine Art* (tr. F. P. B. Osmaston)(London: G. Bell & Sons Ltd., 1920), Vol. I, pp. 125ff.
24. *Ibid.,* p. 108.
25. *Ibid.,* p. 120.
26. Cf. Walter Kaufmann, *Tragedy and Philosophy* (New York: Doubleday and Company, 1968), p. 284.

REJOINDER
MICHAEL MITIAS

It is neither meaningful nor instructive to draw a comparative relationship of inferiority or superiority in Hegel, between art, religion, and philosophy. Why? The Idea objectifies itself concretely in these three types of activity: thus the content of the aesthetic, religious, and philosophical experience is the Idea as such. Accordingly, from the standpoint of content, none of them is higher or lower than the other: "owing to its preoccupation with truth as the absolute object of consciousness, art too belongs to the absolute sphere of the spirit, and therefore, in its content, art stands on one and the same ground with religion (in the stricter sense of the word) and philosophy." Thus the content of these spheres of the Spirit is identical. They differ "only in the *forms* in which they bring home to consciousness their object, the Absolute." (HA, 101) The differences between them, however, are inherent in the nature of the Spirit itself. The Idea, in other words, manifests itself differently in art, religion, and philosophy. Consequently, the experiences associated with these realms of the Spirit are *generically* different. Accordingly there is no logical, or ontological, ground for saying that art (or religion) is inferior to philosophy.

Again, on the basis of what criterion can we say that art is inferior to philosophy? Professor McDonald thinks that the criterion is expressiveness of cognitive or discursive truth; that is, art is inferior to philosophy because it does not express cognitive or discursive truth. It is true that, for Hegel, "thinking is the essence and concept of the spirit;" (HA, 13) but from this premise we cannot infer the inferiority of art, i.e., because art is not discursive the way philosophy is. We can only infer the inferiority of another type of activity which is discursive in character. And Hegel himself never held that art is inferior to philosophy because its essence is not discursive or conceptual; on the contrary, art, for him, is a truly spiritual activity. It expresses a unique aspect of the Idea, viz., beauty, which neither philosophy nor religion can express. And if one misses this element of the Idea he would remain distant from the life of the Spirit. This is exactly why I held that it is a mistake to look at the relationship between art, religion, and philosophy in terms of inferiority or superiority. Each one of them is a distinctive activity in the life of the Absolute.

V

A Re-examination of the 'Death of Art' Interpretation of Hegel's Aesthetics

by

CURTIS L. CARTER

There was a time in our very recent past when we were told that all-encompassing theories of art were unfruitful. But losing one's perspective in the rich field of particularity in art, or in a narrow analytical focus on art concepts, will no more produce significant understanding than will arid theories apart from experiencing the qualities of individual art works. It is possible to retain the insights of both approaches, into particular works with their distinctive qualities and into the analysis of art concepts, by not treating the two activities as ends in themselves. In the philosophy of art there is a need to take up once again the grand scheme that relates art to other aspects of human experience, and connects to a study of art concepts, insights derived from attending to particular works.

What better way to do this than to re-examine the grandest of the grand schemes for a philosophy of art? There is good reason to regard Hegel's philosophy of art as a means to overcome deficiencies found in the two approaches considered above. It relates art to other aspects of human experience, nature, culture, and to the world order. At the same time Hegel's philosophy of art emerges from his own extensive acquaintance with the arts. The possibility that his approach to art fulfills the need to relate the particular perceptions and analysis of concepts to each other in the wider scope of human experience is quite strong. There is no doubt that Hegel provides one of the richest accounts of art given by any philosopher. Yet, there exists a formidable obstacle to the appreciation of his aesthetics. The dominant trend has been to interpret Hegel's *Lectures on Aesthetics* and his other materials on art as signifying the "death of art," or the view that art as a significant human activity reaches its end with the dissolution of romantic art. Erich Heller's statement is representative:

> Both Hegel's Classical and Romantic art emerge from his
> metaphysics as sentenced to death by the very law of the Spirit.
> Classical art had to die because the Spirit could not abide by the
> perfect understanding it had reached with concrete reality; for it lies
> in the Spirit's true nature that in the end it should be rid of all sensu-
> ous encumbrance. . . . Romantic art is the negation of the very idea of
> art . . . as the body of the Idea.[1]

The view is shared by Croce, Israel Knox, and others who have considered the question less carefully:

> The German refused to evade the logical exigencies of his system
> and proclaimed the mortality, nay the very death, of art. . . . He
> passes in review the successive forms of art, shows the progressive
> steps of internal consumption and lays the whole in its grave, leaving
> philosophy to write its epitaph.[2]

> By a process of sheer dialectical deduction Hegel infers the death of
> art; it is necessitated by the conceptual determinism of his
> metaphysical dialectical absolutism.[3]

Even those who have indicated their lack of support for the prevailing
interpretation — Bosanquet, D'Hondt, Findlay, and Harries — have not
offered an adequate examination of the inadequacy of the view that
Hegel intends to signal the death of art. Bosanquet argues that Croce
misunderstands Hegel's logic and mistranslates the term 'Auflösung'
as 'death of art'; he thereby agrees with my position that Croce errs in
attributing the death of art thesis to Hegel.[4] And these words of professor D'Hondt affirm a similar conclusion: "Hegel a-t-il annoncé la
mort de l'art? Impossible de lui imputer un tel crime. . . . Il
n'emploie jamais ces mots, *la mort de l'art,* et il lui arrive d'exprimer
des opinions qui contredisent cette pensée funèbre."[5] Professor Harries
also agrees that Hegel should not be interpreted as proclaiming the
death of art; but Harries does accept a weaker version of the death of
art thesis when he claims that for Hegel art has lost its highest vocation and asserts that art is in a position to offer the modern world no
more than a diversion.[6] Finally, it is surely significant that so notable
an interpreter of Hegel as Professor Findlay makes no mention of "the
death of art" in his own account of Hegel's view of art.[7]

The paper will develop further the notion that the death of art interpretation is unwarranted by critically examining the arguments of
Heller, Croce, and Knox, with reference to the *Lectures on Aesthetics* and

Hegel's other writings on art. The analysis of crucial texts will result in support for the alternative thesis that Hegel did not intend the death of art and that he explicitly and implicitly provides for the continuation and development of art. He explicitly provides for the continuation of art through its participation in the more inclusive accounts of Absolute Spirit offered by religion and philosophy, which are the other two modes of Absolute Spirit. Additionally, Hegel's aesthetics implicitly liberates art from its past forms and from a narrow construing of content. Art is thus free to develop new forms in the light of future creative activity of individual artists acting in relation to the cultures of their times.

The very richness and complexity of Hegel's discussion of art, not to mention the relation of the material on art to the larger themes of Hegel's system, make hazardous any attempt to give a final reading of Hegel's view on the place and future of art. The same richness suggests a many-sided gem that cannot be examined sufficiently from a single perspective. My primary objective here is not to refute conclusively the death of art interpretation but to set forth the problem in a form that will generate further discussion and rethinking that will lead to clarification of an important aspect of Hegel's philosophy of art. The paper will develop the following points: (1) The claim that Hegel's metaphysical dialectical principle necessarily produces the death of art is shown to be based on a misapplication of the principle of the dialectic. (2) A review of the texts most likely to support the death of art thesis establishes sufficient qualifications in every case to support an alternative interpretation of the texts. (3) The death of art thesis misunderstands the dissolution in romantic art of subjective and sensuous elements and confuses changes in romantic art with the demise of all art.

I. Misapplications of the Principles of Dialectic

Characteristic of the death of art interpretation are applications of the principle of dialectic or development which are in one way or another hostile to the welfare of art. Dialectic can be applied to Hegel's view of art at two levels. It is applied to the relation between art, religion, and philosophy, which are the three modes of disclosing Absolute Spirit to man's consciousness. Art is understood to be Spirit's "sensuous manifestation." Religion and philosophy are more "ideal" and more inclusive representations which come closer to the true qualities of Spirit.[8] (HA, 101-105) Dialectic also operates in reference to the states of the idea of art: symbolic, classical, and romantic.

Croce, Heller, and Knox base their argument for the death of art interpretation on a mechanical view of the role of dialectic. According to their interpretation, the death of art is a necessary logical consequence of the dialectical unfolding of Absolute Spirit. As the dialectic unfolds at this level we find that beauty in art is a synthesis of the sensuous and the rational, romantic art is a synthesis of symbolic and classical art, and philosophy is a synthesis of art and religion.[9] Art's demise is projected on two levels. The appearance of philosophy as the most complete and definitive presentation of Absolute Spirit is understood to dispense with the need for art. Analogously, on another level the dialectic manifests itself in the symbolic, classical, and romantic forms of art. These successive forms are said to "pass in review" until art reaches its outer limits as a viable expression of Absolute Spirit, thus drawing to a close the life of art.[10]

A. The dialectic applied to art, religion, and philosophy

The first line of criticism of the death of art thesis can be made with respect to dialectical development in the progression from art to philosophy. It will be necessary to give a brief explanation of Hegel's view on this point to see where the death of art thesis has gone wrong. The thesis is problematic because it presumes that an advancement in the stages of dialectic evolution from art to philosophy results in the annihilation or uselessness of the previous stages. This view is in conflict with Hegel's explanation of the dialectic. Hegel describes the stages of the dialectic in his Preface to *The Phenomenology of Mind* as equally necessary moments of an organic unity that constitute the life of the whole. Hyppolite and other distinguished commentators on Hegel's system have proposed that the stages in Hegel's dialectic move to ever richer developments and "always reproduce within themselves the prior developments and give them new meaning."[11] I shall adopt this interpretation of Hegel's dialectic because it represents Hegel's general philosophical method and because it is in fact the method that he uses to discuss both the relations between art, religion, and philosophy and the various stages in the development of art.

Hegel does distinguish the points of view of the artist and the philosopher, and he clearly differentiates art from philosophy. The artist's task is to grasp reality and its forms through alert eyes and ears. Although reason acts to enable the artist to relate his perceptions to the idea of Absolute Spirit, the artist does not comprehend experience in propositions and representations *(Sätze und Vorstellungen)* as does the philosopher. Rather, the artist brings to consciousness the inner core of reason clothed in concrete forms and the individualities of real life. His representations are so infused with the stamp of emotional life that they make public a part of the artist's own spiritual personality.[12] (HA, 281-82) Art is thereby capable only of presenting those aspects of the Absolute which can be expressed in sensuous form. By contrast, the point of view of philosophy is that of the whole, the absolute, God. Philosophy or thought is the mode of apprehension in which both subject and form are identical. Philosophy is thus the self-reflection of Absolute Spirit.[13] (HA, 101, 105) The model that is suggested is *incarnation* — in philosophy we have the disclosing of God as he knows himself — and the point of view of philosophy thereby becomes the most inclusive account of being.[14]

There is no doubt then that Hegel assigns philosophy, understood in the above sense, a higher place than art as a manifestation of Absolute Spirit. (HA, 10-11) In the *Phenomenology* art is placed very high but not at the highest stage of the dialectical development. Hegel assigns philosophy a higher place than art in his *Aesthetics* too. Art ranks highest in neither form nor content, and Hegel's choice of philosophy as the more inclusive mode of Spirit suggests his preference.[15] But none of these facts warrant the conclusion of Knox and the others that Hegel pronounces the death of art. Hegel's concept of philosophy *incorporates* art into its more comprehensive grasp of things. Both art and religion are united *(vereinigt)* in philosophy where their characteristics are related to the form and subjectivity of thought. Art is neither lost nor abandoned in the more comprehensive synthesis of philosophy, but continues to function as a vital part of the larger unity. The expression of the Absolute in relation to dialectic and philosophy would be incomplete without the continued participation of art as one of the ele-

ments of the whole.[16] There is no need to think of destruction of previous modes, art and religion, because it is characteristic of dialectic
that the higher mode integrates the content of lower ones as aspects of
a wider scope where the previous categories can exist without contradiction.[17] At the same time, the significance of the previous
categories is retained.

B. *The Dialectic in Symbolic, Classical, Romantic Forms of Art*

The manifestation of dialectic in symbolic, classical, and romantic
art forms is another part of the argument for the death of art thesis.
Knox states that romantic art is a consuming synthesis of the other two
forms, and Heller describes the romantic form as the disintegration of
art itself. Its demise is thus offered as evidence for the death of art
thesis. A brief examination of Hegel's discussion of these forms is
necessary to show that support for the death of art thesis is lacking here
too.

Each of the forms is effective in some degree as a representation of
Absolute Spirit. Symbolic art, the first, is closest to nature. The sensuous element in art and Absolute Spirit are brought into proximity at
this level, but they are unable to achieve a unification of the sensuous
form and spiritual content of art.[18] (HA, 655) The earliest forms of
symbolic art, being close to nature, exhibit the principle of the productive energy of generation.[19] (HA, 641) Phallus and Lingam are
examples of organic shapes used in symbolic art. They appear as pillars
and columns constructed in the shapes of male and female sex organs.
These can be seen in the early pre-architectural and architectural forms
in the arts of Syria, India, and Egypt. The height of symbolic art
comes in architectural structures such as the pyramids which in part
abandon the shapes of nature for shapes that derive from the artistic
powers of man's mind. The pyramids, unlike structures which merely
satisfy the physical want of shelter, act as religious and political symbols.[20] (HA, 653, 655) Despite its degree of success, symbolic art
lacks both the form and the adequate grasp of Spirit as its content that
is found in later developments in art.

Classical art advances the development. Its sculpture takes its preferred model from the human body. Unlike the other natural animal

bodies whose bodily frames are animated by animal soul *(Seele)*, the human form also has a quality of spirit *(Geist)*. [21] (HA, 714-15) Spirit is explained here as "being for itself of conscious and self-conscious existence," together with the emotions, ideas, and purposes of that existence. The universal qualities of the human form are ideally receptive to a unity of form and content by which Spirit enters into the sensuous form of the sculpture, analogous to the receptivity of the human body to Spirit. However the unity of classical art bypasses the genuinely subjective aspects of personal self-consciousness and is found to be unstable. [22] (HA, 716-18) The result is the dissolution of the objective unity of the classical form of art.

The emergence of romantic art introduces the last of Hegel's determinate forms of art. A careful understanding of Hegel's view of the romantic form of art is very important to the clarification of the death of art issue. Advocates of the death of art thesis emphasize two themes arising from romantic art. They assert that romantic art consumes the previous forms of art through the workings of dialectic and then point to the alleged disengagement of inner subjective aspects from outer sensuous form as the definitive evidence for the death of art. But I will show that the synthesis of the previous forms of art into romantic art and the changed relation of the subjective and sensuous elements that Hegel finds in romantic art do not entail the death of art. Croce and the others who interpret Hegel's aesthetics according to the death of art hypothesis fail to see that synthesis in romantic art includes the previously independent forms without destroying them. The changed relation of sensuous and subjective elements in romantic art, moreover, is not synonymous with art's demise.

1. Synthesis in Romantic Art

The romantic arts of painting, music, and poetry each provide some synthesis of the previous forms of art. Painting takes representations of environments from architecture and uses them as background settings for the human figure which it borrows from sculpture. (HA, 797f) Poetry then combines "essential qualities" of painting and music to embrace the most inclusive perspective of the arts. Hegel's remarks on dramatic poetry offer another example of the dialectic synthesis in a particular romantic art. There, the synthesis shows the "lesser arts —architecture, sculpture, painting, and music—appearing as vital parts in a theater presentation of dramatic poetry.[23] (HA, 1181f and 1190) Shakespeare's "Hamlet" and Mozart's "Magic Flute," each in its own way, illustrates the synthesis by its use of the lesser arts in the total "poetry" of a dramatic performance.

According to the death of art thesis, we should expect the workings of dialectic to produce the destruction of the lesser and prior stages of art. But quite a different effect is seen. These representative samples of dialectic synthesis taken from Hegel's discussion of romantic arts show that the lesser arts, or principles derived from them, are retained and used in the context of a larger purpose. On the other hand, neither example suggests any use of these arts that would result in their cancellation apart from the synthesis. Nothing in the painter's use of principles borrowed from architecture and sculpture makes painting an adequate replacement of these two arts. And likewise the use of music in a drama does no violence to its status as music. The examination of dialectic in romantic art thus fails to support the death of art thesis; instead, it reinforces the previous point that dialectic incorporates rather than destroys earlier stages of its development.

2. The Changed Relation of Sensuous Form and the Subjective in Romantic Art

The development of romantic art signifies a shift of emphasis from the sensuous or visible form and its relation to Absolute Spirit to self-conscious subjectivity—the inner world of the ideal and of emotions, soul, and contemplation, of the subject. (HA, 792-96) Personal subjectivity and its involvement with Absolute Spirit are the main center of interest for this changed point of view. This shift has been understood by the advocates of the death of art thesis as an irrevocable split between two essential elements of art, resulting in art's permanent dissolution. However, an examination of Hegel's discussion of this point suggests that too great an emphasis has been placed on the alleged disengagement of sense and subjectivity. Hegel is partly to blame, for his language at times does appear to suggest such a reading. Yet careful attention to the full context of the discussion shows Hegel repeatedly reminding the reader of the continuing necessity for a vital relation between the sensuous and the subjective in art. (HA, 795)

Admittedly, there is less attention given by Hegel to the positive role of the sensuous element in romantic art. But the shift has a different purpose than to bring to an end the life of art. The shift is wrought in part to emphasize the differences between classical and romantic art. Hegel finds too little involvement of personal subjective life in classical art. By comparison, romantic art satisfies this lack. Hegel thus gives prominence to the subjective by de-emphasizing the visible. But this does not mean that romantic art can exist apart from its sensuous form. Romantic art is compelled to operate in the realms of the visible and the sensible *(Sichbaren und Sinnlichen)* to communicate the developments of inner life.[24] (HA, 795f)

The need to communicate the inner workings of imagination suggests another way of looking at the changed role of sensuous form in romantic art. In classical art the visible form acts as a *symbol* participating as fully as possible in the ontological meaning of Absolute Spirit. But the visible form in romantic art acts more as a sign, communicating the artistic happenings of subjective life without being the main center of interest. (HA, 795f) The distinction between symbol and sign could be misleading here. It should not be understood to mean simply that the visible has no significance. Hegel is attempting to show that the significance of the visible is not due to its natural sensuous qualities but comes instead from the fact that imagination subjects the natural qualities to its own subjective purposes and thus transforms the qualities of a medium into art.[25]

II. Discussion of Particular Texts

Even those who agree with the first point, that the dialectic argument fails to support the death of art thesis, may puzzle over certain of Hegel's texts that are cited in support of the thesis. The following interpretation of three principal texts will suggest that they do not necessarily uphold the thesis. The texts are taken from representative major divisions of Hegel's *Lectures on Aesthetics*, one each corresponding to the general idea of a philosophy of art, to a particular form of art, and to a particular medium. The first concerns Hegel's justification for a *philosophy* of art and the limits and place of art relative to religion and philosophy; the second considers the nature and implications of the dissolution of the romantic form of art; and the third concerns the role of sensuous or external form in poetry. All three bear directly and critically on the acceptance or rejection of the death of art thesis.

A. "Art is and remains for us, on the side of its highest possibilities, a thing of the past." (HA, 11)[26]

The *larger* context of the quotation is the introduction to the *Lectures on Aesthetics* where Hegel justifies the need for a philosophy of art. Since the statement is a part of his rationale for writing a philosophy of art, it necessarily takes on a function of apology or justification. It shows in part why Hegel is doing philosophy rather than making paintings or poems. More importantly, the statement expresses the larger need for a form of thought to accommodate the deficiencies that he sees in the art of his own age and culture. The statement expresses Hegel's belief that the critical and reflective activities of his own age are not conducive to the creation of significant art; but it should not be taken as a definitive pronouncement on the future of art for all ages. Here I agree with Gray's point that the emphasis in the passage under consideration is on the "for us," and that art will "in the evolution of ages" continue to awaken man to self-knowledge and truth.[27]

The *immediate* context of the quotation is a preliminary account of the reasons for making philosophy the supreme approach to Absolute Spirit. According to Hegel, art is one, but not the only, and not necessarily the most adequate expression of man's highest concerns. It is important for the argument of this paper to note that the limitations placed on art by Hegel are quite specific, rather than general or all-inclusive ones. The limits are in terms of seeing art as the highest approach to the ultimate truths of the religious point of view of Hegel's time, or of Hegel's own Christian religious point of view. He finds art insufficient to bring the "true interests of our spiritual life to consciousness," and "no longer able to discover that satisfaction of spiritual wants, which previous epochs and nations have . . . exclusively found in it," e.g., the good days of Greek art and the golden time of the later Middle Ages.[28] (HA, 9-10) Though art, in Hegel's view, is not as adequate as religion or philosophy for satisfying man's spiritual wants, art nevertheless retains its place as a highly valued activity, both for Hegel and for the future. Here and elsewhere the limitations of art are stated in relative and qualified terms.

Finally, it is a part of a much larger aspect of Hegel interpretation to decide whether the forward progress of the dialectic is a process *in time*.[29] In the *Phenomenology*, the dialectic is, in part, in time, and the moments in the history of a particular civilization are the movements of the dialectic. Hegel wants to speak in such a way that what he says applies to such moments as when religion or art or philosophy is the dominant voice in a particular historical period, say ancient Greece or modern Germany. But he doesn't necessarily want his categories of art, religion, and philosophy to be tied to these particular phenomena in history. Hegel is also timelessly locating art relative to its place in the total assortment of human values rather than asserting that art is dead because still higher values rise above it, e.g., philosophy or absolute knowledge. (HA, 82-90)

Along the same lines, Hegel sees the dialectic manifesting itself in such particular stylistic moments as the classical style of ancient Greece and the romantic style of nineteenth century Germany. But he does not restrict the symbolic, classical, and romantic modes of art to a determined progress of the dialectic in time. These modes are timeless, universal forms of art. They, and possibly others that have yet to emerge, are necessary to provide a view of art in all of its aspects and to show its relation to the whole, which is, for Hegel, the true.

B. *"We find . . . as the termination of romantic art, the contingency of the exterior condition and internal life, and a falling asunder of the two aspects, by reason of which art commits an act of suicide. . . ."*[30]

The second text to be considered occurs in a discussion of the dissolution of romantic art. In this context, Hegel speaks of a "falling asunder" *(Auseinanderfallen)* of the sensuous and the subjective elements of romantic art, with the result that art allegedly dissolves itself in the process *(selbst sich aufhebt)*. Dissolution is interpreted by advocates of the death of art thesis to mean the death or demise of art. And this interpretation has been a part of the basis for the support of the thesis.

Osmaston's translation of the phrase, *"Kunst selbst sich aufhebt,"* into the English, "Art commits an act of suicide," may have inadvertently served to perpetuate the death of art interpretation, especially among English readers of Hegel. However, insofar as I can determine, Hegel never actually uses the phrase, "the death of art." Osmaston's translation is suggestive only in its fanciful and misleading character. Hegel's text neither benefits from nor requires translation in a manner suggesting the suicide image. The translator ignores the fact that in *aufheben* he has one of Hegel's most enigmatic terms. One of the most important notions in all of Hegel, *aufheben* literally means to raise up something; however, as a philosophical notion it can mean "cancel," "dissolve," or "preserve," or all three at once! Hegel may have resorted to a certain amount of punstering to convey the essence of his dialectical method of interpreting the sensuous and the subjective elements of art. Nevertheless *aufheben* with its multiple connotations assembles the several aspects of the dialectic process with admirable verbal economy.

I would like to propose an alternative to Osmaston's translation of *aufheben* based on the idea of *dissolve*. 'Dissolve' includes both the elements of "cancel" and "preserve," and it expresses the appropriate meanings of both *Auseinanderfallen* and *selbst sich aufhebt* which are the principal terms in the text that is under consideration here. In this case, to dissolve is not the same as to destroy. The dissolution in romantic art is more akin to the modern cinematic principles of dissolve. In a film, to dissolve is to fade out one shot or scene while simultaneously fading in the next, overlapping the two during the process.[31] The camera focuses on an object that dissolves in degrees into a near blur, only to re-emerge as a distinctly new object that retains some of the qualities of the object it has replaced.

The analogous process of "dissolve" in romantic art takes place on the level of the relation of visible sensuous form to the inner subjective workings of imagination. Natural qualities of sensuous form "dissolve" into a new image as they are transformed by the qualities and activities of subjective imagination. In the new image, the natural qualities are retained but are "in the service of" the artist's spirit, feelings, and ideas.

The results of my application of the principle of dissolve are visible in a comparison of a Greek "Bust of Zeus" with Rembrandt's "Portrait of a Young Man, 1662."[32] The bust acts as an ideal vehicle for revealing Absolute Spirit to man's consciousness, according to Hegel's category of classical art. Its universal qualities of sensuous form are abstracted from the human form, but they retain their independence from personal subjectivity and also from complete unity with Absolute Spirit. By comparison, Rembrandt's portrait shows the dissolve of the natural sensuous qualities of color and line into a new image. They reveal the human qualities of a sensitive, fragile personality who is enigmatic in his very lack of a distinct focus. The viewer is aware of the painting's rich sensuous qualities primarily through their disclosure of the particular qualities of the subject's inner life.

A similar effect occurs in two different pictorial scenes. Monet's "Charing Cross Bridge, 1903" shows sensuous form in the relative absence of its domination by subjective purposes. Monet arranges color and light in a manner of scientific objectivity and shows the surfaces of both the painting and its representation of the scene primarily for their sensory values. Consider also Doré's "Loch Lomond, 1875." Compared to Monet's "Charing Cross Bridge," "Loch Lomond" displays a strong sense of the artist's subjective vision of the nature scene. Colors and lines are no less present in the Doré painting, but they do not project their sensory values independently of displaying the artist's vision of an aura of mystery and legend.

The differences in both sets of examples are between art works that show the sensuous qualities retaining a high degree of independence and exhibiting forms that are simply extensions of the natural qualities, and works where the artist's subjective spirit dissolves the sensuous in a more personal representation. The sensuous element is not lost or abandoned. It simply becomes more evidently a vehicle to express man's inner life. If I have correctly interpreted the text referred to here, those who understand romantic art to be the death of art misunderstand Hegel's view. Romantic art is not the death of art; it is one more stage, and obviously is not the last stage in the history of art.

C. "Poetry, alone among the arts, completely dispenses with the sensuous medium of the objective world of phenomena."[33]

The third text is in reference to poetry. Its several variations, appearing throughout Hegel's long discussion of poetry, all suggest that poetry is the most successful of the arts in moulding bare sensuous form to the aims of subjectivity. Advocates of the death of art thesis attempt to use such passages to support their view. However, the strength of their argument diminishes when we examine the qualifications and limits that Hegel acknowledges, and when we apply the principle of dissolve to poetry.

Hegel identifies two principal ways in which poetry is superior to the other arts: in its representational powers and in its greater success at moulding sensuous form to the aims of subjectivity. (HA, 960, 966) Only the latter is important for the death of art thesis because superiority in representational powers does not suggest the dissolution of art. The references to the superiority of poetry are expressed negatively by Hegel and are overstated in order to contrast poetry with the other arts. However, for each statement emphasizing poetry's dispensing with the sensuous materials, there are important qualifications that are applicable to one or all.[34] Hegel continues to remind us of the necessary qualifications leading to a correct sense of the negative overstatements.

A most important qualification arises from the necessity to communicate the results of the inner imaginative activity. Sensuous form remains essential for poetic communication as it does for the other arts. It is not seen as bare matter; instead it acts as a sign that is able to transmit the qualities of emotion and idea. The communication is possible because sensuous form is transformed and elevated through the activity of imagination.

A second qualification is with respect to changes in the natural materials of the different arts. When Hegel states that poetry will have nothing to do with gross matter as such, he is simply indicating the difference between the external materials of architecture and poetry. (HA, 960) In architecture the artist struggles with nature's raw materials of wood and stone. By the time art reaches the stage of poetry, its external "raw material" is *language*. Because language is already a product of mind, it requires less "working over" than do the materials of architecture. However, it remains that language is both thought *and* human speech or inscription, and poetry necessarily retains a sensuous form.

Hegel's understanding of the sensuous element in poetry can be seen clearly in examples of English romantic poetry. The English romantic theory of imagination, as it is discussed in nineteenth and twentieth century literary criticism, closely parallels Hegel's view. Analogous to Hegel's idea of dissolve, imagination acts in English romantic poetry to dissolve the oppositions of emotions and ideas to the sensory elements. Coleridge speaks of the "indissoluble union between the intellectual and the material world" in these words:

> The Poet's heart and intellect should be *combined*, intimately . . . and unified with the great appearances of nature, and not merely held in solution and loose mixture with them.[35]

The distinction between undissolved sensory material in art and the successfully dissolved can be seen in a contrast of sonnets with the same theme by William Lisle Bowles and Samuel Taylor Coleridge.[36] The first is Bowles' "To The River Itchin."

> Itchin, when I behold thy banks again,
> Thy crumbling margin, and thy silver breast,
> On which the self-same tints still seem to rest,
> Why feels my heart the shiv'ring sense of pain?
> Is it—that many a summer's day has past
> Since, in life's morn, I carol'd on thy side?
> Is it—that oft, since then my heart has sigh'd,
> As Youth, and Hope's delusive gleams, flew fast?
> Is it—that those, who circled on thy shore,
> Companions of my youth, now meet no more?
> Whate'er the cause, upon thy banks I bend
> Sorrowing, yet feel such solace at my heart,
> As at the meeting of some long-lost friend,
> From whom, in happier hours, we wept to part.

The second is Coleridge's "To The River Otter."

> Dear native Brook! wild Streamlet of the West!
> How many various-fated years have past,
> What happy and what mournful hours, since last
> I skimmed the smooth thin stone along thy breast,
> Numbering its light leaps! yet so deep imprest
> Sink the sweet scenes of childhood, that mine eyes
> I never shut amid the sunny ray,
> But straight with all their tints thy waters rise,
> Thy crossing plank, thy marge with willows grey,
> And bedded sand that veined with various dyes
> Gleamed through thy bright transparence! On my way,
> Visions of Childhood! oft have ye beguiled
> Lone manhood's cares, yet waking fondest sighs:
> Ah! that once more I were a careless Child!

Coleridge's poem is admittedly done in imitation of Bowles', and both deal with the theme of recollecting a childhood experience which is no longer vital. Yet, their differences exemplify an important distinction. Bowles simply sets up an associative relation between emotion and the sensuous elements of the poem. The sensuous is not integrally connected with the emotion. Compared to Bowles' poem, Coleridge's intensifies the color of sensibility with emotion and idea, giving a richness of significance that signals a fusion of ideas and emotions with sensuous material.[37] The poet's imagination transforms the experience of nature into feeling or thought-infused lines, and brings them under the dominion of subjective spirit. Instead of the death of art, I find that the role of the sensory form is changed in accordance with the purposes of romantic art.

Conclusion

My conclusion is that Hegel did not intend the death of art. He uses the principle of dialectic to show the limits of art for communicating the highest religious truths of interest to man. The dialectic also shows the respective differences among the symbolic, classical, and romantic forms of art and gives a basis for comparing them according to their common use of sensuous and subjective elements. The sensuous and the subjective elements fall apart in romantic art only in a metaphorical way of speaking, and only to dissolve into a new image that makes the subjective element more prominent for this form of art. The texts that allegedly support the death of art thesis are less puzzling when the interpreter is mindful of their respective purposes of (1) justifying philosophy of art; (2) defining art's place and limits in relation to other modes of cognition; (3) contrasting and comparing the different forms of art. In effect, the aggregate force of the arguments offered here — the analysis of dialectic in Hegel's aesthetics, the examination of three principal texts, and the interpretation of dissolution in romantic art — recommends an interpretation that includes a future for art and warrants abandonment of the negative thesis of Croce, Heller, and Israel Knox.

NOTES

1. Erich Heller, *The Artist's Journey into the Interior* (New York: Vintage Books, 1968), p. 115.

2. Benedetto Croce, *Aesthetic* (tr. A. Maude) (New York: Noonday Press, 1958), p. 302f.

3. Israel Knox, *The Aesthetic Theories of Kant, Hegel and Schopenhauer* (New York: Humanities Press, 1958), p. 103.

4. Bernard Bosanquet, "Appendix on Croce's Conception of the 'Death of Art' in Hegel," *Proc. of the British Academy* (1919), pp. 20-28.

5. M. Jacques D'Hondt, "La Mort de L'Art," a report in the *Bulletin International D'Esthetique*, 17 (June 1972), p. 4.

6. Karsten Harries, "Hegel on the Future of Art," *Review of Metaphysics* 27 (June 1974), pp. 677-96.

7. J. N. Findlay, *Hegel: A Re-Examination* (New York: Collier Books, 1962), pp. 341-46. Professor Findlay has expressed in private discussions with the author the opinion that Hegel could not have intended the death of art.

8. G. W. F. Hegel, *The Philosophy of Fine Art* (tr. Osmaston), (London: G. Bell & Sons, 1920), pp. 139-44. The new translation of this work by Sir T. M. Knox did not appear until after this essay was presented, but page references to his edition are given in parentheses throughout the present text following the abbreviation HA. My citations to the German text are to Friedrich Bassenge's two volume edition (Berlin & Weimar: Aufbau-Verlag, 1965). Hereafter I will give parallel references to those in the Knox translation by citing the Bassenge edition and the Osmaston translation in the following notes.

9. Israel Knox, *op.cit.,* provides a representative statement. See p. 103.

10. Israel Knox's phrase is ambiguous here. The phrase "pass in review" can apply to either logical or metaphysical stages of the idea of Absolute Spirit, or to stages in art history.

11. Jean Hyppolite, *Genesis and Structure of Hegel's Phenomenology of Spirit* (tr. Cherniak and Heckman), (Evanston: Northwestern University Press, 1974), p. 64. See also pp. 65 and 597.

12. Osmaston translation, I, 381-83; Bassenge edition in the German, I, 275-76.

13. Osmaston, I, 139, 143; Bassenge, I, 108. See also Nathan Rotenstreich, "The Essential and the Epochal Aspects of Philosophy," *Review of Metaphysics*, 23 (1970), p. 714.

14. Rotenstreich, *op. cit.,* p. 714. See *Werke* (Glockner), Vol. 19, p. 686.

15. Hegel differs from Schelling, who gives art the highest place in his *System of Transcendental Idealism*.

16. McTaggart notes in his discussion of the dialectic the inseparability of the dialectic in pure thought and in experience. It is inconceivable that Hegel would destroy art, the essential bridge between the two. J. M. E. McTaggart, *Studies in the Hegelian Dialectic* (Cambridge: Cambridge Univ. Press, 1896) Chapters 1 & 2.

17. *Ibid.,* p. 1f.

18. Osmaston, III, 56; Bassenge, II, 46f.

19. Osmaston, III, 39; Bassenge, II, 33.

20. Osmaston, III, 53-56; Bassenge, II, 44-47.
21. Osmaston, III, 127f; Bassenge, II, 99.
22. Osmaston, III, 130f; Bassenge, II, 101.
23. Osmaston, IV, 278f, 289; Bassenge, II, 535f, 543.
24. Osmaston, III, 224, Bassenge, II, 175.
25. This interpretation is in keeping with Hegel's general philosophical practice of regarding nature as a lower form of reality in need of being transformed by the activity of mind. Nature acquires greater importance for Hegel when it is allied with mind's purposes. By analogy, so should the sensuous in art. Below, I will seek to show that the sensuous in romantic art must retain a positive role.
26. "In allen diesen Beziehungen ist und bleibt die Kunst nach der Seite ihrer höchsten Bestimmung für uns ein Vergangenes." (Bassenge, I, 22; Osmaston, I, 13).
27. J. Glenn Gray, G. W. F. Hegel on Art, Religion, Philosophy (New York: Harper Torchbooks, 1970), p. 18.
28. Osmaston, I, 11f; Bassenge, I, 21f.
29. This point was suggested to me by an anonymous critic of an earlier version of the essay.
30. "Dadurch erhalten wir als Endpunkt des Romantischen überhaupt die Zufälligkeit des Äusseren wie des Inneren und ein Auseinanderfallen dieser Seiten, durch welches die Kunst selbst sich aufhebt und die Notwendigkeit für das Bewusstsein ziegt . . ." Knox translates this text as follows: "Therefore we acquire as the culmination of the romantic in general the contingency of both outer and inner, and the separation of these two sides, whereby art annuls itself and brings home to our minds that we must acquire higher forms for the apprehension of truth than those which art is in a position to supply." (529) Cf. Bassenge, I, 509; Osmaston, II, 296.
31. Random House Dictionary of the English Language (Unabridged edition, 1967), p. 416.
32. The St. Louis Art Museum contains the original works cited here.
33. "Unter allen Künsten entbehrt nur die Poesia der vollen, auch sinnlichen Realität ausserer Erscheinung." Knox translates this: "Of all the arts poetry alone does not appear outwardly in something completely real and also perceptible" [sic]. (1181), Bassenge, II, 535; Osmaston, IV, 278. Variations of the statement are found on HA, 960 and 966 (Osmaston, II, 328, 334; Bassenge, II, 960, 966).
34. See 964-66, 977-78, 1181 (Osmaston, IV, 10-13, 27-29, 278; Bassenge, II, 331-34, 343-45, 535).
35. S. T. Coleridge, Letters (Boston, 1895), Vol. I, p. 404. Cited in William K. Wimsatt, Jr., The Verbal Icon: Studies in the Meaning of Poetry (New York: Noonday Press, 1958), p. 107.
36. I am indebted to Wimsatt's essay "Romantic Nature Imagery" for this example. In Wimsatt, op.cit., pp. 105-10.
37. Ibid., pp. 106-09, 115.

B. The Logic of Hegel

VI
Hegel's Theory of the Concept
by
MEROLD WESTPHAL

"The subject-matter of the philosophical science of right is the Idea of right, i.e., the concept of right together with the actualization of that concept." So begins the Introduction to Hegel's *Philosophy of Right*. Since Hegel defines right in terms of freedom[1], his account of the actualization of that concept is the story of how freedom is actual in the modern world. This occupies almost the entirety of Hegel's text. Thus the concept of freedom is developed for the most part not by itself but in the context of narrating its actualization. But if either the reader or the writer is to have any way of recognizing what counts in the modern world as the actuality of freedom, some prior understanding of the meaning of freedom seems to be required. It is this which the Introduction seeks to provide, a purely conceptual analysis of freedom.

This analysis will of necessity be incomplete, just because of its a priori character. "The shapes which the concept assumes in the course of its actualization are indispensable for the knowledge of the concept itself." (PR, § 1) To repeat, it is only when we grasp "the concept of right *together with* the actualization of that concept" (my italics) that we can adequately grasp that concept. The adequate conceptual grasp of any content can never be reached by conceptual analysis alone. Yet a prior understanding of the concept is needed to guide the discovery of that actualization of freedom which alone can provide us with an adequate conceptual grasp. It is tempting to think of this prior understanding in terms of hypothesis or conjecture, but we know from his discussions of Reinhold that Hegel rejects this suggestion out of hand.[2] Whence this pre-understanding of freedom, then? There can be only one Hegelian answer—from the Logic. For in Hegelian philosophy it is always the Logic which provides the conceptual wherewithal for any truly speculative understanding of nature or spirit.

The conceptual analysis of freedom presented in the Introduction to the *Philosophy of Right* does not disappoint these expectations. It is indeed derived from the Logic, in particular from the analysis of the Concept as universal, particular (or specific), and individual. This triadic structure of the Concept thus becomes the basis for getting at the genuinely speculative element in Hegel's political philosophy. My purpose here, however, is just the opposite. It is to throw a little light on the logic of the Concept by reflecting on Hegel's employment of the categories Universality, Particularity, and Individuality in developing a pre-understanding of freedom.

This procedure will no doubt make some readers feel uncomfortable. The Logic, we will be told, is intelligible in its own right, and is first to be understood by itself as pure thought before any consideration of its employment can be legitimated. That there is something genuinely Hegelian about this response I shall not deny. But there is something equally Hegelian about my own procedure as well. After all, for Hegel the truth is the whole, and no part of philosophical science can be fully understood apart from its detailed relations to the others. I have just quoted Hegel's claim that the concept of right or freedom cannot adequately be understood apart from the shapes of its actualization in the world. I am taking this in the strong sense to mean that even the concepts from the Logic which go into spelling out that prevenient concept of freedom to which the Introduction is devoted cannot be adequately understood in and by themselves but only when we see them at work in the *Philosophy of Right* and elsewhere.

It is in this sense that I understand Hegel's "knowing before you know" (or don't go into the water before you have learned how to swim) critique of critical philosophy. In a paper presented to the Hegel Society of America at Notre Dame in 1972, John Smith reminds us that Hegel praised the critical project of examining the categories and directed his criticism only toward the tendency to separate such criticism from "first order" knowing, thus examining the categories while they were "idling". "Hegel's fundamental complaint, then, is that Kant analyzed the categories as functions of thought, not when they were functioning in actual knowing, but only in their status as necessary conditions for knowing. . . ." In support of this suggestion Smith quotes from Section 41, *Zusatz* of the *Encyclopedia*, where Hegel writes, "So that what we want is to combine in our process of inquiry the *action* of the forms of thought with a criticism of them."[3] This requirement seems to me at best to be only partially satisfied in the Logic itself. Thus it serves as another justification for seeking to understand the Logic in terms of its so-called "application". The activity of the categories of Universality, Particularity, and Individuality in Hegel's political theory belongs to the deduction, analysis, and criticism of them in his Logic.

Methodologically, then, I believe my project has ample Hegelian validation. But I claim no scientific status for my attempt at interpretation. This humility is strategically motivated, I hasten to confess, for it leaves me free to invoke hypotheses and test them out, which is what I intend to do. My initial hypothesis is that the following sentence from the *Zusatz* to Section 7 of the *Philosophy of Right* is the key to the logic of the Concept: "Freedom in this sense, however, we already possess in the form of feeling—in friendship and love, for instance." The meaning of my hypothesis is both a) that the structure of the Concept as Universality, Particularity, and Individuality is necessary to an adequate understanding of friendship and love, and b) that if we think through the meaning of friendship and love adequately we will have developed the structure of the Concept as Universality, Particularity, and Individuality. Since I am trying to work toward the Logic and not from it, it is obviously the latter form of the hypothesis which I shall be exploring.

* * *

The suggestion that friendship and love are the true meaning of freedom follows a summary of Sections 5 through 7, which define freedom in terms of the triadic structure of the Concept. While Hegel once suggests that Universality, Particularity, and Individuality are abstractly the same as Identity, Difference, and Ground (ELW, § 164), they here function as Indeterminacy, Determination, and Self-Determination. Since these categories have an obvious bearing on the question of freedom, the task is to see how the original triad can legitimately be translated into them.

The first equivalence is that of Universality with Indeterminacy. Hegel puts it this way:

"The will contains (α) the element of pure indeterminacy or that
pure reflection of the ego into itself which involves the dissipation of
every restriction and every content either immediately presented by
nature, by needs, desires, and impulses, or given and determined by
any means whatever. This is the unrestricted infinity of absolute
abstraction or universality, the pure thought of oneself."

Freedom involves the ability to abstract from every dependence
upon an other, and since it is always and only in relation to an other
that anything is determinate and not the "indeterminate immediacy"
of pure Being, freedom involves "my flight from every content as from
a restriction." (PR, §5)[4]

There is a freedom which takes this moment of independence as its
whole meaning. Theoretically it is "the Hindu fanaticism of pure contemplation" in which the fundamental structures of the self's being in
the world are systematically undermined. Practically it is exhibited in
the Terror of the French Revolution with its "irreconcilable hatred of
everything particular" [jedes Besondere], i.e., everything determinate in
the social order (Pr, §5-z) "Only in destroying something does this
negative will possess the feeling of itself as existent." This freedom
professes to serve some new and better actuality but cannot do so, for
any such actuality "leads at once to some sort of order, to a particularization [Besonderung] of organizations and individuals alike; while it is
precisely out of the annihilation of particularity [Besonderung] and objective characterization that the self-consciousness of this negative
freedom proceeds." Hegel indicates the one-sidedness of this freedom
as absolute independence curtly by calling it "freedom as the Understanding conceives it" (PR §5).[5]

The second equivalence is already before us, that of Particularity and
Determination, for it matters little whether the content from which
this negative freedom flees as from a restriction is called Besonderheit or
Bestimmtheit. But freedom that would be actual cannot flee forever. For
"my willing is not pure willing but the willing of something. A will
which, like that expounded in Section 5, wills only the abstract
universal, wills nothing and is therefore no will at all" (PR, §6-z).
To will something the will must include the moment of "the finitude
or particularization [Besonderung] of the ego," which is described in
this way:

> "(β) At the same time, the ego is also the transition from undiffer-
> entiated indeterminacy to the differentiation, determination, and
> positing of a determinacy as a content and object. Now further, this
> content may either be given by nature or engendered by the concept
> of spirit" (PR, § 6).

This latter qualification is important, for it indicates that the other
which cannot be excluded from freedom is of two sorts, natural, that
is, the impulses and inclinations *(Triebe und Neigungen)* of immediate
selfhood in their otherness to rational self-determination, and
spiritual, that is, both social institutions and concrete other selves in
their otherness to the independence of the self who would be free. This
second moment, Particularity or Determination, is no less essential to
freedom than the first. For the self which can respond to its own
natural immediacy and to the other selves around it only by withdrawal or destruction cannot be said to be free. On the other hand, this
moment by itself is just as abstract and inadequate as the first. For the
self which is only a function of its impulses and inclinations or of the
other selves it encounters is no more free than the self which flees from
every content as from a restriction. Indeed, it can scarcely be called a
self at all.

Only a caricature of freedom arises, then, when either the moment
of Universality=Indeterminacy or that of Particularity=Determina-
tion is asked by itself to provide a definition. But neither moment can
be eliminated from the concept of freedom. What is needed is a
genuine unity of the two, antithetical as they seem. We already know
that the unity of Universality and Particularity will be called Individuality, and we might guess that the unity of Indeterminacy and Determination will be called Self-Determination, though in both cases, as in
calling happiness the highest good, the task of comprehension lies
ahead and not behind. Hegel writes:

> "(γ) The will is the unity of both these moments. It is particularity re-
> flected into itself and so brought back to universality, i.e., it is indi-
> viduality. It is the *self*-determination of the ego, which means that at
> one and the same time the ego posits itself as its own negative, i.e.,
> as restricted and determinate, and yet remains by itself, i.e., in its
> self-identity and universality" (PR, § 7).

Three comments on this passage may help us get to the heart of the matter. First, it serves to validate the third equivalence, that of Individuality and Self-Determination. Self-determination is defined as the preservation of self-identity in the process of determination. Only that which is in some strong sense individual can endure determination without becoming simply a function of those others through whom this determination is mediated. Such endurance involves the retention of more than that logical self-identity which permits one to be an object of reference or the subject of predication. It requires that real self-identity which is here equated with the moment of universality, which, as we have seen, is the moment of independence.

Second, we are referred directly back to the Logic, where this unity of self-identity and determinateness is central. We can now understand why, when Hegel calls the Concept "the principle of freedom," he goes right on to say, "Thus in its *self-identity* it has original and complete determinateness," and, when defining the structure of the Concept in terms of its three moments, he describes Individuality as the unity of Universality and Particularity, "which negative self-unity has complete and original *determinateness*, without any loss to its *self-identity* or universality."[6]

Third, Hegel calls this unity of self-identity and determination which constitutes Self-Determination or Individuality "the innermost secret of speculation," though the Understanding disdains it as "inconceivable" (PR, § 7). The passage before us indicates both why the synthesis is so easily dismissed as inconceivable and how we may begin to conceive it after all. Self-determination means determination, which means that the self stands in relation to its own negative, to another through whom its determination is mediated. The self is thus *dependent* upon the other for its determinateness. Yet, if this is to be self-determination, it must be a self-mediating activity, and the self must retain its self-identity and universality, i.e., its *independence*. Hegel here uses one of his favorite locutions, *bei sich bleiben*.[7] This means to keep control of oneself, to stay conscious and not pass out. The task, which Understanding finds impossible, is so to remain in control of oneself in giving oneself up to the mediating activity of the other that the whole operation can be called a self-mediating activity and not something which happens to me while unconscious, after which I come to again to learn about my new determinateness. It could then be said that "the ego determines itself insofar as it is the relating of negativity to itself" (PR, §7), or that the self is *Vermittlung* but not *ein Vermitteltes* (WL, II, 241=SL, 602).

This is possible, on Hegel's account, because self-determination means "that at one and the same time *the ego posits itself* as its own negative, i.e., as restricted and determinate, and yet remains by itself . . ." (PR, §7)[8] We have already seen that the self cannot be determinate except in relation to another, and that it cannot be free if this relation is either withdrawal or destruction. But if this other is in some sense itself, the possibility of a more positive relation begins to lose its inconceivability. The only problem is that this solution sounds a bit too Fichtean.[9] The otherness of the other seems compromised.

At this point Hegel's earlier allusion to the categories of Identity, Difference, and Ground is helpful, for it reminds us that for Hegel identity always involves some difference. If the other through whom the self is determined must *in some sense* be identical with that self, we must inquire more carefully what that sense may be. A second formulation from Section 7 calls for our attention.

> "Still, both these moments [self-consciousness as universal and as particular] are only abstractions: what is concrete and true (and everything true is concrete) is the universality which has the particular as its opposite: but [only] that particular which by its reflection into itself has been equalized with the universal."

Here otherness sounds less Fichtean. It has the status of an opposite (*Gegensatz*). But it must have become equalized (*ausgeglichen*) with that to which it stands opposed. We are not told which way the scale must be tipped to bring about this balance. Whether the reflection into itself of the other which confronts the self is a scaling down of its power and activity so that it does not overwhelm the self or a scaling up of its dignity so that its activity is of the same sort as that of the self, the result is that the self and its other are somehow on a par. They are not the same in the sense of numerical identity but of qualitative similarity. This seems the opposite extreme from the Fichtean overtones of the previous formulation. If one thinks of the struggle for recognition in the *Phenomenology*, for example, it seems that neither way of looking at it will do. For if the other from whom the self seeks the determination of recognition is numerically identical with itself, there can be no acceptance of the claim to human dignity but only the repetition of that claim. While if the other is the same as the self in the weaker sense of being qualitatively similar, equal in being another full-blooded human self, we can see nothing in such equality to weaken the Understanding's suspicion that the self must either destroy the selfhood of the other by becoming its master or give up its own by becoming the slave, in neither case achieving freedom.

Turning to the *Zusatz* to Section 7 for help we find a definition of freedom in terms of the three moments of the Concept. It repeats the familiar idea that the self posits itself as its other yet remains by itself in this other; but it provides us with no assistance in making sense out of these Hegelian clichés. Just at this point, however, occurs the sentence which my hypothesis makes central to interpreting Hegel here. "Freedom in this sense, however, we already possess in the form of feeling—in friendship and love, for instance." The explanation continues,

> "Here we are not inherently one-sided; we restrict ourselves gladly in relating ourselves to another, but in this restriction know ourselves as ourselves. In this determinacy a man should not feel himself determined; on the contrary, since he treats the other as other, it is there that he first arrives at the feeling of his own self-hood. Thus freedom lies neither in indeterminacy nor in determinacy; it is both of these at once."

Guided by these descriptions and reminded of whatever experiences of true friendship or love we may have had, we suddenly see how the abstract antithesis between numerical identity and mere qualitative sameness does not exhaust the possibilities. Genuine otherness is preserved, since friendship and love require numerical duality and not numerical identity. Yet we can speak of identity and not mere qualitative sameness, for friends and lovers are not merely different numerical units of the same sort—they constitute together a new reality which they express by saying "We." This whole is more than the sum of its parts. As its co-constituents the parts are identical with each other, for each of them simply is that We just as much as each is also a distinct I.[10]

* * *

Such reflections on the way friends and lovers relate to their counterparts illuminate the kind of identity with difference which the Concept expresses. This confirms Hegel's own view that the theory of the Concept is a theory of freedom, of personality, and of that sense of ego which the slave lacks (ELW, §163-z). When loving intersubjectivity is taken as basic, two conspicuous features of the logical exposition of the Concept appear in a new light, namely the ubiquity of the concept of creativity and the transition from Essence to Concept, more specifically, the development of the triadic structure of the Concept from the category of reciprocity.

The creation motif is never far from sight. The Concept is *unendliche, schöpferische Form, freie, schöpferische Tätigkeit*, or simply *schöpferische Macht*. It is *das Formierende und Erschaffende*; and one can speak of *das Schaffen des Begriffs,* or even of the Idea as *Schöpferin der Natur.* [11]

All this tells us that the Concept is something active and not inert. In its individuality the Concept is *das Wirkende* (EL, §163. Frequently Hegel expresses this central theme in Aristotelian language, the concept being related to its objectivity as soul to body or seed to plant.[12] We are given a theory of development which at first appears to be but a restatement of the Aristotelian theory of substantial form as the merger of formal, final, and efficient causality. But Aristotle's is a theory of life, not of spirit, and while Hegel recognizes the Concept to be "the principle of all life" (ELW, §160-z) and the organic level to be "the stage of nature at which the Concept emerges, " (WL, II, 224=SL, 586), it is only at the level of spirit that its true meaning is manifest. This means that no Aristotelian interpretation of Hegel's creation talk will be adequate. As creative the Concept is *das Wirkende* indeed, but the organic-developmental models of soul-body and seed-plant give at best a partial account of this. For, as we have seen, the theory of the Concept is a theory of intersubjective selfhood and thus of spirit. Its task is to give an account of determinateness through an other such that this "is not a *limit*, as though it were related to another *beyond* it [*einem Jenseits*]. . . ." (WL, II, 245=SL, 605) How does the concept of creation contribute to this central problematic?

The *Zusatz* to Section 161 of the *Encyclopedia* is of special importance in this connection. For while both the original paragraph and the first long paragraph of the *Zusatz* are devoted to the Aristotelian-developmental aspects of the Concept, the final brief paragraph goes beyond this to the level of spirit.

"The movement of the concept is as it were to be looked upon merely
as play: the other which it sets up is in reality not an other. Or, as it is
expressed in the teaching of Christianity: not merely has God
created a world which confronts Him as an other; He has also from all
eternity begotten a Son in whom He, a Spirit, is at home with Himself"
[bei sich selbst ist]

Three models of the self in relation to its other are given here. In
play the other is not really an other, but the figment of the self's active
imagination. Remember Puff?

One gray night it happened, Jackie Paper came no more
So Puff the Magic Dragon ceased his fearsome roar.

His head was bent in sorrow, green scales fell like rain
Puff no longer went to play along the cherry lane
Without his lifelong friend, Puff could not be brave
So Puff that mighty dragon sadly slipped into his cave.

The strength of this model is that it completely removes the *Jenseits*
character of the other for the self; its weakness is that the other is
somewhat ephemeral. The freedom of the child at play is total, but not
very real.

The second model is that of God as Creator in relation to the world.
Since the world depends on God for its continued existence, it is sometimes viewed as no more truly other to God than Puff was to Jackie
Paper. But creation is more often seen as an exercise of omnipotence
voluntarily limiting itself, giving genuine otherness to the world. This
is the view Hegel has in mind, for while the other of play is "in reality
not an other," when God creates the world it "confronts him as an
other." The strength of this model is obviously that otherness gains in-
tegrity; its weakness that otherness can all too easily emerge once again
as a *Jenseits,* outside the reconciliation of the Concept. This possible
obstinate otherness is not incorrigible. As Creator God could either destroy the world he has made, or, alternatively, abandon it. But we have
already seen that destruction and withdrawal are anything but the
freedom Hegel is seeking to grasp; and nothing in the concept of
Creator suggests that God has any options but these in the face of a
world turned hostile.

The third model is that of the eternal love between the Father and
the Son. As eternal the Son is truly other, neither imaginary like Puff
nor contingent like the world. But while otherness is most complete in

this model there is no estrangement or hostility here. For in place of the child's sovereignty over his imaginary playmates and God's over the created world, the relation here is that of reciprocal love. Only in love is even God able to be *bei sich selbst* in his other. Though Hegel doesn't mention it here, this holds for his relation to the world as well. For it is only as Redeemer, not simply as Creator, that God can be at peace with the world. It is the God who loved the world who sent his Son, not to be its Judge but its Saviour (John 3:16-17).

It is now possible to give Hegel's creation talk its proper place in his theory of the Concept. By itself it is not an adequate model of the conceptual structure being developed. But it helps to express two essential elements of that structure. The first is the active, effective nature of the self as *das Wirkende*. The other is that aspect of love which Hegel especially wishes to highlight, the non-otherness of the most genuinely other (PR, § 158-z). Taken together the three models we have just examined are not just a progressive series. The first two belong to the third as part of its meaning. In love the threatening aspects of otherness are as thoroughly eliminated as in play and creation (but without having to eliminate otherness as such and with it the benefits which only real otherness can confer). In love the other does not owe its existence to me, but we are so related that I feel no need of that sort of power over the other in order to be myself. I can live in the real world without resort to the pathological phantasies in which I elevate myself to the role of Creator and reduce the world to a collective Puff with whom I play in childish sovereignty.[13]

* * *

Lest we get carried away here we must remember that the Logic does not try to tell us how or where this freedom as loving reciprocity is to be realized. It only tells us what it is to be free. It does so, however, by calling our attention to the fact that love is only a special form of reciprocity and that there is another reciprocity which is not freedom at all. It is this contrast between two reciprocities which constitutes the transition from Essence to Concept in the Logic.

As a category of Essence Reciprocity expresses a world wholly subject to natural necessity. It is composed of substances, thus of independent and self-sufficient units. It is a world, however, not a chaotic multiplicity, solely because these units do have one mode of relation to one another, causal necessity. Since they are both active and passive, cause and effect in relation to one another, causal necessity has the form , of Reciprocity.

In this world independence and identity are mutually exclusive. Causal necessity involves a special form of identity. The effect, being simply the expression or unfolding of the cause, loses its independence and becomes simply an aspect of the cause's career. As the distinction between them vanishes, they become identical. The attempt to see the world exclusively and consistently from this point of view leads to Spinozism, where the world has only one substance in it, or, alternatively, to the Laplacian way of saying the same thing in different language. If, as the category of Reciprocity itself suggests, some plurality is to be preserved, it must be by viewing the units which make up the world in abstraction from their causal relations, as external and contingent in relation to one another. I have no difficulty, for example, viewing the misfortunes of my beloved and bumbling Chicago Cubs as wholly unrelated to the political climate in Washington. In Reciprocity as a category of Essence I alternate between two incompatible viewpoints, one which views the units of the world as mutually indifferent to one another, and one which views them as so tightly bound together by natural necessity as to lose their independent identity. Clearly neither of these represents freedom in Hegel's sense.

If there is to be a reciprocity which does constitute freedom, it must overcome the mutual exclusiveness of independence and identity. It is in just these terms that Hegel states the transition to the Concept.[14] The truth of necessity is freedom, we are told, and that of substance the Concept. For reciprocity can be seen as infinite, negative self-relation; negative in that it involves the independence of actualities in relation to one another, but infinite self-relation because "their independence only lies in their identity" (ELW, §§157-158). This harmony of independence and identity is crucial to freedom. The old identity excludes independence.

"The identity [*Einheit*] of the things, which necessity presents as bound to each other and thus bereft of their independence, is at first [i.e. while Reciprocity is still a category of Essence] only inward, and therefore has no existence for those under the yoke of necessity"(ELW, §158-z).[15]

Where identity has this character it not only leaves the so-called individuals "bereft of their independence" but also deprives them of any awareness or enjoyment of their identity. There is no experience of love or of community. But there is another kind of identity.

> "It then appears that the members, linked to one another, are not really foreign to each other, being, as it were, at home, and combining with itself [*bei sich selbst ist und mit sich selbst zusammengeht*]. In this way necessity is transfigured into freedom. . . ." (ELW, § 158-z)

Just as we have previously seen Hegel describe love as a contradiction and the unity of the concept as inconceivable to the Understanding, we now are reminded that it is not exactly easy to think this unity of identity and independence. "The passage from necessity to freedom, or from actuality into the concept, is the very hardest, because it proposes that independent actuality shall be thought as having all its substantiality in the passing over and identity with the other independent actuality." Once again, to help us get headed in the right direction, Hegel tells us that love is what he is talking about, love as the liberation which can also be called I, free spirit, and blessedness (ELW, § 159).[16]

* * *

I have been discussing the theory of the Concept as a theory of freedom rather than as a theory of knowledge, as a theory of the practical rather than the theoretical self. Of course, Hegel would not have called this part of the Logic by the name Concept if his theory were not also a theory of knowledge (and the object of knowledge as well). But in spite of saying "Concept" instead of "Freedom" when naming the final level of categorial development, Hegel himself seems to give the epistemological part of his theory a secondary place. "The Concept," he writes,

> "when it has developed into a concrete existence that is itself free, is none other than the I or pure self-consciousness. True, I have concepts, that is to say, determinate concepts; but the I is the pure Concept itself which, as the Concept, has come into existence" (WL. II, 220=SL, 583).

However we interpret this contrast between the self's being the

Concept and its having concepts, a complete analysis of Hegel's theory of the Concept would have to develop its epistemological discussions which are constantly and overtly interspersed throughout the discussion of freedom to which I have limited myself up to this point. My first hypothesis, that love is the key to the structure of the Concept, would be enhanced both in strength and in philosophical interest if a second, corollary hypothesis could be established, namely that the theory of loving intersubjectivity which is the direct meaning of the Concept as a theory of the practical self is the guiding metaphor for the theory of knowledge which has reached the same level of philosophical insight. In other words, knowing, too, is to be understood in its highest form as the non-violent unity of the self and its other. In the space and time remaining to me I can but outline such a reading of Hegel's text.

As a theory of knowledge Hegel regularly contrasts his view of the Concept with that of the Understanding, which views it as an abstract universal, devoid of particularity and individuality. It is thus without content of its own, the mere form of our subjective thought. Two features of this view are especially stressed, the independence of the object and the subjectivity of thinking.

The independence of the object consists in its being unconditioned in relation to the concepts through which it is thought. It is there first, standing ready made over against the concept, possessed of its being and truth prior to any rendezvous with the concept. The content thus falls on the side of the object. The concept is an empty and inert form which comes to it from without. This kind of thinking is subjective, for it is separated from its truth. The truth is supposed to reside in the content or object, while thinking is entirely the activity of the subject. The abstract universals employed in such thinking are generated, as their name suggests, through the activity of abstracting; and it is the knowing subject who must perform this operation of neglecting some features presented to consciousness while focusing attention on others. Since it is the contingent purpose of the knower which directs this process, it can also be said that an interest external to the subject matter presides over this whole domain of thinking.

On this view the truth of the object is not an intelligibility or meaning it can reveal to us but rather a brute otherness which we must forge weapons to overcome. Abstract universals are those weapons, by means of which we hope to deprive the object of its original independence and render it subject to our purposes and interests. Knowing is the desire to master and dominate. Without any specific reference to technological purposes and interests, Hegel has described the essence of calculative thinking.

Knowledge at the level of the Concept contrasts sharply. This highest kind of knowing, attested by both religion and philosophy (WL, II, 225-26=SL, 587-88), assumes that things have their being and truth by virtue of the Concept at work within them. The form by which they are known is identical with the form by which they are what they are. Since the form is already present in the content Hegel can say, *"dass wir die Begriffe gar nicht bilden"* (EL, § 163-z2). We do not need to impose our external purposes on the processes of thought. This is not to say that knowledge, any more than love itself, is entirely devoid of interest. It is to say that the subject no longer seeks to use the object. The guiding interest is no longer the subject's private purpose, but its openness to the object so that the object may reveal both itself and the subject for what they are. In thus giving itself up to the object, the subject does not discover that in ceasing to be the master it has become the slave. The impetus toward domination is undermined as a new identity takes shape. For the form which is the truth of the thing and the form which is the thought of the subject are one and the same.

Hegel, as is his wont, lapses into lyricism.

> "The universal is therefore *free* power; it is itself and takes its other within its embrace [*greift über sein Anderes über*], but without *doing violence* to it; on the contrary, the universal is, in its other, in peaceful communion with itself. We have called it free power, but it could also be called *free love* and *boundless blessedness,* for it bears itself towards its other as towards *its own self*; in it, it has returned to itself" (WL. II, 242=SL, 603)[17]

We might call this the Golden Rule of the Concept. For Hegel it is the norm for philosophical knowledge as well as for life with our neighbor.

NOTES

1. *Philosophy of Right*, §29. The *Philosophy of Right* and the Lesser Logic of the *Encyclopedia* will be cited by the paragraph numbers which are common to all editions and with the abbreviations PR and EL. Where *Zusätze* are indicated, a z will follow the paragraph number. The translations of Knox and Wallace will be followed with minor alterations, mostly pertaining to italics. The *Science of Logic* will be cited with pages from both the Felix Meiner edition, edited by Georg Lasson (WL) and the Miller translation (SL) which I follow with minor alterations. I have regularly substituted *concept* for *notion* as a translation of *Begriff*.

2. EL, § 10; WL I, 55ff.; and *Differenzschrift, Gesammelte Werke,* (Hamburg, 1968), IV, 77ff.

3. "Hegel's Critique of Kant," *The Review of Metaphysics,* Vol. XXVI (March, 1973), pp. 441-45. Italics are Smith's.

4. Cf. WL, II, 220=SL, 583: "Ich aber ist diese *erstlich* reine, sich auf sich beziehende Einheit, und dies nicht unmittelbar, sondern indem es von aller Bestimmtheit und Inhalt abstrahiert und in die Freiheit der schrankenlosen *Gleichkeit mit sich selbst* zurückgeht."

5. It is helpful to recall Hegel's analysis of Skepticism and of the Terror in the *Phenomenology*.

6. EL, §160 and §163, my italics. Cf. WL, II, 219=SL, 582.

7. Hegel uses *bei sich sein* more or less interchangeably with *bei sich bleiben,* though it obviously hasn't quite the active sense of the latter. Present translations frequently render *bei sich* as "at home."

8. My italics.

9. Especially in view of Hegel's critique of Fichte in §6.

10. Cf. Hegel's stress on Rousseau's distinction between *volonté génèrale* and *volonté de tous,* EL, § 163-Z, and his analysis of the We constituted in marriage by contrast with that of contract, PR, No. 75 and No. 158ff., with Zusätze.

11. These phrases occur, respectively at EL, No. 160-Z; No. 163-Z; WL, II, 244-45=SL, 605; WL, II, 242=SL, 603; WL, II, 245=SL, 605; and WL, II, 231=SL, 592. Cf. EL, §163-z: "Rather the Concept is the genuine first; and things are what they are through the action of the Concept, immanent in them, and revealing itself in them. In religious language we express this by saying that God created the world out of nothing. In other words, the world and finite things have issued from the fullness of the divine thoughts and the divine decrees."

12. WL, II, 236=SL, 597; WL, II, 242=SL, 602; EL, §161-z; PR, §1-z.

13. Cf. R. D. Laing, *The Self and Others,* Part One.

14. EL, §157-59. Cf. WL, II, 214-19=SL, 578-82.

15. Cf. WL, II, 218=SL, 581: "Dieser, die aus der Wechselwirkung resultierende Totalität, ist die Einheit der *beiden Substanzen* der Wechselwirkung, so dass sie aber nunmehr der Freiheit angehören, indem sie nicht mehr ihre Identität als ein Blindes, das heisst *Innerliches* . . ."; and WL, II, 224=SL, 586: "Das Leben oder die organische Natur ist diese

Stufe der Natur, auf welcher der Begriff hervortritt; aber als blinder, sich selbst nicht fassender, d.h. nicht denkender Begriff."

16. Cf. the quotation with which this essay concludes.
17. Cf. WL, II, 246=SL, 606, where Hegel uses the same notion of *übergreifen* which Miller here renders as "embrace." Thus, "Das Allgemeine als der Begriff ist es selbst und sein Gegenteil, was wieder es selbst als seine gesetzte Bestimmtheit ist; es greift über dasselbe über und ist in ihm bei sich."

VII
Hegel's Concept of Logical Life
by
MURRAY GREENE

The Absolute Idea alone is Being, imperishable Life, self-knowing Truth, and is all Truth.

In Hegel's mature philosophy,[1] Life obtains systematic treatment twice:[2] as a category in the science of logic, and as organism in the philosophy of nature. That Life should be treated in a philosophy of nature is hardly an occasion for surprise. But what are we to say about "Logical Life as pure Idea"?[3] What is the difference between Logical Life and Natural Life and what is their connection? These questions can only be answered by Hegel's concept of logic itself as "the science of the pure Idea" and by the role of the pure or logical Idea within Hegel's conception of philosophic science generally.

By the time Hegel wrote on Life, several thinkers had rejected Descartes' mechanistic conception of organism and his interactionist view of the soul-body relation in man. In the case of Spinoza and Leibniz, the rejection of interactionism came as part of a whole new metaphysics of substance. But it was doubtful that either thinker wholly overcame Cartesian mechanism. Both of their systems and concepts of Life were regarded by Hegel as untenable and for roughly the same reasons. Spinoza's two attributes of thought and extension, Hegel noted, are "adopted empirically" and the purported mind-body union based on their "correspondence" is termed by Hegel but an "external reflection" in which Life altogether lacks "the *punctum saliens* of selfhood" (SL, 537).[4] Selfhood obtains ampler scope in the Leibnizian monadology, according to Hegel, but the internal determination of the monad and the pre-established harmony come as a "predestination" posited externally through a "dogmatic reflection" (SL, 539-540). A decisive breakthrough against mechanism is seen to have been gained by Kant, among whose "great services" to philosophy was the concept of "internal purposiveness," which "opened up the Notion of Life" (SL, 737). But even more fundamental for Hegel's approach to Life generally was the Kantian original synthetic unity of apperception, which united the opposites: subject and object, in the "objective" judgment. As in the case of the Hegelian position as a whole, the relation to Kant is important for an understanding of Hegel's concept of Logical Life.

In contrast to Kant's "notion of Reason," which is transcendent for all phenomena (SL, 755), Hegel claims his logical Idea to be immanent in all actuality.[5] Hence while Hegel acknowledges his great debt to Kant's transcendental logic, he differs basically from Kant with regard to the concept of logic generally. According to Kant (as Hegel notes), logic is "merely a canon of judgment," and to regard it as "an organon for the production of objective insights" is an "abuse" (SL, 590).[6] But in Hegel's eyes it is the very task of a genuine logic to be the immanent connecting of form and content, and hence his own speculative logic seeks not merely formal correctness of judgment but has "the truth as such" as its "object and aim" (SL, 761 and 38).[7] This claim of immanence of the logical Idea will be central for the notion of Natural Life but can only be validated in the science of the Idea itself, of which Logical Life forms a part. In the course of the science of the Idea, speculative logic brings up for consideration "all possible shapes [*Gestalten*] of a given content" in order to show that "the Notion is everything, and its movement is the universal absolute activity" (SL, 826).

The treatment of Logical Life falls in that part of the science of the Idea which Hegel calls Subjective Logic; and that "the Notion is everything" means at the beginning of the Subjective Logic that it is "subject" as the consummation and higher truth of substance (SL, 580). Substance itself marked the culmination of the preceding Objective Logic which encompassed the categories of Being and Essence. The course of the Objective Logic resulted in the emergence of the Notion as subject and "unconditioned ground" into which the reality of substance "has vanished" (SL, 591). At the commencement of the Subjective Logic, however, the Notion is but "formal" subject; it is not yet "subject-object" or Idea, which alone is the "unity of subjective Notion and objectivity" (SL, 758).[8]

The Notion's elevation to Idea cannot come externally but only insofar as the Notion "builds up in and from itself the reality that has vanished in it" (SL, 591). The building up of this reality, i.e., the Notion's objectification, marks the course of the Subjective Logic in which Logical Life finds its place. In Mechanism and Chemism, the Subjective Logic's initial forms of objectivity, the Notion confronts external materiality as an "other" of which it is implicitly the truth. This implicitness first becomes explicit in the means-end relation of Teleology, which Kant had already conceived in terms of "inner" purposiveness. In Hegel's demonstration the Notion as "subjective end" is shown to possess externality "yet in this external totality to be the totality's self-determining identity" (SL, 754). The "truth" of the teleological relation and its speculative "result" is Life, wherein "the Notion is now the Idea."

The advance from Notion to Idea, from Teleology to Life, consists in an advance in the subject-object relation constituting the end-means relationship in "external" purposiveness. In Life the end-means relationship becomes an inner self-differentiation of the subjectivity wherein objectivity is an "other" as predicate of the subject's own "judgment" (Ur-teil).[9] In Life the Notion first becomes Idea, or subject-object, as

> this absolute judgment [Urteil] whose subject, as self-related negative unity, distinguishes itself from its objectivity and is the latter's being-in-and-for-self, but essentially relates itself to it through itself. . . . (SL, 758).

Hegel's concept of the judgment as inner self-differentiation of the Notion will be a main feature of his purported overcoming of the "external reflection" of the Spinozist metaphysics of substance and the Leibnizian monadology. For the subject-object relation as "self-related negative unity," Hegel is greatly in debt to Fichte's self-dividing Ego, which Fichte employed to show the inadequacy of mechanism and the causal principle for the explanation of sentient nature.[10] That the self-dividing Notion is the "ground" of objective judgment is also Hegel's response to Kant's concept of the teleological judgment.[11] As such an Urteil the Notion is no longer substance as Spinoza's causa sui which, in its identifying of cause and effect, already stands on the threshold of subjectivity.[12] Rather it is more truly subject, as that which is "its own end [Selbstzweck] and the urge [Trieb]" to realize it, i.e., objectify itself. Objectivity is therefore nothing other than

> the realization of the End, an objectivity posited by the activity of the End, an objectivity which, as positedness, possesses its subsistence and its form only as permeated by its subject (SL, 758).

Logical Life will mark the initial stage of the Idea as subject-object and thus the Idea in its "immediacy" (SL, 759).[13] The immediate Idea is the Notion as soul [*Seele*] "realized in a body" of whose externality the inner subjectivity is the "immediate self-relating universality" (SL, 763). As such an immediacy, in which soul and body, Notion and objectivity, are separable, Life as Idea is but the Notion "in itself" and related to itself as "indwelling, substantial form" (SL, 775). But in Cognition and Volition, for which Logical Life is the "presupposition" (SL, 761), the Idea becomes "for itself" (SL, 775) as the True and the Good. Finally as "absolute," the Idea is the truth "in and for itself" (SL, 760),[14] the infinite eternal Idea in which "cognition and action are equalized, and which is the absolute knowledge of itself." In this way the Absolute Idea is a "return to Life" (SL, 824), and thus the Aristotelian divine noesis. (ELW, No. 236-z).

In Cognition and Volition, the Idea has sublated the immediacy of Life. More than substantial indwelling form, the Idea is now "personality": at once "atomic subjectivity" and "for-self universality and cognition" (SL, 824). In this "return" of the Idea to Life, Hegel purports to go beyond Aristotle's divine noesis, as in the subjective Notion he has claimed to go beyond Spinoza's *causa sui*. Hegel's Idea "which thinks itself" is an "eternal intuiting of itself in other" that is simultaneously an "eternal creation" (ELW, §214).[15] Unlike Kant's Transcendental Ideal, Hegel's pure Idea is not merely regulative and not less immanent by reason of its purity. That the Idea is "self-knowing Truth" is one with its absolutely constitutive activity: it is "the Notion which in its objectivity has carried itself out" (ELW, §214).[16]

With this actualization of the Notion as at once "self-knowing Truth" and "universal absolute activity," logic has shown the Idea to be the "sole subject matter and content" of philosophic science generally, the "absolute form" to which no object or content can stand in a "merely external relationship" (SL, 826). In this way logic has marked out the task of the concrete philosophic sciences: to cognize the Idea as universal creative activity particularizing itself and returning to itself in the manifold shapes of nature and Spirit. Among these shapes, and the most important in nature, is Natural Life or organism.

From this brief survey of the role of Logical Life, its import for Hegel's position emerges as twofold: 1) Insofar as logic is "the exposi-

tion of God as he is in his eternal essence before the creation of nature
and a finite spirit" (SL, 50), Logical Life is the Idea as "creative universal soul" (SL, 764). Hereby its exposition is part of speculative philosophy's "ontological proof" of the existence of God; for in the Notion as
Life we see how existence is not merely superadded to essence but how
the Notion "determines itself to objectivity" (SL, 705-06, 625). 2)
But connected essentially with this objectification of the Notion generally, the exposition of Logical Life also provides the conceptual
framework for the comprehension of organism in the *Naturphilosophie*.[17] Here the three moments of the notion of Natural Life are:
the inner "process of Shape" of the organism; the organism's relation to
its outer world or "inorganic nature"; the organism's relation to
another of its own kind. Each of these moments, Hegel claims to
show, displays within itself the self-mediating "closing together with
self" of the speculative syllogism (PNM, §352),[18] and the three together comprising the one total process of organism in its Notion, i.e.,
according to the logical Idea. For this demonstration of Natural Life in
the science of Organics, the exposition of Logical Life provides the
pure notional determinations.

Hegel distinguishes the exposition of Logical Life from that of
Natural Life by their respective "presuppositions" (SL, 761). Natural
Life as considered in the Philosophy of Nature is Life "projected into
the externality of subsistence." It has its conditions in "inorganic nature," and its moments comprise a "multiplicity of actual formations"
[*Gestaltungen*] (SL, 762). Logical Life presupposes no "shapes of actuality"[19] but only the preceding determinations of the Notion in the science of logic.[20] Most proximally, the demonstrated outcome of the
means-end relation in Teleology is the emergence of the Notion as
"simple inwardness" of subjectivity that is at the same time "the urge
which mediates for itself its reality through objectivity" (SL, 762).[21]
In Life, the Notion has arrived at its "truly correspondent externality."
But "externality" here carries a purely logical sense, since Life as a logical category has to do with pure thoughts (SL, 761), and the
"moments of its reality" are not shapes in space and time but remain
"enclosed in the form of the Notion."[22]

The twofold role of Logical Life: in the science of logic and the science of organism, provides the two main tasks of the present paper on
Hegel's concept of Logical Life. Our principal effort must be devoted

to showing as clearly as possible how in Logical Life the Notion first attains to subject-object and in what sense Life is the "immediate Idea." But since Logical Life affords a crucial instance of speculative logic's claim to immanence, we shall also indicate briefly how the logical notion forms the basis of the treatment of organism in the *Naturphilosophie* and how Hegel's speculative approach purportedly advances our comprehension of Life beyond that of Hegel's main predecessors.

A. The Living Individual

1. In the modern view of nature as mechanism, Life has been variously comprehended as a "warmth of the heart" by Descartes, as conatus by Spinoza, and as entelechy and inner purposiveness by Leibniz and Kant, respectively. It is to Kant's notion of *Selbstzweck* in modern times and Aristotle's concept of the soul that Hegel is most indebted.[23] But in Hegel's reconstitution of Kant's transcendental logic, Life as *Selbstzweck* is conceived in terms of the Notion as subjectivity which has itself for object. This is possible through the speculative conception of the Notion as *Ur-teil*. Life, says Hegel, is initially the Notion whose objectivity is "presupposed" as appropriate to it (SL, 764). The presupposition, however, is in fact the outcome of the preceding dialectic of external purposiveness and in general signifies the nature of the Notion itself as inner self-differentiating *Urteil*.

> Consequently the original *judgment* of Life consists in this, that the [living nature] detaches itself as an individual subject from objectivity, and in constituting itself the negative unity of the Notion makes the *presupposition* of an immediate objectivity (SL, 764).

Initially the relation of subject and object in the self-determining Notion is that of "subjective singularity" and "indifferent universality" (SL, 764). This "judgment" governs the movement of the first moment of Logical Life as the process of the living individuality "within itself."[24] It is a process of the abstract individuality's "particularization" into the two extremes of the judgment that "becomes immediately syllogism" (SL, 764).[25] In this first *Schluss* of Logical Life the appropriateness of the objectivity "presupposed" in the Notion will be realized as the subjectivity's inner self-producing activity.

Although the presupposition is that of an "immediate" objectivity, immediacy here will not have the same sense as in the previous processes of Mechanism, etc. For in Life as *Selbstzweck* the judgment of the Notion means that objectivity has now "gone forth" from the Notion, and "its essence is positedness."[26] To be sure, objectivity is universality and "totality" of the Notion,[27] on its face "independent" and "indifferent" to the subject. But the indifference is implicitly a show, the totality "lent," the independence "presupposed" (SL, 765),[28] deriving as "predicate" of the Notion's self-determining judgment that renders the very being of the object an "inhering" in the subject.

> Self-subsistent objectivity, therefore, having proceeded from the Idea, is immediate being only as the predicate of the judgment of the Notion's self-determination—a being that is indeed distinct from the subject, but at the same time is essentially posited as moment of the Notion (SL, 765).

It is in this way that the subject is "self-related negative unity," and it is through this speculative concept generally that Hegel would overcome the soul-body dualism inherited from Descartes and perpetuated, though in altered form, in Spinoza's two attributes and Kant's separation of mechanism and inner purposiveness.[29]

Opposite the objective totality is the subjectivity as the former's negative unity or "true centrality" (SL, 765),[30] not a "lent" totality but the "free unity with itself" inhering in nothing else.[31] As this "simple but negative identity with itself," the subject is the Idea in the form of singularity: the living individual. Life is then in the first place "soul" as "the Notion of itself," wholly determined within itself, "the initiating self-moving principle" (SL, 765).[32]

To a certain extent one can, indeed must, speak of a duality. But the two sides are to be conceived neither as "interactive" nor as somehow coincident or correspondent, as in the case of Spinoza's two attributes. They must be conceived as moments of the negative unity: the Notion that "distinguishes itself from its objectivity and is the latter's being-in-and-for-self" (SL, 758). Enclosed in its simpleness the Notion contains the determinate externality as "simple moment," as "means" of the inwardly self-determining subjectivity as *Selbstzweck*. For to the soul as "immediacy" belongs an objectivity as "the immediately external": the body. The latter is a "reality" that is "subordinated" to the End; as objectivity it is "predicate of the subject" and "immediate means" for the latter's self-realization.

In conceiving the body as means or instrument of the soul, Hegel

employs an old idea in a new context recently established by Kant.[33]
The body is means of the soul as its dialectical opposite: it is means insofar as the Notion as subjectivity is the "urge" to objectify itself in its
externality. The objectivity is no indifferent other; as deriving from
the Notion's own judgment it is fated to be permeated by the subjectivity. The means-end relation of inner purposiveness, as Kant saw,
must be a self-relation. But this self-relation, according to Hegel, can
only be conceived speculatively as the self-determining *Urteil* of the
Notion. The living being in its objective reality is means of itself as
subjectivity. In the present first syllogism of the living individual
"within itself," objectivity is but the "immediate reality identical with
the Notion," i.e., the organism's own body, which it has "by nature."[34]

For the comprehension of inner purposiveness, as Kant noted,
mechanism is utterly fruitless. If such categories as causality, force,
parts and whole (SL, 766, 735, 755; ELW, §136)—the categories
of Mechanism and Chemism—are employed for the living creature,
says Hegel, "then the Notion is regarded as external to it and it is
treated as a dead thing" (SL, 766).[35] In the living being, objectivity is
"completely purposive," the "executed end"; for the Notion is its
"subsistence and immanent substance" (SL, 763, 766). The living
being is not be viewed in terms of an organization of parts, as in Descartes[36] and to some extent Spinoza, but rather "members," i.e., distinctions articulated by the inner subjectivity in actualizing itself as
Selbstzweck.

To account logically for this articulation we must look again to the
Notion as *Urteil*. Since the objectivity as totality of the external manifold is opposed to the subjectivity as negative unity, the latter is the
urge to posit as "real difference" what in the judgment formally is as
yet but "abstract moment" (SL, 766). But insofar as real difference is
in the first instance "immediate," the positing is expressed in

> the urge of each single, specific moment to produce itself and
> likewise raise its particularity to universality, to sublate the others ex-
> ternal to it, engender itself at their cost, but similarly to sublate itself
> and make itself a means for the others (SL, 766).

Thus what in Spinoza is a relation of parts where somehow in their
proportional replacement "they all preserve the same mutual relations
of motion and rest";[37] and in Kant is a relation of parts where each is

somehow "reciprocally both end and means"; is in Hegel a relation of "members" where each in its particularity is permeated by the urge of the subjective totality, and its self-aggrandizement as particular is simultaneously its self-sublation in the subjectivity as negative unity.

2. The positing of real difference, i.e., the logical emergence of members and organs, marks the transition to the moment of particularity. Although the particularization has a certain element of conflict among the particulars,[38] its significance in the syllogism of the living being "within itself" is that of the metabolic process conceived as a self-articulating and self-consuming: the initial moment of the living individuality in its immediacy as a "this." Hegel expressly points out the difference from "finite" teleology, i.e., external purposiveness, and Hegel's effort to explicate the difference logically marks an important step in his endeavor to reestablish the notion of End in speculative thinking. In the case of external purposiveness, Hegel notes, objectivity has the form of "something already there" [*ein Vorhandenes*] (SL, 742), which is approached by the subjective end through interposition of another object (SL, 746). By means of a tool, for example, the subjective end mediates itself with objectivity. Viewed logically, objectivity in the premise of the syllogism is not "in its own self" sublation, so that the mediation has the aspect of a "violence" (SL, 746)[39] and the subjective end only becomes "in and for itself" in the conclusion.[40] But in the organism as internal purposiveness the objectivity is already implicitly its own, and the subjective end makes itself the ruling power over the mechanical and chemical forces in which the processes of the organs with one another are directly the process of the self-producing organism.

In the case of internal purposiveness or infinite end, objectivity as corporeality is not merely a tool but is "immediately means" as predicate of the subject. Through the Notion's original *Teilung* the objectivity as an other has been permeated from the start by the subjectivity as *Selbstzweck*. As for Aristotle, the end is at once the source of the movement and its telos. The difference from Aristotle is in the notion of subjectivity as negative unity: that to which all the members and organs in their conflicting claims, their "restlessness and mutability," return (SL, 767).[41] Unlike the external means-end relationship, the objectivity's show of indifferent subsistence here "reveals itself as self-sublating." In this way the living individuality as Notion

produces itself by its urge in such a manner that the product, the Notion being its essence, is itself the producing agent; that is to say the
product is product only as the externality that equally posits itself as
negative, or is product only in being the process of production (SL,
767).[42]

In this logical demonstration of the living individuality's inner
self-articulation, Hegel claims that his speculative Notion makes possible a comprehension of organism that must remain for the reflective
understanding an "incomprehensible mystery" (SL, 763).

3. While the Idea is thus the living individuality that produces itself in its objectivity as immediately means, it is so as yet only in the
Notion. The self-identical subject has returned to itself in its objectivity; the latter as corporeality is "concrete" totality. But the Notion's
moments as such are not yet determinate externalities, do not yet
comprise the living creature in its "reality." As "ensouled" by the Notion, however, the objectivity as living totality is essentially differ-
entiated into the notion-determinations: universality, particularity,
individuality. In its reality, then, the living being is "shape" [Gestalt],
wherein the logical moments of the Notion are externally divisible into
determinate bodily systems.

The living individual is in the first place universality, which has
emerged as "simple immediacy" that is "absolute negativity" within
itself; or "absolute difference" whose negativity is "dissolved in
simplicity." As this immediate universality the vitality [Lebendigkeit]
of the individual is the pure inner process of Sensibility. Sensibility is
the soul's simple being-within-self [Insichsein], not in the inert, empty
fashion of a tabula rasa but as

infinitely determinable receptivity, which in its determinateness does
not become something manifold and external but is simply reflected
into itself (SL, 768).[43]

Thus for Hegel no approach beginning with atomic impressions can
comprehend Sensibility, whose prior condition and possibility is the
living being as intro-reflected subjective universality. Vitality as Sensibility is termed by Hegel a kind of internal "vibrating."[44] In Sensibility the single "so-called impression" returns from its externality and
manifoldness into this "simpleness of self-feeling." Sensibility is thus
the determinate being [Dasein] of the soul as Insichsein; for in Sensibility the soul "takes up into itself all externality" and brings it back to

the simpleness of the self-identical universality.[45] But in this way the soul is but immediate ideality and its determinateness as yet "simple principle."

Insofar as the soul is Notion, however, its *Dasein* cannot remain the merely *ideelle* but not yet *reelle* determinateness of simple inner feeling. In the notion-moment of particularity the living being is the urge to "open up" the negativity implicit in self-feeling and give its ideal *In-sichsein* determinate reality. This is Irritability, the moment of the living being as "posited difference": its "judgment or finitization [*Verendlichung*] whereby it relates itself to the external as to a presupposed objectivity and is in reciprocal activity with it" (SL, 768).[46] In this interaction with an externality that is not, like its own corporeality, immediately its own, the living being is determined partly as species [*Art*] alongside other species of living beings. From this indifferent diversity the individual is reflected into self in "formal" fashion as the "formal genus and its systematization";[47] and it is reflected into self as "individual" inasmuch as it is the *Urteil,* hence negativity of its determinateness as outwardly directed against the presupposed objectivity, and thereby the self-related negativity of the Notion.

As reflected into self in its very direction outwards, the living being is "its own externality toward itself" and has raised its particularity to individuality. Logically this is seen in the syllogistic connecting of the subjectivity, the "immediate" objectivity (its corporeality) and the "presupposed" external objectivity. In Sensibility and Irritability the subjectivity's relation to its own corporeality has been mediated by the external objectivity so that the first objectivity is no longer "immediately means" (SL, 768).[48] In the direction outwards the corporeality has been externally determined, but by the presupposed externality that is implicitly the individual's reflection into self. Thus objectivity has been elevated from immediate means to external reality in which the subjectivity remains reflected into self and negative unity.[49] This reflectedness has been 1) "theoretical" or ideal, where negativity is the simple self-identity of Sensibility as inner feeling; 2) "real," in the "posited difference" and the subjectivity's positing itself in Irritability as negative unity of the external objectivity. As sublation of the immediate objectivity and negative unity of the external objectivity, the living individual is Reproduction.

In presenting Reproduction as the sublation of Sensibility and Irritability, Hegel once again draws on important themes from his predecessors. But in Spinoza's quasi-mechanistic account of the individual's perseverance as form, the important element of self-feeling[50] is added *ab extra*; and in Kant's teleological account of the self-forming organism the stress on organization leaves scant regard for self-feeling.[51] All these essential moments are united by Hegel in the notion of the reproductive individual as subjectivity and negative unity of its corporeal as well as external manifold. Reproduction is negativity "as simple moment of Sensibility"; and Irritability, which of course includes self-feeling, first becomes "living resistance-force"[52] insofar as the relation to the external other is "Reproduction and individual identity with self" (SL, 769). In Reproduction, says Hegel, Life has feeling and power of resistance; is for the first time truly "vitality." As totalities that are, as such, but abstract moments, Sensibility as "inwardness" and Irritability as "direction outwards" obtain their unity and truth in Reproduction. The individuality reproductive within itself as Shape is "real totality," at once distinguished from the determinate totalities of Sensibility and Irritability and their "implicit essentiality" in which they are "held together as moments and have their subject and their subsistence" (SL, 769).

Thus in Reproduction the living being posits itself as "actual" individuality:

> a self-related being-for-self, but at the same time a real relation outwards, the reflection of particularity or irritability towards an other, towards the objective world (SL, 769).[53]

The immediate objectivity initially "presupposed"[54] in the *Urteil* of the Notion as Life is now "posited."[55] The first syllogism of Logical Life as individuality "within itself" has been demonstrated as a self-mediating coalescing with self wherein the subject in its objectivity as means "only reproduces itself" (ELW, §218). The individuality having consummated itself logically as Shape, the life-process passes from one of self-enclosedness to a process with the external objectivity. This is no longer, as in Irritability as such, a "direction" outwards but a "real relation" outwards. The outer process becomes "actual," for "when the individual posits itself as a subjective totality, the moment of its determinateness as a relation to externality becomes a totality as well" (SL, 769).

B. The Life Process

In the previous process (A), Sensibility, Irritability, and Reproduction were conceived, respectively, through the logical notion-moments of universality, particularity, and individuality. But as process of the living individuality "within itself," the process of Shape constituted the moment of Logical Life as "abstract universality." The present Life Process (B) as a whole[56] will be Logical Life as the moment of particularity. The transition is to be understood again in terms of the *Urteil* of the Notion. As internally organized individuality that has "returned to itself" in its objectivity, the living being as Notion "tenses itself against its original act of presupposing," i.e., posits itself *as* presupposing, and in so doing "opposes itself as an absolute subject to the presupposed objective world" (SL, 769).[57] Thus where in the previous process, particularization signified internal articulation and a producing itself out of its own self, now it will mean the subjectivity's explicit entanglement with external reality. Where before "subject-object" meant identity in difference of soul and body, now it will mean identity in opposition of organism and "inorganic nature." Where before the objectivity was immediate means belonging "by nature" to the subjectivity as *Selbstzweck,* now the subjectivity will still be related to the objectivity as its means but as an "other" against which it must exert its negating activity in order to actualize itself as *Selbstzweck*.

As the moment of explicit opposition, the Life Process has much more the aspect of a struggle.[58] Although there would be here—if we were in Natural, not Logical, Life—an element of contingency for the creature as this existing particularity, the outcome of the struggle is not left open or in doubt.[59] For the relation between the opposites derives from the Notion, which is subjectivity: i.e., one of the opposites. The living subject is inherently the power over its objectivity: it is the self-subsistent Idea against which the presupposed other is in itself but a negative. In its very feeling of itself the living subject has the certitude of the nullity of the other confronting it. But its subjective certainty remains to be objectified; and to this extent the subjectivity is Notion but not yet Idea of Life. Hence its objectifying itself in its immediate objectivity is mediated by its process with "the completely posited externality," the objective totality "standing indifferently alongside it" (SL, 770). In this way the living being becomes a creature of Need [*Bedürfnis*].

Need begins the Life Process as an original self-dividing. In Need the creature is not simply denied, but in determining itself "posits itself" as denied. In this way it relates itself to the indifferent objectivity not abstractly as an other but as *its* other.[60] But by the same token it is "not lost in this loss of itself but maintains itself therein and remains the identity of the self-similar Notion" (SL, 770).[61] As thus Notion that is not yet Idea, the living being is again "urge" to posit the other as its own, "to sublate it and objectify itself."

But objectivity is no longer, as in immediate Shape, directly conformable to the Notion and hence the creature's "good" in which it straightway returns to itself. Since in the Life Process the negative is in the form of "objective particularity," each of the Notion's moments is "realized for itself as totality" (SL, 770),[62] and the Notion is sundered into the "absolute unlikeness" of itself in its very self-sameness. As Notion and hence "for itself" in this its sunderance, the living being has the feeling of its contradiction, which is Pain. Hegel's comprehension of pain affords a prime example of what he regarded to be speculative logic's fundamental insight: that the negative is at the same time positive.

> Pain is . . . the prerogative (*Vorrecht*) of living natures; because they are the existent Notion, they are an actuality of infinite power such that they are within themselves the negativity of themselves, that this their negativity is for them, and that they maintain themselves in their otherness (SL, 770).[63]

Pain is "first" negation, not yet negation of negation. In Need and Urge, the living being moves toward negation of itself "for itself," thereby becoming for itself identity as negation of negation or infinite negativity. In Urge as such, the living creature is the subjective self-certainty which maintains that the indifferent externality is in truth but appearance lacking the Notion. The externality can obtain its Notion only through the subjectivity which alone is "the immanent End."[64] Lacking the Notion[65] the externality cannot preserve itself in its own negative and lies impotent before the penetrating power of the living creature. Insofar as the creature is Urge, the externality is not "cause" but "excitation" of the determination, whose possibility is the creature's finding the externality "conformable" and itself "already in and for itself in it."[66]

Nevertheless the living creature is finite subjectivity, and in relating itself determinately to the externality in Need it must make itself an externality, render itself an instrument of "violence." In this way it employs the object's own forces of mechanism and chemism against it in order to transform it into its own internality. But this relationship of "external End"[67] is directly broken off in the transformation. For the subjective activity is not merely an altering of the object's external form but a positing of the Notion in the object as the latter's very substance and indwelling essence.

In this transition of external appropriation to inner Assimilation, the process with externality fuses logically with Reproduction in the first syllogism of Logical Life. Whereas in the moment of abstract universality the individuality's reproducing itself was a self-consuming,[68] now in the process outwards the externality has been incorporated as an objective moment of the subjectivity itself.[69] Assimilation thus constitutes the living creature's return to self in and through externality, the individual's positing itself as negative unity of the outer objectivity. Having thus mediated its being-for-self through a positive negating of the objectivity, the living being has objectified its subjective certainty. It no longer merely possesses self-feeling as "simple principle,"[70] but in its concrete negating activity has given itself its self-feeling as satisfaction.

This closing together with itself in its objectivity is the subjectivity's overcoming of its sunderance as *Urteil*. As the individual's rendering its universal inorganic nature a means of its own objectification, the Life Process is the syllogism of the living being's sublation of its particularity and its positing itself as "real universal Life" (SL, 772).

C. The Genus

As the demonstration has thus far shown, Logical Life is conceived speculatively by Hegel in terms of the Notion's actualization as subject-object or Idea. The actualization is a process from the abstract to the concrete, from the empty universal to the opposition of particulars and the concrete universality of the self-determining individuality. At each stage of this process the living individuality as Notion obtains increasing dimensionality and concreteness of feature. Each stage is constituted as a logical relation of subject and predicate that establishes itself as a real relation of subjectivity and objectivity. The stages are syllogistic processes wherein the subjectivity "closes together with itself" in its objectivity. The *Zusammenschliessen* is the subjectivity's becoming "in-and-for" itself as a "return" from its "other" that derived from the subjectivity's original self-dividing as Notion. It is this *Urteil* that constitutes the logical relation of subject and predicate as an initial "presupposing." The subjectivity as Notion presupposes its objectivity, thereby also presupposing itself as subject of a judgment by way of its "finding" itself confronted with an other. Inherent in the relationship of the two terms of the judgment, therefore, is the "reflectedness" of each side in the other. In the subjectivity's overcoming of its own sunderance, the mutual reflectedness becomes explicit, the presupposing becomes a positing, the "indifferent" other becomes the subjectivity's "own" in which it objectifies itself and realizes itself as "for itself." Insofar as these moments mark the process of the Notion generally, they appear in each particular syllogism and the *Schluss* movement of Logical Life as a whole.

The first syllogism of Logical Life was the process of internal organization and self-production: the formation of the organism as singularity of Shape.[71] In its *Urteil* as Notion the living individual presupposed its objectivity as immediate natural means in which it proceeded to posit itself as actual. But insofar as this self-enclosed process meant the individual's emergence from the universal Notion of Life, its very positing itself as actual was within the context of a presupposition that was not yet verified through itself. The second syllogism began with the actual individuality and its "inorganic nature" confronting one another as particulars. In its life process with the world thus "simultaneously presupposed with it," the living individual won through to negative unity of its otherness, thereby positing itself as "the foundation of itself" (SL, 772). As thus having brought itself forth from "actuality,"[72] the living being is the "actuality" of the Idea. More specifically, the individual has determined itself as "Genus," whose otherness is no longer an "indifferent" objectivity to begin with, but one with which it is identical from the start.

As actual Idea, the individual is "essentially" self-particularization: its "judgment" is not a distinguishing itself from an other that is implicitly null; but rather its own "doubling" [*Verdopplung*]. This is once again a "presupposing," but of an objectivity identical with itself.

Now the living being relates itself not to an inorganic nature[73] but to itself "as to another living being" as "its immanent moment." Its relation is to an objectivity not "as sublated but as subsisting" and in which, as subsisting, the individual nevertheless has its self-certainty. But for the living being to have its self-feeling in another independent individual is a "contradiction";[74] and in the genus-process the living being is "once again Urge."

As initially within the sphere of immediacy, the universality of the Genus is actual only in singular shape. Hence while the individual is Genus "in itself" it is not Genus "for itself." What is "for it" is another, although at the same time the other is not, as in Assimilation, one that is implicitly null and which it must proceed to infuse with its own inwardness. The other is rather itself an inwardness. Nevertheless the other is not identical with the subjectivity *as* Notion but as external objectivity: another self-subsistent living being with which it is immediately in "reciprocal" relation.

Insofar as the individual is thus at first merely the "inner" or the "subjective" universality of feeling, it has the "longing" [*Verlangen*] to posit its identity with the other and realize its implicit universality. This urge of the Genus in the particulars is a "tension" that can only be satisfied through the sublation of the individuals confronting one another as particulars. Satisfaction of the tension in the realized identity is the dissolution of the particulars as such in the genus-universality: the negative unity of the Genus reflected into itself out of the doubling. Hereby the Genus is the individuality of Life no longer generated from its Notion, as in the first syllogism, but from the "actual Idea". In the Germ as initial outcome of the *Gattungsprozess,* the subjective Notion now has "external actuality." To be sure, objectification *qua* maturation lies ahead. But this process comes wholly as an inner unfolding. The Germ is "the complete concretion of individuality" containing *virtualiter* all its articulated distinctions: it is the "initially immaterial subjective totality" as yet "undeveloped, simple and nonsensuous." The Germ is "the entire living being in the inner form of the Notion," and, adds Hegel, a "visible evidence" to ordinary perception of what the Notion is (SL, 774).

As thus obtaining its actuality in its reflection within self from the doubling, the Genus is the "propagation of the living generations." Since the Idea as Life remains in the sphere of immediacy, that reflection takes the form of an endless succession of the immediately real.[75] But this on-going repetition of the like is only in one respect a *progressus ad infinitum*. Having mediated itself in its "process within immediacy," the Idea in the "realized Genus" has attained a *Dasein* higher than the perishable individual life. In the genus-process the singular individuals "sublate their immediate, indifferent existence in one another" and "die away."[76] As the one process of the generation of individuality and its sublation, the Genus returns to itself as negative identity. In thus positing itself as identical with the Notion, the "realized Genus" is the "for-self-becoming universality" of the Idea; and in the Genus the Idea has given itself a "reality that is itself simple universality" (SL, 774).

As "immediate Idea", the Notion as living individuality has been related to itself "as submerged [*versenkt*] in its subjugated objectivity" (SL, 775). To be sure, the living creature was for itself in its objectivity as means, but it was so as the latter's "indwelling, substantial form." With the sublation of the particularity of Life, the Notion has become "freely for itself" as abstract universality. Its inner differentiation now means that the objectivity is "likewise liberated into subjectivity or the form of simple self-likeness, and hence the object of the Notion is the Notion itself" (SL, 775). Thus the elevation of the Notion above Life means that in its *Urteil* as Notion the Idea is duplicated into the subjective Notion "whose reality is the Notion itself," and the objective Notion "that is in the form of Life."

> Thinking, Spirit, Self-Consciousness, are determinations of the Idea where it has itself for object, and its *Dasein*, i.e., the determinateness of its being, is its own difference from itself (SL, 775).

Insofar as it now "relates itself to itself as Idea," or is "the universal that has universality for its determinateness and *Dasein*," the Idea of Life has become the Idea of Cognition.

In his concept of Logical Life, as we have seen, Hegel has drawn upon major themes of post-Cartesian thinkers. In his viewing organism as that which "only is, in making itself what it is" (PNM, § 352), we can detect Spinoza's divine substance that is not a thing apart from its action, and Fichte's Absolute Ego that is nowise different from its product. Before Hegel, Spinoza had conceived the body as the "object" of the soul, a concept that was even more influential for Hegel in its Leibnizian formulation as the monadic subject wherein the world's "varied multiplicity" is taken up and "in a negative manner preserved" (SL, 539). Among the moderns, Hegel was most directly indebted for his notion of Life to Kant's concept of internal purposiveness, the inner relation of means and end, and the organism as "self-propagating formative power, which cannot be explained by the capacity for movement alone."[77] Not only in this last formulation but in all these thinkers centrally we see a striving against Cartesianism, a repudiation of interactionism, and a rejection of Descartes' view of nature as soulless extension. But since these repudiations for the most part start by accepting mechanism as in some sense absolute, or fail to overcome it, they eventually pay the price of their starting point: in Spinoza, for example, the essentially external "correspondence" of the attributes and the denial of freedom; in Kant, the dualism of nature and freedom and the denial of the possibility of a genuine science of organism. Hegel's alleged *Aufhebung* of mechanism in Logical Life is fundamental not only for his exposition of Natural Life but for his philosophic position generally.

In a certain sense one can say that Hegel too begins with a post-Cartesian,[78] as contrasted with an Aristotelian, view of nature. What for Descartes was soulless extension is for Hegel "the Idea in the form of otherness." The character of "externality," says Hegel, stamps nature as what it is. But to comprehend nature in its Notion, i.e., philosophically, is to comprehend it as the Idea's "return into itself out of its immediacy and externality" (PNM, §251). This means that nature moves toward inwardization, a movement consummated in the sentient organism, which is the prelude to Spirit. Hence the fundamental theme in Hegel's science of Organics is that the spatial asunderness [*Aussersichsein*] of nature and the "mutual outsideness" [*Aussereinandersein*] of its forms are "brought back to the ideal unity" of the soul in the animal organism (PNM, §252).[79]

If Hegel was to build on his predecessors while avoiding their pitfalls, he needed to accomplish a thorough recasting of their concepts. This was to a large extent already provided by Kant's Copernican revolution in philosophy, which transformed the conception of the subject-object relation generally. After Kant's original synthetic unity of apperception that grounded objective judgment, perhaps the most important contribution to transcendental thinking was Fichte's notion

of Ego as negative self-relation. Now the subject-object relation contained the moment of negativity; every objective judgment derived its
logical form from the nature of the subjectivity as an original self-
dividing. Indeed, every "presentation" [*Vorstellung*], and thus sentient
nature generally, must have the condition of its possibility in such a
negative self-relation. This was the great discovery that would
supplant causation and make possible an overcoming of mechanism.
This principle was developed in Hegel's logic with an richness of forms
unexampled in the history of thought. The logical forms of negative
self-relation, in the manner that we have seen, determine the organism
in its three stages of inner self-formation, process with externality, and
relation to another of its own kind.

Of all the thinkers of the Western tradition, Hegel is probably
closest to Aristotle in his concept of the soul. But the thrust of the
Hegelian endeavor in Logical Life is toward resolution of a modern
problem. In the post-Cartesian view of nature as extension there could
be no *entelecheia* of a natural body but only the principles of motion and
rest. However rigorously scientific those principles appeared to early
modern science, they separated materiality irretrievably from spirit,
nature from freedom. There could be no regaining the continuity by a
return to a pre-modern view of nature. To resolve the impasse of the
Cartesian heritage with regard to Life, Hegel summons us to "think
contradiction"; to grasp the negative as at the same time positive and
thereby dissolve the rigidities of *Verstand* that lie at the heart of
mechanistic thinking. In Logical Life, Hegel claims to recast the
post-Cartesian view of nature by conceiving the *partes extra partes* of
materiality as the "objectivity" of the speculative Notion as subjectivity and negative self-relation.

> This multiplicity, as self-external objectivity, has an indifferent sub-
> sistence, which in space and time . . . is a mutual externality of
> wholly diverse and self-subsistent elements. But in Life, externality is
> at the same time present as the *simple determinateness* of the No-
> tion; thus the soul is an omnipresent outpouring of itself into this mul-
> tiplicity and at the same time remains absolutely the simple oneness
> of the concrete Notion with itself. The thinking that clings to the de-
> terminations of reflection-relationships and of the formal Notion,
> when it comes to consider Life, this unity of its Notion in the external-
> ity of objectivity, in the absolute multiplicity of atomistic matter, finds
> all its thoughts without exception are of no avail; the omnipresence of

the simple in the manifold externality is for reflection an absolute contradiction ... an *incomprehensible mystery* for it, because it does not grasp the Notion, and the Notion as the substance of Life (SL, 763).

NOTES

1. The present paper will deal mainly with the concept of Logical Life as presented in the *Wissenschaft der Logik,* 2d ed., 1831 (hereafter WL), which offers a considerably more comprehensive exposition of Life than in the *Enzyklopädie der philosophischen Wissenschaften im Grundrisse,* 3d ed., 1830, (hereafter EL). G. R. G. Mure, whose chapter, "The Idea: Life" (*A Study of Hegel's Logic,* Oxford, 1950, pp. 260-68), is in many ways illuminating, takes the *Encyclopedia* version as his basis, for he finds the presentation in the *Science of Logic* "highly obscure." (p. 264) The chapter on Life in the latter work has been given no detailed exposition of text in English. The subheadings here used are those of Hegel's text.

   The present treatment is based on Hegel's German text (hsg. Georg Lasson, Felix Meiner, Leipzig, 1951, zweiter Teil, pp. 413-29). Page references, however, will be to the English translation by A. V. Miller (*Hegel's Science of Logic,* Humanities Press, New York, 1969) and quotations will also be from this source, although in some instances, as also in the case of other translations of Hegel texts, I have made some modifications. The Miller translation will hereafter be referred to as *SL*.

2. Life is treated from various viewpoints of consciousness and self-consciousness in the *Phänomenologie des Geistes* but to deal with these treatments would raise questions about the relation of this 1807 work to the system proper that are beyond the scope of the present paper.

3. *Das logische Leben als reine Idee* (WL, II, 415).

4. See also *Hegel's Philosophy of Nature*, trans. by A. V. Miller, (Oxford, 1970), §359 Remark. Hereafter PNM with section number.

5. "When anything whatever possesses truth, it possesses it through its Idea, or something has truth only insofar as it is Idea." (SL, 755).

6. For the Kantian conception of logic that Hegel is here criticizing, see Kant's *Logic,* trans. by Hartman and Schwarz (Bobbs-Merrill, 1974), 15 ff.

7. In fact Hegel's whole Introduction to the *Science of Logic* is one sustained argument against the separation of form and content in logic and the demand for their immanent connection.

8. The Idea is the "absolute unity of the Notion and objectivity." *The Logic of Hegel,* trans. William Wallace, (2d ed., Oxford, 1892, §213); hereafter ELW with number of paragraph and -z for the *Zusatz* where it is referred to.

9. "The judgment is the self-diremption of the Notion; this unity is, therefore, the ground from which the consideration of the judgment in accordance with its true objectivity be-

gins. It is thus the original division [*Teilung*] of what is originally one. . . ." (*SL,* 625) See also ELW, No. 166.

10. See "First Introduction to the Science of Knowledge," Section 6, J. G. Fichte, *Science of Knowledge,* ed. and trans. Peter Heath and John Lachs (New York, 1970), pp. 16ff. "Nobody who ever understands the words can deny that all causation is mechanical and that no presentation comes about through mechanism" (pp. 19-20).

11. Since the teleological judgment can only be reflective and regulative, it cannot provide objective knowledge as in the case of the determinative and constitutive judgments regarding mechanism. Human reason cannot unite mechanism and teleology in scientific knowledge, hence no Newton will ever make a blade of grass intelligible from natural laws: i.e., in the strict sense of science there can be no theoretic science of Life. (See Kant's Preface and Introduction to the *Critique of Judgment,* trans. James C. Meredith, Oxford, repr. 1969; and Part II, pp. 38, 54. See also Kant's *Metaphysical Foundations of Natural Science,* trans. James Ellington, Bobbs-Merrill, 1970, pp. 6 ff., 105-06.) Hegel criticizes Kant's concept of the "reflective judgment" in which "only the particular is given for which the universal is to be found." This is mere "external reflection," says Hegel, as is Kant's whole view of judgment as a "subsuming" of the particular under the universal. In inner purposiveness, Hegel claims to show, End is not an "abstract universal," as for Kant, but a "concrete universal, which possesses in its own self the moment of particularity and externality and is therefore active and the urge to repel itself from itself". (SL, 404, 739; see also Mure, *op. cit.,* pp. 197ff.)

12. The Subjective Logic as noted has "behind it" the sublation of substance to subject, of the causal relation as one of blind necessity to the relation of free self-determination. Hegel's recapitulation of this movement elucidates certain meanings of "positing" and "presupposing" that play a key role in Logical Life. Substance as "absolute power," says Hegel, differentiates itself into "passive substance," which is "only an original positedness," and "active substance," which relates itself to this "other" that the active "has presupposed for itself as condition." But as "for itself" in this its very presupposing, substance has posited itself as "self-related negativity," in this way sublating what was presupposed: i.e., where before it presupposed, now it posits, acts, and thus appears as "cause" and positedness as "effect." But as effect the positedness receives only the determination of the cause, thus becoming cause; and the cause reveals itself in the effect as precisely the absolute power that it is. Hereby each side "becomes the opposite of itself, so that the other, and therefore also each, remains identical with itself": the absolute identity of the opposites precisely in their posited duality. This "infinite reflection-into-self," says Hegel, is the "consummation" of substance, but a consummation that is "no longer substance itself but something higher, the Notion, the subject." (SL, 579-80)

13. See also ELW, §216.

14. See also ELW, §213.

15. Aristotle neither seeks to demonstrate the divine Life as "creative" of materiality, nor does he try to show the forms of nature as proceeding from the divine active intellect in the way Hegel claims to demonstrate the forms of nature and Spirit as proceeding from the Idea.

16. Speculative logic shows the elevation of the Idea "to that level from which it becomes the creator of nature." Hegel regrets that Kant did not go further with his concept of the "intuitive understanding" (SL, 592).

17. For the general concept of "the Idea as Nature," see PNM §§245-52.

18. As inner self-dividing, the Notion becomes judgment, which becomes syllogism. The speculative syllogism is "the completely posited Notion; it is therefore the rational" (SL, 664). Every rational process has the form of syllogism in which "the universal nature of the Notion gives itself external reality by means of particularity, and thereby, as a negative reflection-into-self, makes it an individual" (ELW, No. 181, Remark). Hegel claims that his speculative *Schluss* is the logical form par excellence for comprehending Life as *Selbstzweck*: "the antecedent End which is itself only result" (PNM, §352).

19. In Logical Life there is no separate treatment of geological, vegetable, and animal organism, as in Natural Life (see PNM, §337); the logical exposition is closest to that of animal organism, which is "veritable organism" and most truly "subjectivity." (PNM, §§349ff.) The nervous, circulatory, and digestive systems, which comprise the "reality" of the moments of animal organism (PNM, §354) are not separately dealt with in Logical Life. Neither is there discussion of specific organs or the organism's relations to specific features of its outer world, as for example in the particular senses.

20. Logic "as the formal science cannot and should not contain that reality which is the content of the further parts of philosophy, namely, the philosophical sciences of nature and of Spirit" (SL, 592).

21. For Hegel's brief characterization of the relations of subjectivity and objectivity in Mechanism, Chemism, Teleology, and Life, respectively, see SL, 710.

22. Thus in Logical Life—where Hegel must perforce discuss the body, yet strictly speaking should not deal with actual configurations in space and time—we have a test case, so to speak, of how logic as "the science of absolute form" can "possess in its own self a content" that is not that of the sciences of nature and Spirit, while at the same time claiming its pure notions are immanent for all of nature and Spirit. (See SL, 592ff., 763, 782)

23. See PNM, §358 Remark, SL, 737ff.; *Hegel's Philosophy of Mind,* trans. William Wallace and A. V. Miller (Oxford, 1971), §378; hereafter cited as PMW.

24. The process of (A) The Living Individual "is restricted to that individuality itself and still falls entirely within it." (SL, 767; ELW, §218) It is the process whereby in the action of its several organs the living subject is the one act of self-reproduction. In the *Naturphilosophie* the first moment of animal organism is to be considered "as individual Idea which in its process is only self-related, and inwardly coalescesces with self—Shape" (PNM, §352).

25. The moments of the Notion are universality, particularity, individuality: but every moment is "the very total which the Notion is" (ELW, §160, 163).

26. In contrast to the meaning here of objectivity, its meaning in Mechanism consists in the fact that the moments of the objective totality "exist in a self-subsistent indifference as objects outside one another" and in every combination "external" to one another as well as to the subjective unity of the Notion implicit in their relation. (SL, 710, 711) It is basically in terms of such mechanism that Spinoza deals with "compound" bodies or individuals that are identities insofar as they retain "the same mutual relations of motion and rest" among their "parts." (*Ethics,* Part II, especially Prop. XIII and its Lemmata, etc.) Spinoza's concept of the mind as the idea of the body, and the latter as "object" or "ideatum" of the mind, is formally akin to Hegel's concept of the body-soul relation, as is Leibniz's development of the Spinozist concept in terms of the "windowless" monads. Neither earlier thinker, however, conceives the body-soul relation as an *Ur-teil* in Hegel's sense.

27. With regard to the objective totality, the teleological relation has proved that "in this ex-

ternal totality" the Notion as subjective inwardness comprises the "totality's self-determining identity." (SL, 754) Thus Hegel will seek to show the body as more than a persevering union of parts, as in Spinoza. As in Aristotle's *entelecheia* of a natural organized body, for Hegel the body as objectivity is "permeated throughout" by the subjectivity of the Notion and "has the Notion alone for substance." (SL, 763) Spinoza does not conceive the soul as "negative unity" of its objectivity (an idea that first emerges with Fichte) and has rejected the concept of organism as substance. One can agree with those commentators who view Spinoza's concept of organism as an advance beyond Cartesian mechanism and interactionism (in the case of man). Hans Jonas claims that in Spinoza "for the first time in modern speculation, an organic individual is viewed as a fact of wholeness rather than a mechanical interplay of parts." ("Spinoza and the Theory of Organism," *Journal of the History of Philosophy*, vol. iii, no. 1, Apr. 1965, p. 50.) While the parts "come and go," the persevering identity of the form, says Jonas, testifies to the "self-affirming 'conatus' " as a "common conatus of the whole" (p. 48). But that the form testifies to (or "bespeaks" or "evidences", p. 47), the conatus of the whole does not mean that the latter accounts for the former as *this* organization of parts. "Organization" in terms of motion and rest, and "conatus" appear connected, as Hegel says, only by an "external reflection."

28. Presupposing does not yet have the "within-self reflected unity" of a positing.

29. For Hegel's critique of the mind-body dualism, see PMW, §389.

30. Cf. the centrality of Mechanism (SL, 721ff.), whose logical outcome is a falling asunder of the center into a relation of "reciprocally negative objectivities in a state of mutual tension": this then is Chemism (SL, 726).

31. Already Teleology, which "has proved to be the truth of Mechanism," exhibited the Notion "in free existence." (SL, 735) But in End as external purposiveness the side of objectivity was still independent and not yet predicate of the Notion's *Urteil*.

32. The soul is the self-moving not only in the Platonic and Aristotelian senses of locomotion or actualization, but more specifically as the movement of the subject's "objectification." In Natural Life this will include the animal's faculty of locomotion (PNM, §351).

33. See Aristotle's *De Anima* 407b26. Kant of course does not accept Aristotelian *entelecheia* and its soul-body relationship. For Kant an organism is "an organized natural product . . . in which every part is reciprocally both end and means." This entails that the parts "are only possible by their relation to the whole" and "combine of themselves into the unity of a whole by being reciprocally cause and effect of their form." (*Critique of Judgment*, ii, 22ff.) Such a formulation goes beyond Spinoza but, according to Kant, leads reason completely outside the domain of mechanism where alone it can make constitutive judgments about nature. In Kant's conception of internal purposiveness, says Hegel, "he has opened up the Notion of Life, the Idea," but "the end-relation is more than judgment; it is the syllogism of the self-subsistent free Notion that unites itself with itself through objectivity" (SL, 737, 739).

34. Hegel notes that objectivity is also the "middle term" of the syllogism so that "the corporeality of the soul is that whereby the soul unites itself with external objectivity." (SL, 766) Here the influence of Spinoza is traceable. (See pp. 130-131.)

35. It is precisely the aim of the Subjective Logic to provide the forms of thought for a content beyond mere mechanism.

36. For Descartes the mind does not change with its changing "accidents," i.e., thinking, willing, etc., but the body "is no longer the same if a change takes place in any of its parts." ("Synopsis," *Meditations on First Philosophy*) On this view, which in effect denies organisms a continuing identity, Spinoza undoubtedly made an advance.

37. *Ethics*, Part II, Proposition XIII, Lemma V.

38. See the account in ELW, No. 218 and PNM, §352-z.

39. In finite teleology the means "is broken up into two elements external to each other, (a) the action and (b) the object which serves as means." (ELW, §208) But in the organism there is "nothing merely there"; the living being only "is" as this "self-reproductive being, *nicht als Seiendes* . . . it only is, in making itself what it is" (PNM, §352-z).

40. Later on, however, in the process with externality posited as actual, the means-end relation initially will also have the aspect of a violence: in the organism's mechanical seizure and appropriation of the object. But this external means-end relationship will become transformed directly to the inner process of Assimilation. (See p. 135).

41. As "infinite negativity" the soul is the "dialectic" of its *auseinanderseienden Objektivität*, conveying the externalities "away from the semblance of independent subsistence, so that all the members are reciprocally momentary means as well as momentary ends." (ELW, No. 216) We see here Hegel's debt to Kant, with the decisive difference that Kant does not conceive the organism's parts as self-sublating in the whole as their negative unity. As we noted, Hegel said that such a conception was inaccessible to Kant because of the Kantian notion of judgment (see above, fn. 11).

42. Cf. Fichte's concept of the Ego as *Tathandlung* which is at once "the active, and what the activity brings about." (*Science of Knowledge*, ed. and trans. Peter Heath and John Lachs, New York, 1970, p. 97)

43. The plant in its particularization does not fully come back to itself as subjective one. Hence not the plant but the "veritable organism," i.e., the animal, has feeling; for "in the actuality and externality of immediate singularity," the animal nature is equally "the inwardly reflected self of singularity, inwardly present subjective universality" (PNM, §350).

44. This *Erzittern* is also used by Hegel to characterize sound *(Klang)* as a "transition of materialized space into materialized time" (PNM, §300). Vibrating thus seems to suggest the temporal nature of Sensibility, but more specifically as an overcoming of the spatiality of the corporeality in the veritable organism, "in which the outer formation accords with the Notion, so that the parts are essentially members, and subjectivity exists as the One which pervades the whole" (PNM, §349). For Voice as a dialectical unity of space and time, and thus an *Erzittern*, see PNM, § 351.

45. CF. the characterization of Sensibility in Natural Life: PNM, §353.

46. On self-limitation, see SL, 113-14, 132. In Natural Life, Irritability is "just as much a capacity for being stimulated by an other and the reaction of self-maintenance against it, as it is also, conversely, an active maintenance of self, in which it is at the mercy of another" (PNM, §354).

47. I am uncertain of Hegel's meaning here. The formal introreflectedness of the genus would seem to have two possible significations, perhaps not mutually exclusive. In his lectures Hegel at one point terms the genus-process in the plant "formal" insofar as "the plant's

relationship with the outer world is already a production of the plant itself' and the genus-process is not truly a sexual relationship (PNM, §348-z). But in Logical Life, Hegel is not dealing with the plant, whose process outwards does not involve Sensibility and Irritability. (See PNM, §347.) Possibly by formal introreflectedness Hegel is referring to the formalistic tautological explanation often characteristic of the physical sciences (see SL, 458). Thus contemporary ecologists use the term "niche" for the relation of an organism to a specialized physical environment, including other species. In his lectures, Hegel notes that: "The drive is completely determinate in particular animals; each animal has as its own only a restricted range of inorganic nature, which is its own domain, and which it must seek out by instinct from its complex environment. . . . The animal can be stimulated only by means of *its* inorganic nature, because for the animal, the only opposite is its *own*. The animal does not recognize the other in general, for each animal recognizes its *own* other, which is precisely an essential moment of the special nature of each." (*PNM* §361-z: Hegel's italics) Like the animal's "niche" or generic habitat, the "formal genus and its systematization" would be the formal reflection into self from the outer diversity. But as explanation, "formal genus" (like "niche") would be as tautological as explaining a crystalline form by saying "it has its ground in the particular arrangement which the molecules form with one another" (SL, 458).

48. Cf. Spinoza: "The human mind does not perceive any external body as actually existing, except through the ideas of the modifications of its own body" (*Ethics,* Part II, Proposition XXVI).

49. For Hegel, not only is the subjectivity related to external body through its own (as for Spinoza), but the relation to the external is a higher form of the subject-object relation than that of soul and body. Hegel's effort in this regard first becomes fully evident in the soul-body relation of Subjective Spirit. (See Murray Greene, *Hegel on the Soul,* The Hague, 1972, pp. 141ff.)

50. See Jonas, *op. cit.,* pp. 55ff. Jonas notes that in Spinoza "for the first time in modern theory, a speculative means is offered for relating the degree of organization of a body to the degree of awareness belonging to it" (p. 52). When all is said and done, however, the "relating" can be no greater than the "correspondence" of the attributes.

51. See Kant's comparison of the organism and the watch (*Critique of Judgment,* ii, 22) which curiously leaves out the element of self-feeling (perhaps because Kant wants to speak of organism generally, which would include plants). With regard to animals, Kant held in opposition to Descartes that animals have a certain consciousness. (See H. J. Paton, *Kant's Metaphysic of Experience,* 2 vols., Humanities Press, 1936, vol. 1, pp. 332ff.) But in arguing against the possibility of grasping organism by the categories of mechanism, Kant does not especially stress inwardness and subjectivity as does Hegel.

52. In Reproduction the living individual makes a stand and is not a mere *vis inertiae* that lies in the background of Spinoza's conatus. (See Frederick Pollock, *Spinoza,* New York, repr. 1966, pp. 109ff.)

53. In Natural Life, Reproduction is "the animal subject's negative return to itself from its relation to externality, and, through this, the engendering and positing of itself as a singular." (PNM, §353.) In his detailed treatment of the three systems (Sensibility, Irritability, and Reproduction) and their respective organic formations, Hegel tries to show how the three "unite in a general concrete interpenetration in Shape" and how each formation contains the systems "linked together in it" (PNM, §355).

54. See above, pp. 126-127.

55. If we would try to translate this movement into the terms of substance (of the Objective Logic), we would probably regard the corporeality as objectivity in the role of passive substance "presupposed" by the active. Having become "for itself" in its presupposition, the active substance is now "cause" that posits the passive as "effect"; and the demonstration will go on to show the sublation of the posited as an other. (See above, fn. 12.) But of course Hegel's claim is that the causal relation as such is inadequate for Life, and the Subjective Logic is the sublation of *causa sui* to the *Begriff* as self-producing subjectivity.

56. This too will be distinguished according to the moments of the Notion.

57. In ELW, §219 the *Urteil* is characterized as the Notion's free "release" [*entlassen*] from itself of its objectivity as an independent totality. For a similar characterization of the emergence of objectivity on the level of consciousness in Subjective Spirit, see PMW, § 413.

58. Although Life is not yet Spirit proper, nature is a manifestation of Spirit, and "the strength of the Spirit is measured only by the extent of the opposition it has overcome" (PNM, §365-z).

59. For a different point of view, an existential dialectic where Life is not eternally necessitated but remains in principle a question, see Hans Jonas, *The Phenomenon of Life* (Harper and Row, 1966).

60. See ELW, §119-z.

61. "Only what is living feels a lack; for in Nature it alone is the Notion, the unity of itself and its specific opposite. Where there is a limitation, it is a negation only for a third, for an external comparison. But it is a lack only insofar as the lack's overcoming is equally present in the same thing, and contradiction is, as such, immanent and explicitly present in that thing. A being which is capable of containing and enduring its own contradiction is a subject; this constitutes its infinitude" (PNM, §359 Remark).

62. For example, Irritability is inherently self-preservation, but it could also mean the organism's lying "at the mercy of an other" (PNM, §354). In the Life Process as moment of *Be-sonderung* this element is posited. The powers of external objectivity "are as it were continually on the spring, ready to begin their process in the organic body; and Life is the constant battle against them" (ELW, §219-z).

63. The logical principle that the negative "is just as much positive," Hegel claimed, is "all that is necessary to achieve scientific progress" (SL, 54). Organics is par excellence a science that requires a thinking of contradiction. "It is said that contradiction is unthinkable; but . . . in the pain of a living being it is even an actual existence" (SL, 770; see also 135).

64. The "destiny" of the plant is to "sacrifice itself to the higher organism" which actualizes the Notion that is only implicit in the plant (PNM, §§349 and 349-z.) But in the same way the plant makes use of the "geological organism" which is "only the corpse of the life-process, the organism as totality of inanimately existing, mechanical and physical nature" (PNM, §337.) Hegel is here undoubtedly influenced by Kant's notion of "a vast system of natural ends" but seeks to show a hierarchy wherein the Notion as immanent End is increasingly realized on ascending levels of subjectivity.

65. See above, fn. 61.

66. For Hegel, "nothing whatever can have a positive relation to the living being if this latter is not in its own self the possibility of this relation, i.e., if the relation is not determined

by the Notion and hence not directly immanent in the subject" (PNM, §359 Remark).

67. See above, p. 129.

68. See above, *ibid*.

69. For the conversion of the process outwards "into the process of the organism with itself" in Natural Life, see the discussion of Assimilation as digestion in PNM, §365 and Remark. Here Hegel notes that the syllogism of the organism is "not the syllogism of external teleology," for "the process outwards into external difference is converted into the process of the organism with itself, and the result is not the mere production of a means but of the end — union of the organism with itself."

70. That is, as Sensibility in the self-enclosed process of the Living Individual. (See above, p. 131.)

71. In Natural Life the geological organism or "inanimate organism of the earth" has but the one process of Shape. The plant is the first "vivified organism": "the subjectivity which differentiates itself into members and which excludes from itself, as an objectivity confronting it, the merely implicit organism" in which it has "the condition of its existence" and the "material of its process." Thus the plant has the processes of Shape and Assimilation, but its Reproduction is only "an adumbration of the genus-process." The animal as "veritable organism" has all three processes as fully developed moments of the Notion. (See PNM, §338-350, but especially §342.)

72. I.e., not merely, as previously, arising from the Notion. Initially the individual's self-producing presupposed its objectivity as immediate means belonging to it "by nature." This presupposition is sublated in Assimilation, wherein the organism converts its very process with externality to a process with itself. Hereby the means is no longer merely immediately its own but mediated through negation of the process against the other, i.e., negation of negation.

73. In Natural Life, Hegel maintains, the plant can only go this far and "does not attain to a relationship between individuals" (PNM, §348).

74. For love as such a "contradiction" on the higher levels of Spirit, see PMW, No. 397; and *Hegel's Philosophy of Right,* trans. T. M. Knox (Oxford, 1942) §158-z, hereafter PR. Here too, Hegel claims, for a comprehension of the relation we need to "think contradiction," which is impossible for the non-speculative logic of *Verstand*. [See also the previous essay, Eds.],

75. For Hegel's discussion of the "spurious" and the "genuine" infinity: "the infinite of the understanding" and "the infinite of reason," see SL, 137ff.

76. Hegel links sexual reproduction in positive fashion with death (see PNM, §§367ff). "In copulation the immediacy of the living individuality perishes; the death of this Life is the advance of Spirit" (SL, 774). In Spinoza's concept of conatus the individuality endeavors to persist in its own being and its destruction is seen to come only from outside itself (*Ethics,* Part III, Proposition IV ff.). For Hegel the passing of the singular Life is not merely a violence coming from the outside. With the "self-induced destruction of the individual," i.e., its giving itself up as particularity to the higher universal life of the Genus, "the last self-externality of nature has been sublated" and nature has passed over into its "truth" as Spirit. (See PNM, §§375ff.)

77. *Critique of Judgment,* ii, 22.

78. The "genuine refutation" of a philosophical position, says Hegel, "must penetrate the opponent's stronghold and meet him on his own ground" (SL, 581). It is actually Newton and the Kantian principles supportive of Newton with which Hegel most often takes explicit issue. "Gravity is the universal determination of matter" but "the whole of Physics is the form which develops in contradistinction to gravity" (PNM, §351-z).

79. Insofar as the organism in its very "process outwards preserves inwardly the unity of the self," the "asunderness of spatial existence has no truth for the soul" (PNM, §350-z).

COMMENT: HEGEL AND EVOLUTIONARY THEORY

H. S. HARRIS

I have no quarrel with Murray Greene's exegesis of Hegel's concept of "life". I doubt whether any serious student of Hegel's text will quarrel with it. But I am not happy with it, all the same, because it leaves the fundamental question of Hegel's relation to and relevance for our own time and our own science of life unanswered. I cannot help suspecting that this is because he regards this "fundamental" question as being much easier to answer than I do. (He would certainly not be alone in that conviction).

My question is: What is the relation between Hegel's concept of the infinite or divine life, and our *evolutionary* theory of all finite life, and indeed of non-living nature as a whole? The *Aristotelian* inspiration of Hegel's concept both of nature and of God is plainly acknowledged throughout his work. Hegel saw that it was impossible to reconcile a Newtonian philosophy of nature with a Christian conception of human existence. He found in Aristotle, and in the main tradition of Greek speculation, the basic concepts that he needed for a properly coherent account of experience; and in the *Encyclopedia* he showed us the kind of coherence that a thoughtful contemplation of our life and our world can reveal. To me his achievement remains immensely impressive. But the more I appreciate it, and the more that I seem to myself to be gaining understanding of it, the more worried I become about the comfortable conviction, which is prevalent far beyond the ranks of professed Hegelians, that the Hegelian logic will stand unshaken no matter what happens in the sphere of what Hegel called "real philosophy". The revolutionary upheavals caused by Marx in the philosophy of spirit, do not appear to be *logically* threatening, because as far as *logic* is concerned "it's all in the family". In the same way, many students seem to feel—whether they have examined the problem closely or not—that there is a natural affinity between dialectical logic and evolutionary science. This may be the case, but it needs to be shown and the consequences must be properly assessed.

The issue between Hegelians and Marxists boils down to the simple question, "Which party is *really* looking at the world upside down?" And it is, of course, possible that the proper "speculative" answer *may* well be: "Both and/or neither, according to context". *No* answer—least of all this maximal reconciliation—will be achieved, certainly, without "the patience and the labor of the negative". But it is clear that the dialectic, together with *some* conception of "speculation" or "absolute knowledge", will survive whatever the answer may be. It is by no means equally clear that Hegel's ideal of speculation can survive the triumph of Darwin over Aristotle and of Einstein over Newton; and nothing could be more un-Hegelian than placid confidence about this. For this reason, I applaud Greene's paper because it focuses our attention in the right place. But I am unhappy because he seems only to pose the question in its most trenchant form. As far as I can see, he gives no hint of an answer.

Greene says that he wants to deal with the *transcendental* side of Hegel's doctrine rather than its *ontological* side. I think myself that to raise the question of biological evolution would have been the most appropriate way to focus on the transcendental aspect of the problem. But I find that he has *not* focused effectively on this side of the problem at all. At any rate, speculative theology has carried him away from *my* "transcendental problem" about life. But I suppose that is only because there are so many different transcendental problems. My problems start, like Kant's, with my cognitive and practical experience of life in this world. "For Hegel, as for Aristotle, life is divine," says Greene in his concluding paragraph. Some of the time, at least, I *think* that I know what this meant for Aristotle; and because I fully recognize that Hegel's philosophy of nature is a reworking of Aristotle's views, I find Hegel very helpful to me here. But if Hegel's concepts of "life" and of "divinity" are *only* consistent with an Aristotelian philosophy of nature (or, more exactly, with an Aristotelian philosophy that has been rendered concordant with some of the principal exigencies of Platonism), then the Hegelian concept of "logical life" will have to be rejected, just as surely as the Aristotelian concept of nature must be set aside by anyone who takes the theory of evolution as the foundation stone of his biological science. For it is quite clear that Aristotle's concept of nature cannot be effectively conciliated with an evolutionary interpretation of biological phenomena; and although, because of his heritage from Heraclitus, the ontology of Plato probably *can* be reconciled with an evolutionary theory of nature, Plato's *logic* of collection and division, like the theory of genus and specific difference that Aristotle developed from it, will not serve the needs of modern biology (and the enormous influence of this Platonic-Aristotelian heritage upon our practical common sense interpretation of the world becomes truly baneful when it is reflected—as it often is—in the disputes of working biologists about the definition of a "species").

Hegel's attachment to the Aristotelian philosophy of nature was natural and inevitable since Aristotle was the *only* thinker before Hegel himself who had framed a concept of nature which made the unity of reason and life, or even the unity of physics and biology intelligible. The greatest minds of the modern scientific revolution, Newton and Descartes, had conceived their own achievements in the philosophical context of dualism and scepticism. Hence Descartes, the dualist, was obliged to claim that non-rational "living" organisms were really complex *machines*, and Kant was forced to declare on behalf of Newton that there never could be a Newton for the blade of grass.

But even as we recognize how natural Hegel's adherence to Aristotle was, we must acknowledge that his return to the Greeks in his philosophy of nature has proved to

be an enormous cultural stumbling block set up against the proper appreciation of
his philosophy of nature. His reverence for Greek thought combined with his violent
antipathy to Newton's metaphysical assumptions create in Hegel's mind a prejudice
which led him to espouse the wrong side in practically every major scientific controversy that he had to deal with, in an incidental way, in his philosophic labors
upon the concept of "nature". As the controversies got settled, and Hegel was found
to be always on the wrong side, the idea was bound to grow up, even in the most
"Hegelian" minds of the following generations, that there was something absurd in
the very *project* of a "philosophy of nature". The publication of the *Origin of the Species*
appeared to provide conclusive evidence of this, by overthrowing the Aristotelian
foundations of biology. There were, indeed, some Hegelians who welcomed it because Hegel's "philosophy of spirit", his evolutionary account of human consciousness and human culture, seemed intuitively to be in harmony with an evolutionary
concept of nature. But they did not seek to establish their contention logically. It
remained simply a general idea which served, for them, *in the place of* the real labour
of the concept. On the other hand, those who took the Darwinian revolution seriously—Dewey, for example—simply abandoned their faith in the possibility of
"speculative" knowledge altogether.

What has changed the picture for us, and made us see once more both the un-
avoidable necessity of a philosophy of nature, and at least the possibility of establishing one that will not be fatally dependent on some existing status of natural science
that is destined to become historically outmoded, is the triumph of relativity theory
in cosmology and of quantum theory in mechanics. Now that Newton's theory of
gravity has taken its place *within* the context of science, instead of *constituting* the
context of all other scientific endeavors as it used to do, the *need* for a philosophy of
nature is apparent, and it seems eminently worthwhile to re-examine the views of
Newton's philosophical opponents. The real Newtonians—Laplace is the greatest
example—felt that they had dispensed with speculation—even Newton's own
speculation—altogether. Kant was the only one among them who recognized what
they were giving up. He at least could give grounds for the sacrifice which made it
seem as sensible as it was safe.

But if we can now see that the concept of nature, and of our place in it, is *not* finally established and safe, and hence that we cannot afford to give up on it as a
philosophical problem, we can also see that a return from Newton to Aristotle is not
an option that is open to us as it was to Hegel. To have recognized this possibility in
the heyday of Newtonian physics was an outstanding feat of speculative imagination;
to have *realized* the possibility almost single handed, in a state of scientific culture
that had moved so far from the world of Aristotle, was a feat of intellect that is no
less remarkable. To try to *maintain* that achievement in the present state of scientific
inquiry would only testify to our obtuseness, and to our utter failure to comprehend
what Hegel really did achieve. It would be far more stupid, for instance, than

Hegel's attempt to revive the Greek theory of the four elements, which is perhaps the most comical of his scientific follies. We must now address ourselves to the task of constructing a philosophy of nature, and especially a philosophical theory of organic life, that corresponds properly to what is actually known.

It is obvious that I cannot hope to contribute significantly to that task at all since I do not have more than a smattering of the requisite empirical knowledge. No one could sensibly set out, nowadays, as Hegel did in his day, to do it single handed. The new Hegelian philosophy of nature — if it is possible at all, as I believe it is — will be the result of a collaboration of many minds and of more than one pen. The most that I can do now and here is to point to that aspect of Hegel's logic which gives us grounds for thinking that it will pass the test when it is properly put to it.

Hegel's concept of "life" is, in his terminology, the "genus". The relation of "genus" and "species" in his view is a dialectical one, such that the genus is in a certain sense, *identical* with its own highest species. I shall not try to expound the logic of genus and species here. I only want to point out that it constitutes a *Platonic*, rather than an Aristotelian inheritance in Hegel's *Logic*. Hegel needed this "speculative" interpretation of the genus-species relation, if his logic was to be adequate for the formulation of our self-conscious experience. His concept of "logical life" as the ultimate "genus" is the rational form for the experienced identity of "the living God", (the absolute genus) with man as rational species. The "logic" of "logical life" is the logic of the Incarnation — which is a very *different* matter from the religious *pictures* of it that our tradition has bequeathed to us. Hegel's logical concept can accommodate the evolutionary theory of organic life quite simply, by extending the scope of the "identity". Continuity replaces discreteness. But this accommodation can only take place consistently, I believe, if its scope is made universal. The Aristotelian "scale of nature", as a ladder with discrete steps, must be given up altogether. Some extremely radical consequences follow from this, with respect to our speculative conception of "God" or the "absolute genus". What the Aristotelian systematic theory of "species" did was to guarantee individuality through the abiding permanence of a natural hierarchy. Among other things it guaranteed the individuated independence of God at the peak of the hierarchy. This was a point of vital importance for the evolution of Christian theology. I may be wrong, but I believe that in his doctrine of God as *spirit*, Hegel already broke decisively with the orthodox faith in this respect. It is hard to feel certain, and impossible to be dogmatic, because orthodoxy has certainly always involved a mystical reconciliation of several opposing points of view. But these high theological matters do not concern me very much in any case. What does concern me is that when "discreteness" yields pride of place to "continuity" throughout the whole range of the philosophy of nature, the a priori certainty that there is a *hierarchical* relation between nature and spirit has to be given up. This has momentous consequences for the whole controversy between Hegelians and Marxists. Hegel, if I am right, already established finally, the speculative identity of "God" with "human historical consciousness". For this reason a great part of what the "left" Hegelians conceived of as *criticism* of Hegel was really just correct philosophical interpretation; and a great part of Marx' polemic against the Hegelian technique of "mystification" only testifies to the fact that Marx was himself mystified by Hegel. The speculative interpretation of evolutionary theory will bring us to the further recognition of the *identity of man with nature*. When that speculative identity is grasped we shall be able to see that a great part of the polemic of Hegelians (and others) against Marxian "materialism", on behalf of "spiritual" values, is mistaken in its turn. The solution of the question, "Which party is *really* looking at the world upside down?", which I suggested earlier as a mere hypothesis: "Both and/or neither, according to context", will then be found to be no mere hypothesis but a necessary truth of speculative reason. Hegel's logic will survive but some of the dearly cherished shibboleths of Hegelian philosophical piety will not.

COMMENT: BIOLOGY AND THE HEGELIAN ABSOLUTE

ROLF AHLERS

Professor Greene's paper is extremely stimulating because it indicates the manner in which Hegel dealt with an issue which may presently be central to our culture's intellectual life. If a generation ago physics was the science *par excellence*, the science of life *(bios)*, biology, has undoubtedly taken its place today. Great theoreticians, such as Werner Heisenberg and Hans Jonas, have pointed to this shift as well as to the philosophical problematic inherent in the contemporary theoretical physics and biology. Hans Jonas has indicated that the science of life shows great promise, but also danger. The danger arises in a problematic approach to its object, "life." The theoretical basis of its approach he has earlier referred to as an "ontological dominance of death."[80] In such a context life itself cannot be adequately grasped because that science does not arise out of life itself as life's own self-differentiation. Hence life cannot be determined, as the great theologian Wilhelm Herrmann had already noted fifty years ago in his *Ethik*, by the traditional, limited scientific theory which reduces *Leben* to mere *Lebensmittel,* the reduction of life to a mere "means to life." In such an approach, life has not found itself as its own end. In the same vein Professor Greene mentions in his excellent paper that "no Newton will ever make a blade of grass intelligible from natural laws; i.e., in the strict sense of science there can be no theoretic science of life." (See above, fn. 11.) Professor Greene's paper is laudable, therefore, because the "grave potentials" of the "ontology of death"[81] promise not only boon but also bane for man, as long as the science of life is not understood as a self-differentiating and logical *Ur-teilung* within life itself. That Hegel could make a valuable contribution to this problem was hardly apparent twenty or even ten years ago. But it becomes apparent now that it is well worth-while considering Hegel's thoughts on life as the "science of the pure Idea" in this context.

What is of interest to us in Greene's paper is Hegel's claim that the science of Logic and the science of Life must have a common ground in the Life of the Idea, if both Logic and Life are to be recognized in their truth adequately. Hegel says that this common view *seems* to mix realms (i.e., Logic and Biology) apparently incompatible in the sense of *Wissenschaft*. But he insists that an understanding of Logic as unrelated to life conceives of that science as nothing but "empty, dead forms of thought"(WL, II, 413). Furthermore, one could not even speak of "life" out of the context of a logic conceived as undifferentiating, empty thought. Certainly "life" can be viewed from "other scientific perspectives" (WL, II, 414f.), but Hegel claims, to our satisfaction correctly, that if those other perspectives are to have content, truth

155

and specificity, then they must be rooted in logic as the living self-differentiation of the Idea itself. The origin of that differentiation and specification is Life itself, which is by itself as yet undivided. "The immediate Idea . . . is Life."

The process by means of which the concept of life posits as subject its objective other in the Idea of Life, a positing which is the self-dividing *Ur-teil* or judgment, has particular relevance at a time when a viable theory of communication is to be sought. The shortcomings of traditional scientific approaches to "life" not only fail to give an adequate account of biological life as such, but in a broader sense threaten, in conjunction with technological and industrial implementation of these approaches, to destroy the totality of life on the globe. A more adequate understanding of life is therefore necessary, one in which life communicates with itself, and creates, in that process of communication and differentiation reasonable judgments which have a greater reasonableness than the undifferentiated whole prior to this process. I believe that Professor Greene makes a valuable contribution in this direction in highlighting Hegel's understanding of the Logical Life.

The great advantage of the Life of Hegel's *Logic* for these purposes rests in his transcending the Spinozistic substance which had to be characterized as volitional subjectivity in order to invest it with vitality. Although Hegel understood Spinoza's intentions, he understood also the problematic in this approach. The Life of the Logic, in which the concept differentiates in the judgment is Hegel's answer to this problematic, but it depends, as Michael Theunissen has shown, intimately on Hegel's concept of the Absolute. Those who have rejected Hegel's understanding of Life have done so because they have understood correctly that this concept of the Absolute is the key to Hegel's philosophy. The vitality of the Life of the Logic remains impotent apart from the Absolute Concept; as Hegel states at the end of the Logic of Essence: Both causality and necessity have disappeared in the Absolute Concept (WL, II, 203), while in that disappearance they receive both the immediate identity as connection and relation and the absolute substantiality of the differentiation. It is fitting therefore that the entire *Logic* ends with the chapter on the Absolute Idea, just as the description of the phenomenon of consciousness in the *Phänomenologie* ends with the chapter on Absolute Knowledge. The Absolute becomes thus the centre of Hegel's central work, the *Logic*. But precisely this centrality has been the stumbling block of the Younger Hegelians both on the left and the right, and is the basis of the critique of the inadequacy of Hegel's thought by such thinkers as Habermas,[82] who charges that in Hegel's concept of the Logical Life of the Absolute the reasonable and enlightening dialogue has *already* taken place, and has taken place *vicariously* in the Absolute, so that it need not take place anymore in the universities and on the political platform. In his essay on Hegel's concept of *Erfahrung*, Heidegger[83] has correctly seen that the Absolute Idea is central to Hegel's thought, and has rejected Hegel on that account. So, too, have Gadamer[84] and Otto Pöggeler.[85] Gadamer, for example, insists that Hegel has suspended history with his thought that, in the Idea of the Absolute, philosophy comes to complete elucidation.[86] It is Murray Greene's great contribution to have shown that historicality and temporality, or non-repressive dialogue cannot even be thought outside of the context of the Logical Life which differentiates itself in the judgment into the subject concept and the objective Idea of Life. The question remains, therefore, whether the radical temporality of Being and the "herrschaftsfreie Dialog" envisioned respectively by Gadamer and by his pupil Habermas, are realizable outside of the historical process which takes place in the Absolute Idea as self-differentiation, self-identification and self-reclaiming. Murray Greene's paper admirably reconstructs this vitality of Hegel's divine life of the Absolute Idea, and if any fault is to be found in it, it can be only that he has not answered from the substantial foundation of his analysis those critics just mentioned. Such an answer is necessary today because a proper appraisal of Hegel's Logical Life is impossible without paying heed to these rather significant charges.

NOTES

80. *Phenomenon of Life*, (New York: 1966), p. 12.
81. Hans Jonas, "Technology and Responsibility" in *Technology and the Humanizing* of Man, ed. Jas. M. Robinson, (Council on the Study of Religion, Waterloo, Ontario, 1973), p. 14; also in H. Jonas, *Philosophical Essays* (Englewood Cliffs, N.J.: Prentice Hall, 1974), pp. 3 ff., esp. p. 16.
82. *Theorie und Praxis*, (Berlin, 1963), p. 107.
83. *Holzwege* 4th edition (Frankfurt: 1963), pp. 105-192.
84. *Wahrheit und Methode*, (Tübingen 1965²), pp. 461, 285, 325f., 327, 353f., 433, 437, 444, 451, 511.
85. "Hegel und die Griechische Tragödie," *Hegelstudien*, Beiheft I, Bonn, 1964, pp. 285ff., especially p. 302.
86. *Op . cit.,* p. 285.

LIFE AS ONTOLOGICAL CATEGORY: A WHITEHEADIAN NOTE ON HEGEL
GEORGE L. KLINE

Hegel distinguishes three forms, or levels, of life: (1) life as generalized *ontological* category, (2) life as specialized *biological* category, and (3) life as specialized *culture-historical* category.[86] Instances of (2) would be: individual ferns, fleas, and foxes, and the species fern, flea, and fox; of (3) the historical and cultural life of Periclean Athens, Renaissance Florence, and Elizabethan England. Pure instances of (1) are difficult, if not impossible, to find—since "logical life" is precisely life as *generalized* ontological category.

The life of what Hegel sometimes calls (unfortunately, in my judgment) the "organism" of socio-political culture[87] does not include the life of its attendant biological organisms, although some of the latter serve, in part, as means for the actualization of given cultures (SL, 762).

In spite of the fact that birth, growth, decay, and death—in a broad sense of all of these terms—characterize life at all three levels, the birth, growth, decay, and death of a culture is a process quite distinct from the births, growths, decays, and deaths of "its" flora and fauna, considered either as individuals or as species. With the collapse of Periclean Athens or the Fall of Rome, the ferns, fleas, and foxes of Athens and Rome continued to flourish; or, if they did not, their non-flourishing was a process independent of the non-flourishing of the historical cultures "in" (or "beside") which they lived. (The "life" of the *flea* which became a part of Elizabethan culture when John Donne wrote his celebrated metaphysical poem of that title is of course metaphorical or symbolic, not biological. That life would not have been threatened even by the total success of a Royal Exterminating Service!)

Hegel's attempt to develop a theory of life or "living process" as a general ontological category strikes me as a pioneering effort, but one which is only partly successful. It seems to me that Hegel succeeds in distinguishing the ontological category of life from the culture-historical category, but that he does not entirely succeed in distinguishing it from the biological category. (Hence the biological focus of Mr. Ahlers' remarks has a basis in Hegel's own thought.)

According to Hegel, life as generalized ontological category is characterized by: process,[88] actuality, *An-und-für-sich-sein*, immanent purposiveness (every living being, for Hegel, is—as Mr. Greene has reminded us[89]—a *Selbstzweck*), subjectivity, inwardness, feeling, self-feeling *(Selbstgefühl); self-related negative—that is, exclusive or excluding—unity; the *Konkretion der Individualität*, the appropriation *(Aneignung)* of object by subject, the adaptation of means to end, self-determination, (partial) self-creation, and freedom.[90] It seems to me highly significant that *all* of these

158

characteristics also apply to Whitehead's units of living process, his "actual entities," or "concrescent occasions." Whitehead sees "the origination of conceptual novelty"[91] as essential to life, and lists among the characteristics of life "absolute self-enjoyment, creative activity, [and] aim."[92] What Mr. Greene accurately describes as the "inner self-producing activity" of "atomic subjectivity"[93] is close to what Whitehead calls the "internal adventure of becoming" of the (partially) self-creative atomic concrescence.

Unfortunately, Hegel goes on to say that life as ontological category is *also* characterized by need and urge or drive *(Trieb)*, as well as by pain, sensitivity, irritability, and reproduction, i.e., reproductive power. Need and urge—in a broad sense—*may* characterize ontological as well as biological life, but pain, sensitivity, irritability, and reproductive power surely do not.[94] For Whitehead such properties as pain, irritability, and reproductive power would characterize only *biological* organisms, i.e., certain organized nexūs—structured societies of societies—of (present) concrescences and (past) ex-concrescences (what I have elsewhere called 'concreta').[95]

Hegel fails to consider the relation of living beings to time, except for an almost passing mention in the subsection, "Prozess der Gattung." If Mr. Greene is right and Hegel is there referring not—or not primarily—to biological individuals and species but to the "speculative ascent of the individual into the concrete universal," then Hegel is taking time even less seriously than I had thought he was. For Hegel the individual dies, but the species lives on: "In copulation [or 'procreation'] the immediacy of the living individuality perishes; the death of this life is the procession [or 'emergence'?] of spirit" (SL, 774).[96]

The living Hegelian subject "has" or "appropriates" its own objectivity as object. One might say that the Whiteheadian "concretum," as object, is a kind of Hegelian "other" to its concrescence; that the latter has the concretum, "its own objectivity," as its object. But the crucial Whiteheadian distinction between subject as *present* and object as *past* (or in the case of "eternal objects"—*timeless*) seems to have no counterpart in Hegel. The "having" or "appropriation" is a speculative or dialectical, not a temporal, process.

It seems to me that Whitehead advances the Hegelian account of living process in two ways: (1) He makes a categorial distinction between living and no-longer-living units of process, between present actual entities and past actual entities, that is, between concrescences and concreta. (2) He overcomes the Hegelian gap between nature and life, and between spirit (culture) and life, by developing a radically "pansubjectivist" position.[97] A word on each of these points:

(1) Concrescences are *subjects*: "processive," active, non-objectifiable, non-recurrent. Concreta, in contrast, are *objects*: static, passive, objectifiable and re-objectifiable, and, in this sense recurrent. Concrescences as units of living process are concrete in Whitehead's special sense of the term, i.e., experient and actively self-relating; concreta are abstract (neither experient nor active), or, more precisely

"quasi-abstract" — if one wishes to distinguish their status from the full abstractness of the forms or "eternal objects." Whiteheadian concrescences are also concrete in Hegel's rather different sense of the term, i.e., many-sided and complexly mediated.[98] Thus living beings (or processes) in the ontological sense, for both Hegel and Whitehead, are "many-sided, adequately mediated, experient, and actively self-relating."

(2) Hegel remains within the Cartesian tradition, broadly conceived. For him living beings, like Descartes' *res cogitantes,* stand isolated in a lifeless world—the world of sheerly physical and chemical processes, which is void of subjectivity, inwardness, purpose. And this despite what Mr. Greene has rightly stressed as a Kantian-Hegelian *Umkehrung*: the reinterpretation of externality as objectivity rather than extendedness. Although the living being is not, for Hegel, a *res cogitans* in a world of *rēs extensae*, it is a *subjectum* in a world of *objecta*. For Whitehead, in contrast, whatever is is ultimately either itself a subject or else an organized nexus—a "society," in the ontological sense of the term—of subjects (concrescences) and objects, both ex-subjects (concreta) and non-subjects (forms).

Hegel's position — for Whitehead — involves an assumption of "vacuous [i.e., non-subjective or non-experient] actuality," and thus falls into an unacceptable dualism. Whitehead's own view is that even those entities which for common sense are non-living are in fact ultimately constituted of units of living process: a stone, no less than a person, though in a different way and at a different level, is a "society of societies of societies" of concrescences and concreta.

Hegel's move, in the *Logic*, from life to knowledge, from the more general living relation to the more specific cognitive relation has a parallel in Whitehead's distinction between the general case of "prehension," as taking account of, and the special case of "apprehension" as taking cognitive account of. For Whitehead all instances of life as ontological category prehend, but only some ("higher") instances apprehend.

Whitehead's monistic ontology — at the "microcosmic" level — is a panpsychism, or "pansubjectivism." Admittedly, it entails certain theoretical difficulties, the chief of which is the rendering precise and detailed (something which Whitehead himself did not do) of the relationship between the evanescent individual units of living process and the relatively stable things and persons of the macro-world. It is *persons*, i.e., "societies of societies," which speak, reason, are responsible, although individual *concrescences* "feel," "decide," and realize their purposes ("subjective aims").

In Hegel's ontology living and non-living beings, Spirit and Nature, are ultimately included — at the "macrocosmic" level — in the "divine life" of the Absolute Idea.[99] This position entails its own theoretical difficulties, the chief of which seems to me to be the neglect of temporality. The past-present distinction, crucial to Whitehead's account of life as ontological category, appears not to be significant for Hegel's account.

Whitehead's position on this question seems to me both more subtle and more adequate than Hegel's, and its difficulties less severe. But I recognize and applaud Hegel's incomparable contribution to the philosophical conceptualization of life, or "the living" (das Lebendige), as an ontological category.

NOTES

86. Hegel calls them, respectively, (1) das logische Leben, (2) das Naturleben or natürliches Leben, and (3) das Leben des Geistes (WL, II, 415). In the chapter on Life Hegel uses the prima facie puzzling expression das logische Leben — 'logical life' — only twice. In contrast, he uses the term Begriff (which Miller translates as 'Notion' but which I will render as 'Concept') dozens of times, more than any other philosophical term. —I recognize that there is a certain artificiality in considering Hegel's category of Life apart from his categories of Spirit, Idea, and the Absolute. For purposes of the present analysis, however, this artificiality seems justified.

87. Hegel refers in the Philosophy of Right to the 'organism of the state' (cf. §§ 267 and 269). In the Encyclopedia he is more careful, referring to the state as a lebendiger Geist and as an organisiertes . . . Ganzes (§539). In general, it would seem to me preferable to characterize aspects or institutions of objektiver Geist as "organized wholes" rather than "organisms."

88. In both the Science of Logic and the Encyclopedia Hegel uses the term Prozess frequently to characterize life as both ontological and biological category. He speaks less often of a Prozess of Geist, rather of the Werden, Hervorgehen, or Fortgang of Geist.

89. See Murray Greene, above, fn. 18 and pp. 126-7, 128, 130, and 133.

90. In the Encyclopedia Hegel says that life is characterized by a fortdauernde Erhaltung der Gestalt (§ 351), adding that das Lebendige "ist nur, indem es sich zu dem macht, was es ist" (§352).

91. A. N. Whitehead, Process and Reality, (New York, 1929), p. 156.

92. A. N. Whitehead, Modes of Thought, (New York, 1938), p. 208.

93. Greene, above, pp. 124, 126.

94. Hegel took over the rather schematic triad "Sensibility-Irritability-Reproduction" from the Naturphilosophie of his time, expounding it at length in 1807 in the section on "Observation of Organic Nature" in the Phenomenology. (See PhM, 302ff.)

95. See my "Form, Concrescence, and Concretum: A Neo-Whiteheadian Analysis," Southern Journal of Philosophy, vol. 7 (1969-1970), 351-60.

96. The original reads: "In der Begattung erstirbt die Unmittelbarkeit der lebendigen Individualität; der Tod dieses Lebens ist das Hervorgehen des Geistes" (WL, II, 429).

97. Of course Hegel would claim to have closed both of these gaps at the inclusive and reconciling level of Absolute Knowledge and Absolute Idea. But the claim remains controversial.

98. I have developed these parallels in another paper, "Concept and Concrescence: An Essay in Hegelian-Whiteheadian Ontology" (forthcoming).
99. It is in this sense that Hegel defines (ontological) life as an "immediate," i.e., one-sided, inadequately mediated, form of the "Idea"(Cf. SL, 761; WL, II, 414).

VIII

Hegel's Absolute as New Beginning

by

RAYA DUNAYEVSKAYA

In the beginning was the Word (*das ursprüngliche Wort*), not as a command, but as the philosophic utterance which vanishes into thin air. The release of the self-movement of the Absolute Idea unfolds, not as if it were in repose, but so totally infected with negativity that throughout the twenty seven paragraphs that constitute the final chapter of the *Science of Logic*, starting with the very first paragraph, we learn that the Absolute Idea contains "the highest opposition in itself." (*den höchsten Gegensatz in sich*). (W. V,327; SL 824)[1]

The dialectic would not be the dialectic and Hegel would not be Hegel if the moment of encounter with the Absolute Idea was a moment of quiescence. Thus, far from the unity of the Theoretical and Practical Idea being an ultimate, or pinnacle, of a hierarchy, the Absolute Idea is a new beginning, a new beginning that is inevitable precisely because the Absolute Idea is a "concrete totality" and thus entails differentiation and impulse to transcend. To follow Hegel, step by step, without for a single moment losing sight of negativity as the driving force toward ever-new beginnings, it may be best to divide the twenty seven paragraphs into three principal areas. The first three paragraphs, centering around that highest contradiction contained in the Absolute Idea at the very moment of the unification of the Theoretical and Practical Idea, shows its self-determination disclosing not a new content, but its universal form, the *Method*, i.e., the dialectic.

Once Hegel asserts (in the fourth paragraph) that "*Notion is everything* and its movement is the *universal absolute activity,* the self-determining and self-realizing movement," (SL, 826) Hegel divides his field of concentration in what I call the second subdivision into two: a) paragraphs 5 to 7, stressing the new beginnings, immediacy that has resulted from mediation, and b) further opens the scope wider (paragraphs 8 to 15) as he sketches the development of the dialectic historically, from Plato to Kant, and differentiates his concept of second negativity as *the*

> turning point of the whole movement of the Notion . . . the innermost
> source of all activity, of all inanimate and spiritual self-movement, the
> dialectical soul that everything true possesses and through which
> alone it is true; for on this subjectivity alone rests the sublating of the
> opposition between Notion and reality, and the unity that is truth. (SL,
> 835)

The third subdivision I make, covers the last twelve paragraphs. These disclose concreteness both in its totality and in each sphere, in each of which, as well as in the whole, inheres the impulse to transcend. And this includes the *system* itself. The intimation of totally new beginnings is not restricted to the fact that there will be other spheres and sciences Hegel plans to develop, — Nature and Spirit. Inherent in these intimations are the consequences of what we will have been grappling with in the whole of the *Science of Logic*.

The Absolute Idea as new beginning, rooted in practice as well as in philosophy, is the burden of this writer's contribution. While this cannot be "proven" until the end of Hegel's rigorous and yet free-flowing final chapter, it is necessary here, by way of anticipation, to call attention to the three final syllogisms in the *Encyclopaedia of the Philosophical Sciences* which had not been included in the first edition of the work. To this writer, these crucial additions to the 1827 and 1830 editions constitute the summation, not alone of the *Encyclopaedia,* but of the whole cycle of knowledge and reality throughout the long tortuous trek of 2,500 years of Western civilization that that encyclopaedic mind of genius, Hegel, was trying to bring to a conclusion. Just as the first of those syllogisms (*Enc.* §575) *shows that the very center of its structure,* —Logic, Nature, Mind—is not Logic but Nature, so does the very last paragraph in the *Science of Logic*.

Whether one conceives Nature as "externality" in the Hegelian sense, or "exteriority" in the Sartrean manner, or as "Practice" in Lenin's World War I view, the point is that Hegel, not Sartre, nor Lenin, conceives Nature as mediation. When I develop this further at the end of the paper, we shall see what illumination our age casts on the movement from practice that helps us in grappling with the dialectic. But here it is best to continue with the three central divisions I suggested:

(1) The same first paragraph of the Absolute Idea that riveted our attention to the highest opposition, cautioned against imposing an old duality on the new unity of opposites reached, —the Theoretical and Practical Idea. "Each of these by itself is still one-sided. . . ." The new, the highest opposition, rather, has to self-develop: "The Notion is not merely *soul,* but free subjective Notion that is for itself and therefore possesses *personality.*" This individuality is not "exclusive", but is "explicitly *universality* and *cognition* and in its other, has *its own* objectivity for its object." (SL, 824) All that needs to be done, therefore, is for the Absolute Idea "to hear itself speak", to "outwardize" *(Äusserung).* Its self-determination is its self-comprehension. Or, put more precisely, "its own completed totality" is not any new content. Rather it exists wholly as *form* and "the universal aspect of its form—that is, *method.*" From that moment on Hegel will not take his mind's eye from the dialectic for, as he puts it, "nothing is known in its truth unless it is totally subject to method" *(als der Methode vollkommen unterworfen ist).*

(2) No less than eleven paragraphs follow the pronouncement that the Absolute form, the Method, the Notion is the whole. The pivot around which they all revolve, Hegel stresses over and over again, is the *"universal absolute activity"*, the Method which "is therefore to be recognized as . . . unrestrictedly universal". (SL, 826) In a word, this is not just another form of cognition; it is *the unity* of the Theoretical and Practical Idea we have reached. Far from being a "merely *external* form" or the instrument it is in inquiring cognition, the method is no "mere aggregate" of determinations but "the Notion that is determined in and for itself", the middle, the mediation, *because* it is objective and it is "posited in its identity", namely "subjective Notion." (SL, 827)

To be swept up by the dialectic is to experience a plunge to freedom. Since, however, the rigor of thought cannot be allowed to dissolve into a "Bacchanalian revelry", it is necessary to work through these paragraphs without missing any links. The first is the beginning, —the *Absolute as beginning.* When Hegel refers us to the very start of the Doctrine of Being, where he first posed the question: "With What Must Science Begin?", it is not for purposes of proving that the Absolute is a mere unfolding of what was implicit from the start, the manifestations. It also becomes a totally new foundation—absolute negation. Although from the beginning, Hegel emphasized that everything, no matter how simple it sounded contained equally immediacy and mediation (SL, 68), it is now so permeated with negativity that it is no mere remembrance of things past when Hegel writes, *"there is* nothing, whether in *actuality* or in *thought*, that is as simple and abstract as is commonly imagined." (SL, 829)

The long passageway through "concrete totality" of diverse, contradictory forces and relations from the Doctrine of Being through Essence to Notion makes it clear that though every beginning must be made *with the Absolute*, it becomes Absolute "only in its completion." It is *in* the movement to the transcendence of the opposition between Notion and Reality that transcendence will be achieved in subjectivity and subjectivity alone. In a word, this new beginning is both in thought and in actuality, in theory and practice, that is to say, in dialectical *"mediation* which is more than a mere beginning, and is a mediation of a kind that does not belong to a comprehension by means of thinking." Rather "what is meant by it is in general the demand for the *realization of the Notion*, which realization does not lie in the *beginning* itself, but is rather the goal and the task of the entire further development of cognition." (SL, 828)

Whether or not one follows Marx's "subversion"[2] of the Absolute's goal, the "realization of philosophy" as a "new Humanism," the unity of the ideal and the real, of theory and practice, indeed, of philosophy and revolution,[3] one cannot fail to perceive Hegel's Absolute advance *(Weitergehen)* and "completion" as the conclusion *and* fulfillment, as the beginning anew *from* the Absolute for he never departed from conceiving all of history, of human development, not only as a history in the *consciousness* of freedom, but, as we shall see, as achievement in *actuality*. Even here, where Hegel limits himself strictly to philosophic categories, to history of thought, he maintains the need to face reality. In tracing the conceptual breakthroughs of the dialectic from Plato to Kant to his own view of second negativity, he calls attention to Plato's demand of cognition "that it should *consider things in and for themselves*, that is, should consider them partly in their universality, but also that it should not stray away from them catching at circumstances, examples and comparisons." (SL, 830)

Considering things "in and for themselves", Hegel maintains, has made possible the working out of ever-new unities and relations between practice and theory. That is the achievement of Absolute Method. To whatever extent the method is analytic, to whatever extent synthetic as it exhibits itself as Other, the dialectic moment is not reached until (as the unity of the two), the "no less synthetic than analytic moment" determines itself as "the *other of itself*." The point is that it is the power of the negative which is the creative element. It is not the synthesis, but the absolute negativity which assures the advance movement. Since this is what separates Hegel from all other philosophers, and this philosophic ground, how a "universal *first, considered in and for itself,* shows itself to be the other of itself," this idea will dominate the last twelve paragraphs following the encounter with

> the turning point of the movement of the Notion ... the dialectical soul that everything true possesses and through which alone it is true; for on this subjectivity alone rests the sublating of the opposition between Notion and Reality, and the unity that is truth. (SL, 835)

Before, however, we go to those paragraphs developing second negativity to its fullest, I should like to retrace our steps to the threshold of the Absolute Idea, "The Idea of the Good," and call attention to the Russian Communist celebration of the one hundredth anniversary of Lenin's birth, which coincided with Hegel's two hundredth. This will illuminate the problematic of our day. Academician Kedrov, Director of the Institute of History of Science and Technology, embarked on still another attempt to "disengage" Lenin from Hegel with the claim that the word, "alias," before the quotation: "Cognition not only reflects the world but creates it," shows Lenin was merely restating Hegel, not bowing to Hegel's "bourgeois idealism".[4]

The simple truth, however, is that the most revolutionary of all materialists, Vladimir Ilyitch Lenin, witnessing the simultaneity of the outbreak of World War I *and* the collapse of the Socialist International, felt compelled to return to Hegel's dialectic as that unity of opposites which might explain the *counter*-revolution *within* the revolutionary movement. Absolute negativity became Lenin's philosophic preparation for revolution, as Lenin's *Abstract of Hegel's Science of Logic* shows.[5] By the time his notes reach the Doctrine of the Notion, Lenin states that none of the Marxists (and the emphasis on the plural makes it clear he includes himself), had fully understood Marx's greatest theoretical work, *Capital*, "especially its first chapter" since that is impossible "without having thoroughly studied and understood the *whole* of Hegel's *Logic*."[6] His passion at the approach of the Doctrine of the Notion—"NB Freedom = Subjectivity, ("or") End, Consciousness, Endeavor, NB"—had made it clear that Lenin at this time, 1914, saw in freedom, in subjectivity, notion, the categories with which both to transform the world and to gain knowledge of the objectively real *because* he had already, in the Doctrine of Essence, recognized, in Hegel's critique of causality, the limitation of "science" to explain the relation between mind and matter.

Lenin then proceeded to grapple with the role of practice *in Hegel*, especially when Hegel writes of the Practical Idea as having "not only the dignity of the Universal, but also the simply actual." Lenin's quotation about cognition that the Communists are presently trying to expunge is significant, *not* because he accords such "creativity" to cognition but rather because Lenin, in "granting" that creativity to cognition, had followed it up by calling attention to the fact that Hegel had used the word, Subject "here suddenly instead of 'Notion'".[7] And to make matters still worse for those Russian epigoni, it was all in the sentence about "the self-certainty which the subject has in the fact of its determinateness in and for itself, a certainty of its own actuality and the *non-actuality* of the world."

Vulgar materialists are so utterly shocked at Lenin writing about the *"non-actuality* of the world" and the "self-certainty of the Subject's actuality" that, they quote, not Hegel, as Lenin did, but Lenin's "translation": "i.e., that the world does not satisfy man and man decides to change it by his activity." But the point is that, after that "translation", Hegel is quoted in full, on the contrast between inquiring cognition where "this actuality appeared merely as an objective world, without the subjectivity of the Notion, and here it appears as an objective world whose inner ground and actual subsistence is the Notion. This is the Absolute Idea." (SL, 823)

It is this appreciation of the Absolute Idea, not as something in heaven or in the stratosphere, but in fact in the objective world whose very ground is the Notion, that has statist Communism so worried about Lenin, ever since the East German Revolt of June 17, 1953, and the emergence of a movement *from practice* to theory *and* a new society. They have rightly sensed that Lenin's break with his own philosophic past of the photocopy theory of reality plus voluntarism produced the

Great Divide in the Movement that has yet to run its course.[8] We will take up the illumination the actual movement from practice (these past two decades) sheds on the problematic of our day at the end of this study. Here it is necessary to resume Hegel's own concentration on and development of "second negativity" in those last twelve paragraphs of Absolute Idea.

(3) Beginning with paragraph 15, and all the way to the end of the chapter, we no sooner face the subjectivity that has overcome opposition between Notion and Reality than we learn that, since this subjective is the *"innermost"*, it is also the *"most objective moment"* (SL, 836), and it is this subjectivity as objectivity which is *"subject,* a *person,* a *free being . . . ."* Clearly, free creative power assures the plunge to freedom. It is the unifying force of the Absolute Idea. And since absolute negativity, the new foundation, is not "something merely picked up, but something *deduced* and *proved"* (SL, 838), this subjective could not but be objective, so much so that it extends to the *system itself.*

There too we learn that the content belongs to the method, is the *extension of method* so that the system, too, is but another "fresh beginning" which has been arrived at through an infinite remembrance of things past *and* advance signposts *(Weitergehen).* This is why the discussion in paragraphs 20 through 25 not only never departs from absolute negativity as the transcending mediation, but shows that every advance in the system of totality becomes *"richer and more concrete."*

The expression, "richer and more concrete", no more than the categories of subjectivity, reason, freedom, may not have led the reader to think of any such "materialistic" movement as the movement by which man *makes* himself free, but here is how Hegel spells out "Free Mind" in *The Philosophy of Mind* of his *Encyclopaedia*:

> When individuals and nations have once got in their heads the abstract concept of full-blown liberty, there is nothing like it in its uncontrollable strength, just because it is the very essence of mind, and that as its very actuality . . . . The Greeks and Romans, Plato and Aristotle, even the Stoics did not have it . . . .
>
> If to be aware of the Idea—to be aware, i.e., that men are aware of freedom as their essence, aim and object—is a matter of *speculation*, still this very Idea itself is the actuality of men—not something which they *have*, as men, but which they *are*. (Enc. § 482)

The fact that, in the *Science of Logic*, the stages in dialectical advance are not shown as so many stages in the historic development of human freedom, but, in the end, unwind as a circle, become a circle of circles, is, however, a constant reminder that every absolute is a new beginning, has a before and an after; if not a "future", surely a conse-quence, a "*successor* — or, expressed more accurately, *has* only the *antece-dent* and *indicates* its *successor* in its conclusion." (SL, 842) Whatever Hegel said, and meant, about the Owl of Minerva spreading its wings only at dusk simply does not follow from the *objectivity* of the drive, the *summation* in which the advance is immanent in the present. While he neither gave, nor was interested in, any blueprints for the future, he was not preoccupied with death, the "end" of philosophy, much less of the world. His philosophy is "the end" only in the sense that "up to this moment" philosophy has reached this point with "my" philosophy of absolute negativity. From the beginning, when his first and greatest elemental work, *The Phenomenology of Mind*, ended with nothing short of the Golgotha of the Spirit, Hegel had succeeded in describing the final act as if it were an unfolding of the everlasting. When subjected to the dialectic method from which, according to Hegel, no truth can escape, the conclusion turns out to be a new beginning. There is no trap in thought. Though it is finite, it breaks through the barriers of the given, reaches out, if not to infinity, surely beyond the historic moment.

In the final two paragraphs we see that there is no rest for the Abso-lute Idea, the fulfilled Being, the Notion that comprehends itself, the Notion that has become the Idea's own content. The negativity, the urge to transcend, the ceaseless motion will go into new spheres and sciences and first then achieve "absolute liberation." The absolute lib-eration experienced by the Absolute Idea as it "freely releases itself" does not make it ascend to heaven. On the contrary, it first then ex-periences the shock of recognition, "the *externality of space and time* exist-ing absolutely in its own without the moment of subjectivity." (SL, 843)

So much for those who consider that Hegel lived far away from the concrete objective world, in some distant ivory tower in which he "de-duced" Nature from the Idea. Equally wrong, however, are those who, while recognizing that Hegel presents the transition to Nature as an actual process of reality, conclude that Hegel is standing on his head. Proud as Hegel might have been of the feat, we need to turn both to the *Science of Logic*, and the *Philosophy of Mind*, especially the three final syllogisms, to see what Hegel was telling us.

What was an intimation in the Logic about Nature being the mediation is spelled out as the first syllogism at the end of the *Encyclopedia*: Logic, — Nature, — Mind. In that paragraph Hegel further assures us that "Nature, standing between Mind and its essence, sunders them, not indeed to extremes of finite abstraction, nor stands aloof from them." (*Enc.* §575)

One of the most relevant of the scholarly studies of the 1960's is Reinhart Klemens Maurer's *Hegel und das Ende der Geschichte: Interpretationen zur Phäenomenologie*. He holds that it may very well be true that the first of these final syllogisms (in §575), which has Nature as the mediation, gives the appearance that "Hegel turns to Darwin, turns to dialectical materialism and other nature-geneses of man," and also means to turn "to Liberty", there leading the "course of necessity", but Hegel himself brings in a "correction" in his next paragraph. Here the sequence reads: Nature — Mind — Logic. Professor Maurer then proceeds to "appropriate" that syllogism as expressing the dialectic of the *Phenomenology*. Whatever one may think of that analysis as a philosophy of history or whatever, the point most Hegel scholars do agree with regarding the final syllogism (§577), is this, in Otto Pöggeler's words of 1961: "In opposition to the usual interpretations of the Hegelian text, I should like to propose the following: that the actual science of Spirit is not the Logic, but the philosophy of Spirit."

Thus the focus of the third syllogism has shifted and the stress has been correctly placed on the fact the Logic has been replaced and, in its stead, we get, not the sequential but the *con*sequential *Self-Thinking Idea*. To Hegel this has resulted from the fact that "it is the nature of the fact, the notion, which causes the movement and development, yet this same movement is equally the action of cognition." (*Enc.* §577)

Hegel's Absolutes never were a series of ascending ivory towers. Revolutionary transformation is immanent in the very form of thought. As we saw from the chapter on Absolute Idea, the unifying force was free creative power. By the time we reach the mediated final result, Absolute Mind, the absolute negativity that was the moving force in Logic, in Nature, in *Geist* where we saw them as concrete stages of human freedom, there no longer was any difference between theory and practice. This is why our age can best understand Hegel's

Absolute. It has been witness to a *movement from practice* for two long decades, — (ever since the death of Stalin lifted the incubus from the heads of the masses in East Europe). To this writer, Hegel's genius is lodged in the fact that *his* "voyage of discovery" becomes one endless process of discovery *for us*. The "us" includes both Marx's new continent of thought of materialist dialectics, and Hegel scholars, as well as the movement from practice that was itself a form of theory once its spontaneity discovered the power of thought along with its physical might. This writer has followed very closely this movement of revolt ever since June 17, 1953, and saw in it a quest for universality because she had already discerned in the dialectical movement of the three final syllogisms in Absolute Mind, a new point of departure in the Idea and in the movement from practice.[9]

This movement from practice hardly had the ear of contemporary Hegelians, orthodox or Marxist, as evidenced in the erudite, Leftist director of the famous Frankfurt School, the late Theodor Adorno. His very reason for being, for thinking, for acting, was Dialectics, that is to say, for negations of what is. He entitled the summation of his life's thought, his intellectual legacy, *Negative Dialectics*.[10] This book, however, has little to do with the dialectics of negativity, and least with the concept of Subject, by which Hegel distinguished his view from all other philosophers who left the search for truth at Substance only. As "concretized" by Marx for the proletarian class, Subject is supposed to have been accepted also by Adorno, but again, Adorno keeps his distance and originality locked up in what he calls *Negative Dialectics*. From the very beginning of the Preface of his work (p. xix), Adorno informs us that the positive in the negative, — "the negation of the negation," — is the enemy: "This book seeks to free dialectics from such affirmative traits without reducing its determinacy." The so-called "theoretical inadequacies of Hegel and Marx" revolve around what he sees as the all-encompassing evil, the concept, that "subsuming cover", its "autarchy".[11]

Naturally, Adorno keeps his distance from "positivists" and the vulgarisms of the knighted Karl Popper and his infamous "Hegel and Fascism" school. Nevertheless, Adorno, almost out of nothing, suddenly brings in Auschwitz and introduces some sort of kinship between it and absolute negativity. He writes: "Genocide is the absolute integration . . . .. Auschwitz confirmed the philosopheme of pure identity as death . . . . Absolute negativity is in plain sight and has ceased to surprise anyone."[12]

By "almost out of nothing", I naturally do not mean that Auschwitz was not the reality of Fascism, nor do I mean only the suddenness and shock of introducing such subject matter in the climax of a book called "Meditations on Metaphysics". Rather, I mean it is wrong. That is to say, it is totally illogical and non-dialectical, considering that Adorno devoted an adult lifetime to fighting fascist ideology as the very opposite of Hegelian dialectics and had seen the very death of dialectics in Nazi Germany. Perhaps a better word than "wrong" would be Adorno's own curse-word "naive." I mean that as late as 1957, in his *Aspects of the Hegelian Dialectic*, he almost defended a subject-object identity.

> Subject-object cannot be dismissed as mere extravagance of logical absolutism. . . . In seeing through the latter as mere subjectivity, we have already passed beyond the Speculative idealism. . . . Cognition, if it is genuine, and more than simple duplication of the subjective, must be the subject's objectivity.

And, indeed, in his *Negative Dialectics,* he reiterates the same idea when he writes that, despite the fact that Hegel "deifies" subjectivity, "he accomplishes the opposite as well, an insight into the subject as a self-manifesting objectivity."[13]

Why, then, such a vulgar reduction of absolute negativity? Therein is the real tragedy of Adorno (and the Frankfurt School). It is the tragedy of a one-dimensionality of thought which results when you give up Subject, when one does not listen to the voices from below, —and they were loud, clear, and demanding between the mid-fifties and mid-sixties. It is a tragedy once one returns to the ivory tower and reduces his purpose to "the purpose of discussing key concepts of philosophic disciplines and centrally intervening in those disciplines".[14] The next step was irresistible, the substitution of a permanent critique not alone for absolute negativity, but also of "permanent revolution itself."

Now, whether the enduring relevance of Hegel has stood the test of time because of the devotion and analytical rigor of Hegel scholars, or because a movement of freedom surged up *from below* and was followed by new cognition studies, there is no doubt that *because* Absolute Negativity signifies transformation of reality, the dialectic of contradiction and totality of crises, the dialectic of liberation, Hegel's thought comes to life at critical points of history, called by him "birth-times of history." In addition, there were Marxist scholars, revolutionary dissidents, who built on new ground. While a scholar from the West, like Reinhart Maurer, was pre-occupied with Hegel's concept of where to end, the Czechoslovakian philosopher, Karel Kosik, was pre-occupied with where to begin anew. Of the Eastern European studies that accompanied the revolts, and revolved around Marx's Humanism, especially Marx's "Critique of the Hegelian Dialectic", one of the most rigorous studies was Karel Kosik's *The Dialectics of the Concrete*.[15]

Nor were these serious studies limited to the "East".[16] As Frantz Fanon saw it, the African struggle for freedom was "not a treatise on the universal, but the untidy affirmation of an original idea propounded as an absolute."[17] There is no doubt, of course, that once action supersedes the subjectivity of purpose, the unity of theory and practice is the form of life out of which emerge totally new dimensions. To this writer, this is only the "proof" of the ending of the *Science of Logic*, the absolute as new beginning, the self-bringing forth of liberty. Because Hegel's great work had new horizons in sight, Nature and Spirit, the Absolute Idea had to undergo "absolute liberation" *(Befreiung)*. No mere transition *(Übergang)* here; Freedom is unrestricted. It will "complete" *(vollendet)* its liberation in the Philosophy of Mind *(Geist)*. But there is no doubt either in the *Science of Logic* about the Notion being Subject, being Reality, and not some sort of closed ontology. To think that Hegel referred only to the idea of Christianity in the Graeco-Roman world when he wrote about "the pivot on which the impending world revolution turned at that time"[18] is both to forget the Christians thrown to the lions, and that it was the "resigned" Hegel of the *Philosophie des Rechts* who wrote about the "impending world revolution" and not the young Hegel who had earlier toasted the great French Revolution.

Is it mere accident that, after 150 years of indifference, two simultaneous translations of the *Philosophy of Nature* appeared in English? Or is it mere accident that in the new studies on Hegel, a thinker like Professor Riedel suddenly sees *in Hegel* an equal primacy of the Theoretical and the Practical Idea? Or that new studies in Hegel cover East and West, North and South, and that many of the world conferences on Hegel coincide with Marx and Lenin as philosophers? Is it not rather, that the problematic of our crisis-ridden world impinges in no incidental way on the whole question of the relationship of theory to practice not just on the immediate level, but one grounded in philosophy? No doubt, as Hegel put it, to accept a category at face value is an "uninstructed and barbarous procedure". But it is also a fact that the single dialectic process surges up from thought as well as from actuality. It would be equally "uninstructed" for philosophers to act as if the relationship of theory to practice is merely a "job for politicos." Just as the objective world and the elemental quest for universality have a crucial meaning for students of the dialectic, so do the students of the dialectic have a crucial meaning for the movement from practice. Just as the movement from the abstract universal to the concrete individual through the particular, *necessitating* a double negation (and that, after all, comprises the whole movement of the *Science of Logic*), so does the "comprehension" of it. If philosophers learn to eschew elitisms, then the unity of theory and practice, of absolute as new beginning, will not remain an abstract desire, or mere will, but philosophy itself will become action.

In his *Hegel: A Re-examination,* Professor Findlay was right when he stated that Hegel's exegeses can seem "arid and false to those who see nothing mysterious and god-like in the facts of human thought." But is it not equally true that philosophers who stand only in terror before revolution not only do not "comprehend" *it*, they cannot fully comprehend the revolution *in thought*? And Hegel did revolutionize philosophy. Absolute Idea as new beginning can become a new "subjectivity" for realizing Hegel's principle, that "the transcendence of the opposition between Notion and Reality, and that unity which is truth, rest upon this subjectivity alone." This is not exactly a summons to the barricades, but Hegel is asking us to have our ears as well as our categories so attuned to the "Spirit's urgency" that we rise to the challenge of working out, through "patience, seriousness, suffering and the labor of the negative," a totally new relationship of philosophy to actuality and action as befits a "birth-time of history." This is what makes Hegel a contemporary.

NOTES

1. The SL designation together with a number refers to the A. V. Miller translation of Hegel's *Science of Logic* (London: Allen & Unwin, 1969).

2. Karl Löwith writes: "Marx takes over the task of the philosophy which ended with Hegel and puts revolutionary Marxism, as reason becoming practical, in the place of the whole previous tradition." Then Prof. Löwith footnotes his comment by referring to Manfred Riedel's *Theorie und Praxis im Denken Hegels* (Stuttgart: 1965). It is there, continues Löwith, "where it is established for the first time that, for Hegel, theory and practice share an equal primacy, since spirits as will is a will to freedom and freedom is the origin of all historical practice" (from Löwith's "Mediation and Immediacy in Hegel, Marx and Feuerbach" *in* W. E. Steinkraus (ed.), *New Studies in Hegel's Philosophy* (New York: Holt, Rinehart & Winston, Inc., 1971,) p. 122 and note).

3. See Chapter Two, "A New Continent of Thought, Marx's Historical Materialism and its Inseparability from the Hegelian Dialectic," in my book, *Philosophy and Revolution*: (New York: Delacorte Press, 1973).

4. See the article by Academician Kedrov printed in *Soviet Studies in Philosophy*, Summer, 1970.

5. This is my own translation which was published as an Appendix to my *Marxism and Freedom* (New York: 1958). However I am cross-referencing here the "official" translation which was published out of context, in 1961, as "Conspectus of Hegel's Book, the Science of Logic" *in* Lenin's *Collected Works*, Vol. 38.

   See also footnote numbered 221 on page 317 of my *Philosophy and Revolution* for evidence of the interest Lenin displayed in the study of Hegel by Prof. Ilyin who was then sitting in jail for opposing the Bolshevik revolution, and whom Lenin freed. The reference to this in the Archives of the Lenin Institute for the year 1921, was included in Russia only in the first publication of Lenin's *Philosophic Notebooks,* specifically in the Introduction by Deborin.

6. Lenin, *op. cit.,* p. 180.

7. *Ibid.*, p. 213.

8. Elsewhere I have developed more fully the ramifications and break in Lenin's philosophic development. See Chapter Three, "The Shock of Recognition and the Philosophic Ambivalence of Lenin" in my *Philosophy and Revolution*, pp. 95-120.

9. The letters on the Absolute Idea and the three final syllogisms of Absolute Mind (dated May 12 and May 20, 1953), I have turned over to the Labor History Archives of Wayne State University in Detroit. These comprise part of the collection on "Marxism-Humanism, its Origin and Development in America, 1941-1975." They are available on microfilm for other libraries and are listed as "The Raya Dunayevskaya Collection".

10. The original German edition was published in 1966. Quotations will be made from the English translation by E. B. Ashton published in 1973 by the Seabury Press of New York.

11. Adorno's accusation of "conceptual fetishism" against Marx's famous "Fetishism of Commodities" as "truly a piece from the heritage of classic German philosophy" (p. 189f) is not relevant here. Contrast it with Karel Kosik's analysis of the very same section in a work described below in footnote 15.

12. T. Adorno, *Negative Dialectics*, (tr. Ashton, New York: Seabury Press, 1973), p. 362.

13. *Ibid.*, p. 350.

14. *Ibid.*, xx in Preface.

15. Two of the chapters of his *Dialectics of the Concrete* have been published in English in *Telos* (Fall, 1968 and Fall, 1969). While in the second issue, Kosik contrasts the empty absolutes of Schelling with those of Hegel, who characterized the absolutes of the Romantics as having got to the Absolute "like a shot out of the pistol," in the earlier, 1968 issue, Kosik wrote that Marx's beginning of Capital with 'Commodity' means "it can be characterized in Hegelian terms, as the unity of being and non-being, of distinction and similarity, of identity and non-identity. All further determinations are richer definitions or characterizations of this 'absolute' of capitalist society. The dialectic of interpretation or of exegesis cannot eclipse the central problem: how does science reach the *necessary beginning of the exposition.* . . . The dialectic is not a method of reduction, *but the method of spiritual and intellectual reproduction of reality*."

   The only one in the academic world in Hegel studies in the West who has dealt seriously, not with *existing, given,* established, *state* Communism, but with Marx himself and sees the transformation of the commodity as phenomenon into Notion is Karl Löwith in his *From Hegel to Nietzsche* (tr. by David Green, New York: 1964). The original German edition appeared in 1941. [*Von Hegel bis Nietzsche* (Zurich, 1953).]

16. I have limited myself to Eastern Europe, but of course I really mean the East, the Orient, and Mao's perversion of Hegelian dialectics, especially the concept of Contradiction, with which I have dealt elsewhere. (See Chapter Five, "The Thought of Mao Tse-tung," in my *Philosophy and Revolution*, pp. 128-150.)

17. Frantz Fanon, *The Wretched of the Earth*, p. 33.

18. Hegel, *The Philosophy of Right* (tr. Sir T. M. Knox)(Oxford: Clarendon Press, 1942), Preface, p. 10. See also the translator's note No. 26 on page 301.

IX

The Category of Contingency in the Hegelian Logic

by
GEORGE DI GIOVANNI

I

The immediate aim of the present study is the relatively narrow one of analyzing a section of Hegel's "greater Logic" which deals with the modal categories in order to understand what Hegel means by "contingency". The study should be viewed, however, in the context of a problem which is as old as the history of Hegelian criticism; but which recently has been brought again to the centre of scholarly attention because of new research done on the development of Hegel's thought during the crucial formative years of the Jena period. I shall now try to indicate the problem, and to show how the study that follows relates to it.

It appears that even at the beginning of his stay at Jena, when Hegel was closely collaborating with Schelling, he had already assumed an attitude towards philosophy that set him quite apart from his mentor, and even put him on the side of Fichte. In the *Differenzschrift* Hegel had assigned to philosophy (not to art, as Schelling had) the function of reconciling thought with nature, reflection with immediacy.[1] However, as Heinz Kimmerle has rightly pointed out, in taking this step Hegel had in fact accepted Fichte's criticism of Schelling.[2] He had admitted to the futility of trying to gain a standpoint that transcends the limits of reflection. Schelling's Philosophy of Nature still remained *philosophy*; and his appeal to art was done from the side of thought and in order to resolve a problem created by reflection. At best Schelling had mediated the thought of thought with the *thought* of nature. He had left untouched the issue of how reflection can overcome the disproportion that separates it from the *fact* of nature. It does not follow, of course, that Hegel could have accepted Fichte's notion of na-

179

ture as a surd which perpetually eludes the reflection of thought. For him, just as much as for Schelling, thought must be able to recognize itself in nature. However, the subtle modification brought to Schelling's position in the *Differenzschrift* indicates that for Hegel the ground for the reconciliation (i.e., the moment of identity between thought and nature) must be sought from within the standpoint of reflection.

Now, we know that at Jena Hegel repeatedly lectured on Logic and Metaphysics; and that at first he conceived the Logic as an introduction to Metaphysics. We also know that he quickly came to the realization that the two sciences ought to be combined into a single one (a new "Logic") which would be at once logic *and* metaphysics. Hegel thus withdrew from the Logic its introductory role; and assigned it to a Science of Experience on which he had been working, and which finally took the form of the *Phenomenology of Spirit*.[3] It is clear, therefore, how Hegel moved to counter Fichte's objection. To Schelling's philosophy he opposed the idea of a science which, as the elaboration of the concept of thought (viz., as logic), would equally be science of being (viz., metaphysics). In order to break out of Fichte's impasse *vis-à-vis* nature, he did not try to assume a standpoint that transcends thought. He proposed to show, instead, that it is possible for thought to recognize the *fact* of nature as a moment of its life as thought.

At Jena, therefore, the idea is already present for the later System. Also present, however, are the elements for the objection that the critics of the System have constantly raised against it.[4] If it is granted to Hegel that the essence of nature is thought, it is indeed undeniable that the difficulty facing both Schelling and Fichte disappears. No opposition is possible between *real* mediation of thought with nature and the merely reflective synthesis of the concept of one with the concept of the other, for the distinction between real and ideal has lost its force. However, Hegel's feat in removing the difficulty is accomplished only at the price of idealizing even the *fact* of nature. And while to Hegel's eyes the idealism of Fichte and Schelling might have appeared inconsistent for having allowed the difficulty to stand, Hegel's own System can be charged with lack of seriousness precisely because it pretends to have made the mediation between thought and nature complete. The System undercuts all problems of mediation by the simple device of removing within the magic circle of idealistic thought all the material we normally look for in the real world.[5]

I am ready to introduce at this point the theme of the paper. In classical metaphysics contingency has always denoted a limitation of reason. A contingent event (as contingent) is an element of reality impervious to full rationalization. Its occurrence must be accepted without explanation; and any theory suggesting that it is possible to account for it would in fact be denying that "contingency" has objective meaning. However, as Dieter Henrich has so well argued in an article of 1958, Hegel's philosophy is unique in that it maintains the necessity of contingency.[6] It claims that it is possible to comprehend it in thought. Hegel thus tries to avoid the classical alternative posed by contingency (viz., either "contingency" has only subjective meaning, or reality is not fully rational) in the same way in which he tries to resolve the impasse reached by the idealism of his contemporaries. He re-introduces *within* reason what would otherwise appear as a limitation affecting it from without. And this move is only to be expected. For contingency is the essential feature that distinguishes the fact of nature from the thought of it. And if Hegel's System is to comprehend the fact of nature, it must be able to comprehend it precisely as contingent.

The case of contingency thus offers an excellent test by which to measure the seriousness of Hegel's claim to "complete mediation". It also provides, however, a criterion by which to judge the accuracy of whatever notion *we* might have of what Hegel means by that claim. If Hegel can show that contingency need not be merely presupposed, but that the inevitability of its presence can be understood; moreover, if he can show that in thus comprehending contingency, he does not reduce it to necessity — then Hegel has managed to break free from the circle of idealistic thought. He has demonstrated that it is possible to recognize the *reality* of contingency without having to step outside the limits of logical reflection. But a reflection that accomplishes a feat of this sort must be of a very special kind. And one can enquire in all fairness whether, rather than bringing to its logical conclusion the idealism of his contemporaries, Hegel has not in point of fact grounded it on a completely new basis.[7]

There are indications that clearly point in the latter direction. Consider, for instance, how thought develops in the Logic. Its movement depends on the tension created within each category between what the category *intends* to signify (or signifies *formally*, or *explicitly*), and what it signifies *in actual fact* (or *implicitly*). Let me elaborate on this point, using an example which will also allow me to introduce the two categories of *possibility* and *actuality* with which we shall be concerned later.[8] Consider how these two categories differ from two others—viz., the categories of *essence* and *immediacy*, which appear at an earlier stage of the Logic. There is obviously very much in common between the two sets of categories. Both presuppose, as a condition for signifying an object, that a distinction be recognized between the *presence* of the object as mere fact, and the *reflection* which justifies its being present. However, the degree to which the distinction has become part of the formal signification of the four categories differs considerably from one set to the other. The explicit intention of essence and immediacy is to each signify one side of the distinction to the total exclusion of the other. Essence intends to signify the object exclusively as reflection within itself: as pure explanatory ground; immediacy, for its part, intends to signify it exclusively as mere fact. But the formal intention of the two categories is clearly self-defeating. For if it were ever realized, it would destroy upon realization the context within which alone it makes sense to refer to an object as either essence or mere fact. The two categories, therefore, are made to suffer a strange fate at the hands of Hegel's dialectic. Although each *means* to express one side alone of the distinction, in actual fact both are shown to signify one side as well as the other. Essence can just as well be mere fact, while any fact can be taken as the basis for an explanation. In the course of the dialectic, in other words, a disproportion is revealed between the *formal* intention of the two categories and what they signify in *actual* fact.[9]

With actuality and possibility, the situation is quite different. The object they both signify is one which, on presenting itself to an observing subject, does not remain mere fact but proffers a reason for its presence. But possibility refers to the object taking its starting point from the explanatory ground which the object would offer were it to become actually present. Actuality, on the other hand, refers to it starting from the opposite direction. It signifies the object as already present—but with a presence achieved on the basis of a ground which (albeit not obvious in some cases) can in principle always be adduced. The relation that holds between the two categories is *explicitly ambiguous*. Their meaning is definitely not identical. On the contrary, it is true to say that to the extent that an object is only possible, it is not actual; and to the extent that it is actual, it is no longer merely possible.

The meaning of one category excludes that of the other. Yet, it is equally true to say that the two categories are complementary—that each points to the other as completing its own line of signification. Actuality is still possibility: but possibility as achieved; and possibility is already actuality: but actuality as merely adumbrated. One can also legitimately claim, therefore, that the more possible something is, the closer it is to being actual; and the more actual, the more entitled to the claim of being possible.

Possibility and actuality thus overcome the abstractness of essence and immediacy. They include in their formal signification the ambivalence which for the other set of categories had been a *de facto* result. In this way they manage to express *formally* what they would otherwise signify only in *actual fact*; and are no longer subject, therefore, (at least, not in the same sense) to the same process that has reduced to mere abstractions the previous expressions of the logical object.

Now, a discrepancy between the intention of any given category in the Logic, and the determination which it actually brings to the logical object, manifests itself under one form or another at every stage of the Logic. The discrepancy conditions the logical development by injecting into it an element of immediacy. I do not mean to say that the movement of thought in the Logic is subject to the same historical vicissitudes as the development of consciousness in the *Phenomenology*.[10] The Logic is the science of pure thought. From beginning to end it is nothing but a reflection of thought upon itself. However, I must stress that for Hegel even pure thought is at first present to itself only immediately. In fact, its appearance at the beginning of the Logic is so immediate that it can be articulated only indirectly.[11] Moreover, until the final reflection takes place which reinterprets all the categories that have appeared up to that point as the content of the Idea,[12] the logical movement tends to fall (because of the immediacy by which it is affected) into a series of abstract thought expressions only implicitly connected with one another. The sense of the whole movement is made explicit only by the comments provided by the concrete subject engaged in the Logic—viz., the philosopher.

The whole effort of the Logic is directed at shaking off the immediacy of its beginning, and at incorporating within the explicit content of the Idea all the unofficial comments made along the way by the philosopher. It would be wrong, however, to take lightly either the immediacy with which logical reflection is affected; or the presence (albeit unofficial) of the philosopher. The two provide the link between thought and reality which is at issue in the System. I should indicate that I am assuming at this point a crucial position with regard to the Hegelian System. Hegel's Logic is a moment in the experience of an individual (viz., the philosopher) engaged in history and nature. It is not a thought-construction which, starting from *a priori* principles, should rejoin a concrete set of experiences which stand outside of it. In fact, Hegel's Logic has hardly anything in common with the Transcendental Logic of Kant, or the constructions of either Fichte or Schelling. It is to be understood, rather, as the re-enactment in the medium of pure thought of experiences which have already been lived. In the play between immediacy and reflection witnessed in the logical movement, the philosopher should recognize his own effort as a historical individual engaged in overcoming the immediacy of nature. It is only in the Logic that the possibility of his experiences is finally understood. It is important to stress, however, that the Logic operates from the start within the limits of those experiences; and that it is not intended to comprehend anything else but their possibility. The transition, therefore, from thought to reality which Hegel's Logic is supposed to perform is not as formidable a task as it might appear to be at first—not because Hegel has idealized reality, but because with his Logic he only intends to complete an experience which has begun in the immediate presence of history and nature.

These comments bring us back to the problem of contingency. For the immediate is contingent; and if the logical movement is affected by immediacy, it follows that it is in some sense contingent. The essential task of the Logic is to overcome the contingency to which its beginning and its progress are subject. But what does Hegel mean by contingency, and in what sense does one overcome it? This is the question to which we must now turn.

II

The dialectic to be considered falls into the three stages common to the Logic. The first consists in the exposition of the formal meanings of *possibility, actuality, necessity,* and *contingency*. At this first stage, the four concepts are considered *in abstracto* — only inasmuch as they form a system of related meanings and provide the basis for the thought of an object in general. At the second stage, a distinction is introduced between the object and the categories. The object thus begins to function as a material to which the categories bring particular determinations. In the third and final stage, an attempt is made at overcoming the distinction introduced in the second. The meaning of the categories is so reformulated as to allow them to regain the generality they enjoyed at the first stage, but without losing the concreteness they gained when operating in relation to an assumed content.[13]

I have already commented indirectly on the formal meaning of actuality and possibility. I have pointed out that the two categories have independent meaning; yet each expressly points to the other for the fulfillment of its own signification. The existence of what is actual should be justifiable; and what is justifiable, should be actual. However, it does not necessarily follow from the fact that something is possible, that it will actually exist. Nor does it follow from the fact that it exists that an explanation for its existence can actually be given. At the formal level of analysis, the transition from one category to the other (even though expressly required by both) remains immediate. It must be performed on the strength of considerations extrinsic to the logical play of the categories. Hegel argues, moreover, that the immediacy is due to the present abstractness of the two categories. Possibility signifies a mere self-reference on the part of an object (a justification only in principle); and actuality, a mere presence. Neither category characterizes an object concretely enough to reveal just *how*, on being possible, it must be actual; and on being actual, possible. And the abstractness of each is directly related to the abstractness of the other.[14] It is because the possibility of an object is a *mere* possibility, that the object will appear only as a "possible" (". . . nur ein Mögliches . . .") — the sort of actual, in other words, that might as well have not been. Conversely, it is because an actual is (as Hegel puts it) an *immediate first*[15] (i.e., something merely present and still open to determination) that the possibility it establishes remains formal.

The first result, therefore, of the dialectic of actuality and possibility is an ambiguity regarding the character of the object which the two categories signify, and which they are both expected to determine. The object is neither quite actual yet, nor possible; or again, it is at once actual and possible, precisely because it is neither of them determinedly. This ambiguity is expressed by Hegel with the category of *contingency*: "The unity of possibility and actuality is contingency."[16]

I ask you to look at this text carefully, because it is in passages like this that one can appreciate the distance that separates Hegel's Logic from classical metaphysics. In classical metaphysics, contingency was thought to be the result of a discrepancy between possibility and actuality. Hegel now defines it as the unity *(die Einheit)* of the two. Implied by this move is a radical innovation in the understanding of the nature of possibility, and also of the relationship that thought (which expresses the possibility of reality) holds to reality itself. For Hegel, possibility is not a ground that transcends actuality. It is not (if I may make my own a comment of G. R. G. Mure)[17] like a reservoir of yet unrealized being upon which God chooses either to draw or not to draw. It is instead a determination of formal actuality. It is actuality inasmuch as it is expected to result in yet more actuality. And formal possibility is a determination of actuality. It is actuality inasmuch as it is still open to determination. For Hegel, in other words, the distinction between actuality and possibility falls exclusively within the limits of phenomenal existence, and is a characteristic of its phenomenality. To express the possibility of reality in thought, therefore, does not mean to transcend its immediate appearance (as if there were anything to reality except its appearing), but to give a description in pure thought form of its structure precisely as appearance. The formal play of the categories of possibility and actuality which Hegel has just unfolded must be understood as the conceptual expression of the unrest of phenomena which leave undetermined on their first appearing exactly what form they will finally take.

Hegel proceeds, therefore, to develop the concept of contingency in terms of the ambiguity inherent in all phenomenal existence.[18] A phenomenon, upon its first appearing, cuts itself off from the process that has led up to it. As Hegel puts it, it abstracts from the reflection that establishes its possibility. For this reason (". . . insofern sie [viz., the reflection] in ihm aufgehoben ist . . ."), it appears as something which has no ground. Like anything which *de facto* is, it parades itself as self-sufficient. It has its own presence to guarantee for its possibility; and seems to dispense, therefore, with any reference to anything outside of it justifying its existence. It is, simply because it is. However, a simple self-reference is hardly a satisfying justification for the existence of anything. The same abstraction, therefore, that brings out the irrevocability of a phenomenon once it has occurred also detracts from the completeness of its appearance. It bestows upon it the character of something, the reality of which is still in need of developing. The phenomenon is thus a mere possible which must find its fulfillment in something else (*in Gesetztsein*). Now, this ambiguity inherent in the first appearance of anything—its cutting itself loose from justifying grounds, and yet its need for such grounds—is what the category of contingency signifies.

The ambiguity of phenomenal existence is not, however, altogether unmitigated. After the analysis of the category of contingency, Hegel goes on to argue that anything contingent is in principle something necessary.[19] His argument can be re-phrased in this way.[20] The simple self-reference of immediate existence, in spite of the ambiguity that it generates, is nonetheless a real one. However abstract and admittedly insufficient as a principle of explanation, it entails a real distinction within a given event between the event "in itself" and a manifold of determinations which, although belonging to it, cannot be identified with it *tout court*. It also entails a real distinction between the given event and some other possible one. And on the basis of these distinctions, one can begin to relate one determination to another, and the event to yet another event; and obtain thereby a more satisfactory explanation for the presence of the original event than any previous appeal to its mere self-reference. The immediate presence of the event on its first appearing can thus be developed into an explanatory system—viz., a system of explanatory references such as the category of necessity signifies.

Hegel's first explicit statement, therefore, on the nature of contingency and necessity is that both follow with equal strength from the interplay of formal actuality and possibility.[21] Contingency is the result of the abstractness of the two categories which makes their determination of an object a mere adumbration—the first sketch for an object rather than a concrete determination. Contingency, however, does not stand exclusively for irrationality. For the ambiguity with which it is synonymous is such that all the elements are already present in it for the development of an explanatory system. *Contingency is the matrix out of which necessity arises.* As developed so far, in other words, possibility and actuality establish the possibility for the determination of an object in general. The system of thought that they define ensures that, upon being given, an object will have *some* explanation for its being. But they leave unspecified exactly what form such an explanation will have to take. The system still fails to yield the idea of an actual world.

The task that Hegel must face next is to remedy the abstractness of the formal play of categories. This he does in the second stage of the dialectic by introducing the notion of a material content to which the formal categories of actuality and possibility are applied. In being thus related to it, the two categories are expected to be concretized, and finally to yield the idea of an individually recognizable world.

I shall have to call your attention again later in the paper to this material content. Right now I only want to bring out the function that it plays in the new stage of the dialectic that follows. Hegel subsumes its notion under the general rubric of actuality. Since the content is something merely present, it is something actual. However, as applied to it, "actuality" carries explicitly the extra note of "indifference to determinations". It means a manifold of existents, each indifferent to the presence of any other.[22] The formal categories of actuality and possibility are now expected to introduce within it the first determinations. And they, in turn, will become *real* to the extent that they discharge their determining function.

First, what do possibility and actuality come to mean when they are referred to a manifold of existents and become *real* possibility and *real* actuality. In the transition, the two concepts must retain all the notes included in their formal signification—viz., actuality: the immediate presence of an object which is nonetheless referred to a process of mediation; possibility: the reflection of a thing upon itself (its lack of contradiction) which should yield actual presence. Yet, they must also be so modified as to function effectively as the determining principles of a given content.

Now, Hegel introduces two new concepts which he believes will fill the bill. One is the notion of a "power to effect", with which he replaces the formal category of actuality; the other, the notion of "circumstance", with which he replaces the former possibility.[23] These two new concepts, while still signifying actuality and possibility, add to them connotations which the previous two failed to convey on their own. A power to effect is something actual — but with an actuality that can be measured by given results. And a circumstance is a source of possibility — but one immediately related to a particular situation.

What is, moreover, the nature of the relationship that obtains between possibility and actuality thus re-interpreted? The crucial question is whether the new relationship can avoid the ambiguity of the previous formal one. Hegel proposes two formulations for it. According to the first, the relation is one of "identity of content".[24] The same manifold of existents which can serve as manifestation of a power (i.e., as real actuality) can also be determined as a set of conditions and circumstances which occasion certain events to take place (i.e., as real possibility). It is clear, however, that material identity cannot suffice as an exhaustive determination of the relationship — for it abstracts altogether from the distinction between the two notions which it is supposed to relate. When we say that a given manifold can be determined either as something already actual or as a possibility for things to come, we introduce the alternative by reverting back to the formal level of signification. It is to the formal distinction that we appeal. And the same element of indefiniteness present at the formal level makes its appearance again. Insofar as the material content of either one of the two notions is concerned, it is a matter of indifference which side of the distinction is made to apply. The choice remains subjective.

With the second formulation, Hegel tries to introduce the distinction *within* the manifold of existents, and to free it in this way of its formality. He appeals to the notion of a situation in which all the conditions and circumstances are present that fully determine the coming to be of a certain event. Apparently Hegel has in mind the case of a process which is so far advanced as to have become irreversible. And its results, therefore, albeit not actually present, are already irrevocably committed to existence.[25] The determination of a process that has reached such a stage of development would call for both the concepts of possibility and actuality. The process itself would constitute the real possibility for certain events to take place. However, since the process is so complete that its reality is virtually equivalent to the presence of the event or events it is supposed to usher in, it can also be determined as real actuality. Moreover, the process needs *both* concepts for its determination. It retains, therefore, a distinction between the two. But again, it retains it only in a relative sense—for as real possibility, the process is taken precisely as ushering in something actual; and as something actual, as immediately resulting from a possibility. Hegel, in other words, tries to concretize the formal interplay of possibility and actuality by re-interpreting it as the moment of tension in the transition from an antecedent cause to a subsequent effect, when the effect has not yet acquired full independence *vis-à-vis* its cause, and precisely for this reason its whole reality consists in its being related to a cause. And the cause, for its part, is also totally defined (*qua* cause) by its effort to achieve an effect. The two terms (cause and effect) are indeed distinct. But they are *significantly* distinct precisely because the reality of each is exhausted by its relation to the other; and apart from the distinction, it would disappear.

There is nothing formal, therefore, about the necessity that binds the two terms. In a situation such as we have just defined, real possibility is already equivalent to real necessity.[26] When the possibility is at hand, the actuality which it determines *must* come to be. Any hesitation as to which term should be given primacy of determination—whether actuality determines possibility or contrariwise—is strictly academic. For the one significant reality is the emergence of an event as process; and not the abstract determinations under which the event can be subsumed either before or after its advent.

Yet even real necessity does not remain unaffected by contingency.[27] Hegel has easy play showing how the latter makes its appearance again. For we must remember that real necessity is conditioned by the presupposition of a manifold of existents which lacks *per se* all limits. And while it is true that the notion of dynamic tension between power and its manifestations introduces a form which affects it intrinsically, the structure which is thus realized does not extend beyond limits which are still accidental. The amorphousness of the manifold is not absorbed by form; its indifference not dissolved in dynamic tension. The material content still persists as a general matrix in which the coincidence of form and content occurs only sporadically. Outside the immediate limits of any such occurrence, the manifold remains an aggregate of material elements *which might have been* or *might yet be* actual cause or effect, but which are *per se* neither cause nor effect. The determinations of actuality and possibility apply to them only formally.

Real necessity is equivalent, therefore, to an indefinite series of events — none of which counts as ultimate limit. The "reality" of any of them is recognizable only on the strength of an abstraction — i.e., only on condition that an observer limit his field of observation to a given situation, and consider *it* as if it were a complete world. Hegel argues that real necessity is essentially relative. It is predicated only on the assumption of a situation, the presence and limits of which remain in point of fact contingent.

The situation, therefore, at the end of the second stage of the dialectic of actuality and possibility stands as follows: the formal categories of actuality and possibility have provided the limits within which any object can be determined *in principle*. They have provided the basis for a system. However, exactly *which* world (in terms of individual, actual objects) is the system they establish an expression of, still remains an open question. In the first stage of the dialectic, in other words, the possibility of *determinateness* in general has been established — not of individual determinations. In the second stage, on the other hand, the real categories of actuality and possibility have indeed provided the basis for the conceptual determination of individually recognizable objects — but only on condition that the latter be taken as single events which never quite amount in actual fact to a complete world. At the end of the second stage of the dialectic, we are faced by the unhappy choice between a world which is complete as world, but must remain only a possibility; and an indefinite number of situations which are recognizably real, but which do not necessarily belong to a world of which we recognize the possibility.

Contingency erupts, therefore, at every level and in every respect of the dialectic. The world of which the formal categories are the expression is such that no distinction within it has more than a merely momentary (i.e., strictly relative) significance. The structure for which the real categories provide the schema admit of sharpness of detail only on condition that the background be blocked out. In either case, the connection between any category and the reality it intends to define remains *per se* indeterminate; and requires for its completion the intervention of a subject (viz., the philosopher doing the Logic) whose relation to the categories remains in turn also accidental. Translated into the language of the *Phenomenology,* the play of logical notes we have just witnessed would correspond to the busy work of a consciousness which believes itself to have grasped the essence of reality simply because it has developed a system of concepts which exhaust among themselves all the possibilities of being; and alternates between formally applying the concepts in question to every object at hand, and being concerned with the detailed mechanism of certain situations. And when challenged to produce concrete results from its theory, the consciousness would point to the single situations it has analyzed. And upon being further challenged to show how its particular explanations amount to a complete theory, it would point back to the formal system—without realizing that the system and the particular explanations belong to different orders of reflection, and that the actual connection between the two is due *in point of fact* to its own subjective contribution.

Of course to an enlightened observer of all this busy work of explanation, it is clear that abstract theory and detailed analysis of situations do in some sense coincide. And the same applies for the philosopher doing the Logic. To him it is clear that the first and the second stage of the dialectic have a common intention. But its true nature is first made explicit only in the category of absolute necessity which Hegel introduces in the third stage. And, as we shall now see, it is quite different from anything that a consciousness might expect which simply operates with the modal categories without bothering to trace their logical origin.

III

The move with which Hegel rids the logical process of its contingency is so simple that it runs the risk of going unnoticed. Hegel's claim is simply this: ultimately, reality needs nothing else but itself in order to account for its own presence. To conceive it absolutely, therefore, means to define it precisely as a presence that constantly re-asserts itself. The immediacy that affects our experience of it should not be looked upon as detracting from rationality, but as providing for it the limit which alone makes it possible. Reality is the immediate presupposition *(Voraussetzung)* from which all our reasoning must start; and which, upon returning to it as the result *(Gesetztsein)* of a reasoning process *(setzen)*, will appear precisely as that which necessitated our presupposing it *(gesetzt als vorausgesetzt)*.[28] Or again, reality would not be conceived absolutely were it not understood both as the source as well as the resolution of any problem of determination. *Qua* absolute, it must generate its own irrationality—viz., the need for explanation. The ultimate test of any system of thought is not whether it dispels irrationality, but whether it shows that irrationality is contained within reality itself.

In *actual fact*, therefore, by the end of the first stage of the dialectic of actuality and possibility, the point has already been made that the relation that holds between the two categories is a constant source of indetermination because the two categories have indeed defined reality absolutely—not because (as hitherto assumed) they still fall short of a true system of thought. Still needed, before the point is accepted as official doctrine, is only a change in expectation as to what it means to determine reality absolutely. It does not mean to enumerate exhaustively the ready-made qualities which supposedly make up its content, but to define it precisely as generating *its own* problems of determination. Or again, it means to define the terms of the general problem of determining it; and to establish, therefore, the limits within which any particular problem of determination must remain in order to be a significant problem.

The new awareness of what thought accomplishes in determining the concept of reality is forcefully brought home at the end of the second stage of the dialectic. At that point, the frustration that the philosopher doing the Logic can envisage as following upon the endless process of overcoming the contingency that re-asserts itself at the end of any process of explanation forces a change in expectations. It leads to the realization that the contingency does not derive from factors extrinsic to whatever line of necessity has been established. It is instead the result of such a line *having been* established. As Hegel puts it, the philosopher sees that contingency *becomes* in necessity; that it is the contingency *of* necessity.[29]

The category of absolute necessity which is thereupon introduced

proceeds to express reality precisely as generating its own irrationality[30]—as giving rise to contingency as well as necessity:

> Absolute necessity is, therefore, the truth into which actuality and
> possibility as such, and formal and real necessity withdraw. . . . That
> which is simply necessary only *is* because it *is*: [hence, the
> contingency] it has neither condition nor ground: but equally it is
> pure *essence*; its being is simple reflection-into-itself; it is, *because
> it is*. [Hence, the necessity].[31]

It does not follow from this definition of "absolute necessity" that it
is not possible for Hegel to comprehend reality in some ultimate sense.
But it is important to realize that any such final comprehension is possible only in the medium of pure thought—i.e., as Logic. The commentators who have seen in Hegel's idealism the most dogmatic of all
dogmatic positions have very likely failed to give this point its due
weight. I suspect that they all suffer from the same misapprehension
which is also the lot of the busy consciousness we described at the end
of the preceding section. They seem to believe (like the busy consciousness) that to explain the occurrence of any single event (be it of
nature or of history) is the same as to fill out one more detail in a system of explanatory causes for which the abstract categories of the Logic
give a first outline, and which leaves no room for any element of indetermination.

In point of fact, Hegel's Logic does not add anything to the content of the knowledge acquired by either the scientist or the historiog-
rapher.[32] Its only contribution is the *concept* of the experience gained
while acquiring such knowledge—i.e., the purely reflective awareness
of the nature and the limits of the experience. And essential to the
awareness (this is the all-important point) is the realization that the
immediacy that affects all experience of reality, far from detracting
from its rationality, is in actual fact both its ground and consequence.[33] The Logic itself is the exhaustive comprehension of reality
that it is claimed to be—the system of thought unbroken by any resi-
due of unrationalized content—precisely because in it the recognition
is made of the true speculative value of immediacy. In other words, in
the Logic Hegel avoids the classical alternative of either denying that
contingency is real or merely acknowledging it as a fact which does not
admit comprehension but expresses it as a genuine category of
thought, and finds the proper place for it in the universal idea of reality.

We are now in a position to understand why Hegel could start the second stage of the dialectic we have been examining (in fact, the second stage of the dialectic in any section of the Logic) with the notion of a content which he claims to derive from the interplay of formal categories just completed in the first stage. The move has at first a certain air of mystification about it. It gives the impression that Hegel is trying to conjure up a material reference out of purely formal considerations by a play of conceptual trickery. Yet, all misgivings disappear once we understand exactly what Hegel does at the first stage of every dialectical cycle. He simply defines reality (with varying degrees of explicitness) as the inescapable context within which all problems of determination must fall. But once we have understood reality in this way, we can proceed without further ado to presuppose it as fact; and to devise techniques which will bring out the rationality implicit in it. Or again, once we have understood why reality must appear as fact, we have comprehended it absolutely. And there is nothing left for us to do except to deal with the problems that its immediacy presents. The point is indeed obvious. But it is not trivial — for losing sight of it might lead to the illusionary belief that thought needs fulfilling (as thought) in a medium other than conceptual; or conversely, to the equally illusionary belief that the fulfillment of thought on reflective terms alone would render superfluous any non-conceptual apprehension of reality.

As the dialectic of actuality and possibility concludes, therefore, the philosopher detects a new order emerging out of the apparent state of disarray into which the logical process had landed itself by the end of the second stage. At that point, the intention of the formal categories (which was to provide a complete determination of reality) seemed checked by the immediacy that erupted from within their play. And the real categories, which were expected to remedy the abstractness of the formal ones, seemed in fact to lose sight of any systematic plan. Now, at the end of the third stage, the singleness of purpose of the logical process re-asserts itself. It is clear now that the intention of the formal categories has indeed been realized — but not in the manner one might have hitherto expected. It has been realized by the formulation of a complete disjunction (e.g., something is either possible or actual), the terms of which define the limits of any significant problem of determination. As for the real categories, our busy consciousness (to return once more to it) was not altogether misguided when it believed that upon explaining any single event, it was fulfilling the intention of the system of thought defined by the formal categories. It only failed to realize how close indeed is the connection between formal and real level of reflection. The latter simply repeats the former. It does not complete it or extend it—as if the formal categories had not already expressed reality *in toto*. The real categories only elaborate on the special problems of determination that arise granted the definition of reality given at the formal level.

Moreover, the disproportion between the official results of the play of categories and the unofficial comments made by the philosopher regarding their meaning is overcome. For the realization is finally made that the determinations which have accrued to thought unexpectedly in spite of its efforts to be pure thought have been in fact the result of its own reflectivity. The immediacy of the determinations were in fact contained within the reflection of thought. In the third book of the Logic, therefore, the dialectic folds upon itself. All the previous categories reappear, but modified in order to appear explicitly as the determination *of* thought. And the immediacy which accompanied their previous appearance is now revealed as the freedom that thought has with regard to itself while determining its own appearances. But in that immediacy one can also recognize the facticity with which reality presents itself to any observer. In one single stroke, therefore, official cognizance is made of the sense in which reality must remain an ultimate presupposition; and any alleged opposition between the reflection of thought and the immediacy of being is also removed. As the thought of thought, logical thought is recognized as the thought of reality.[34]

V

In Chapter 9 of *De Interpretatione* Aristotle calls attention to the case of events, such as a battle at sea, which are contingent up to their occurrence, but which become necessary once they have taken place.[35] Their "having occurred" then becomes an irrevocable fact. Within the context of Aristotelian philosophy, this circumstance leads to the recognition of two different meanings of necessity. There is a necessity that follows upon the rational ordering of the cosmos—e.g., the necessity that accompanies the cyclical movement of the heavenly spheres; and a necessity which follows upon the indetermination of matter—i.e., the blind necessity of chance. The two meanings (I must add) are for Aristotle quite disparate.

Now, if I were asked to state in a few words the result of the dialectic of actuality and possibility, and also what I believe to be the main thesis developed by Hegel throughout the Logic, I would say that Hegel has shown the interdependence of the two meanings of necessity. Both are required in order to conceive reality as a self-contained process. For Hegel reality would not be self-sufficient if it did not contain its own irrationality. The only order which it exhibits is one which takes shape out of the contingency of facts; and which, upon being realized, leads to a renewal of immediacy. And the only wisdom possible lies in the recognition that there is no situation too irrational to serve as the basis for a new order; and no degree of order which does not generate its own opposite.

NOTES

1. Cf. *Differenz des Fichte'schen und Schelling'schen Systems der Philosophie*, in *Jenaer Kritische Schriften*, eds. H. Buchner and O. Pöggeler, pp. 75-76. Also, the interpretation of this passage by H. Kimmerle in *Das Problem der Abgeschlossenheit des Denkens*, Hegel-Studien, Beiheft 8 (Bonn, 1970), pp. 27-28.

2. *Das Problem der Abgeschlossenheit* . . ., pp. 29-30.

3. See the work of O. Pöggeler on the development of Hegel's thought at Jena; e.g., "Hegels Jenaer Systemkonzeption", *Philosophisches Jahrbuch*, LXXI (1963-1964), pp. 286-318; "Die Komposition der Phänomenologie des Geistes", *Hegel-Studien*, Beiheft 3 (Bonn, 1966), pp. 27-74.

4. For a statement of the objection as it has been recently raised again, cf. L. Puntel, *Darstellung, Methode und Struktur*, Hegel-Studien, Beiheft 10 (Bonn, 1973), pp. 15ff; note 7a (p. 18) is particularly interesting. The problem that the system of Hegel poses is especially felt in the relationship of the *Phenomenology* to the System. It seems that upon reaching the idea of the System, Hegel in fact withdrew the possibility of an introduction to it such as the *Phenomenology* is supposed to provide. Fulda's book, *Das Problem einer Einleitung in Hegels Wissenschaft der Logik* (Frankfurt/Main, 1965), is dedicated to this problem. For a criticism of his approach to the problem and the conclusions he reaches cf. Puntel, *Darstellung, Methode und Struktur*, pp. 308 ff. See also, Stanley Rosen, *G. W. F. Hegel*, (New Haven and London, 1974).

5. C. L. Reinhold had already raised this objection against the idealism of Fichte and Schelling. Cf. Pöggeler, "Hegels Jenaer Systemkonzeption", pp. 296-97.
6. Dieter Henrich, "Hegels Theorie über den Zufall", *Kant-Studien*, L (1958-1959). Henrich's article deals with contingency at every level of the System, but only briefly with its meaning in the Logic. The article is admirable. However, it leaves the definite impression that Hegel only adds to the position of Kant and Fichte a better reflective understanding of what that position entails. It is certainly true (as Henrich points out) that "Die Notwendigkeit setzt sich wohl selbst die Bedingungen, *aber sie setzt sie als zufällige* . . . Die Notwendigkeit kann gerade deshalb gleichgültig sein dagegen, welche besonderen Dinge an ihr zugrunde gehen, weil schon, ehe sie gesetzt sind, es gewiss ist, dass sie ihr nicht widerstehen können . . ." (p. 135). Necessity is identical with the negative power of reflection, and contingency is its immediate result. It must be added, however, that contingency is the *only content of necessity*. Unless this point is made clear, Hegel's full position is not appreciated. Thus, in Henrich's article it is difficult to see exactly how Hegelian ethics differ from Stoicism. It does not suffice, in order to remedy the abstractness of the Stoic attitude, simply to add a public dimension to the personal virtues of self-control. What must be overcome is the very attitude of indifference to the contingent. The prototype of Hegel's moral ideal must be sought rather in Christian doctrine. In both cases salvation is to be sought in some historical (and contingent) event. Or again, for Hegel it is not possible to dispose of sin simply by rendering it indifferent to the plan of salvation. Sin itself must be incorporated within that plan through redemption.
7. But then, of course, "system" would have to mean something very peculiar. I am inclined to accept the position that the whole *Enzyklopädie* represents only the first of the famous three Hegelian mediations (viz., the logical one); and that the other two would have to be sought in some more historical and empirical science. (Cf. Puntel, *Darstellung, Methode und Struktur,* pp. 322 ff.) However, when a system becomes so broad and inclusive that its limits are difficult to determine, it ceases being a system. Emil L. Fackenheim has also a very "unsystematic" view of Hegel's System. (Cf. *The Religious Dimension in Hegel's Thought* (Bloomington, 1967), pp. 15-30; 214-15.)
8. WL II, 169 ff. By "greater Logic" or "Logic" I shall mean *Wissenschaft der Logik,* and shall refer to it in the notes as WL in the edition of G. Lasson (Hamburg, 1963; reprinted from the edition of 1934). References to the English translation by A. V. Miller, *Hegel's Science of Logic* (George Allen & Unwin, London, 1969) will be designated SL. Hegel uses the term "actuality" in two senses: a broader and a narrower one. According to the broader meaning, "actuality" means a process of self-manifestation. It denotes an object, in other words, the only content of which is its own process of manifestation. (WL II, 169: *"So als die Manifestation . . ."*) One could say that its essence consists in its being *present*. According to its narrower sense, "actuality" is used by Hegel in contradistinction to "possibility". Together with "possibility" and also "contingency" and "necessity", it then appears as a moment in the dialectic of "actuality" understood in the broader sense. In the present paper, we shall use "actuality" in the narrower sense alone.
9. For a detailed analysis of "reflection", "essence", and "show" *(der Schein)*, cf. my paper, "Reflection and Contradiction: A Commentary on Some Passages of Hegel's Science of Logic", *Hegel-Studien*, VIII (1973), pp. 131-61. Hegel compares "actuality" (understood

in its broader sense) with earlier categories in WL II, 169: "Das *Sein* ist noch nicht wirklich; . . . "SL, 541: *"Being* is not yet actual. . . ."

10. There is no question of the presence in the *Logik* of a dialectic of the *subjective* "meinen" as in the *Phenomenology.* Cf. H. G. Gadamer, *Hegels Dialektik* (Tübingen, 1971), p. 57.

11. Cf. Dieter Henrich, "Anfang und Methode der Logik", *Hegel-Studien* I (1964), p. 28.

12. Cf. WL II, 485 ff.

13. Cf. Hegel's general remarks about the dialectic in WL II, 494 ff: "Ganz allgemein aufgefasst . . ."; SL, 834: "Taken quite generally . . ." WL II, 498: "Näher ist nun das Dritte . . ."; SL, 834: "Now more precisely than the third. . . ."

14. WL II, 173: "Das Wirkliche als solches ist möglich . . ."; SL, 544: "The actual as such is possible. . . ."

15. WL II, 173; SL, 544.

16. WL II, 173; SL, 545.

17. *A Study of Hegel's Logic* (Oxford, 1959), p. 136.

18. WL II, 174: "Das Zufällige hat also darum . . ."; SL, 545: "The contingent, then, has . . .", WL II, 173-74: "Das Zufällige bietet daher . . ."; SL, 545: "The contingent therefore presents.. . ." I am using "phenomena" and "phenomenal existence" in a rather broad sense not to be confused with the meaning of the category of *Erscheinung* which Hegel has analyzed and superseded earlier in the Logic. By "phenomenon" I mean any event or state of affairs precisely as it occurs or is given. A phenomenon does not make pretense of revealing any reality but its own. In brief, I am using the term synonymously with "actuality" in Hegel's broad sense of the category (cf. note 3 above).

19. WL II, 174: "Aber darum weil jede unmittelbar in die entgegengesetzte . . ."; SL, 545: "But just because each immediately.. . ."

20. Cf. WL II, 174-75: "Das Notwendige ist ein *Wirkliches*; so ist es . . ."; "Das Zufällige ist also notwendig . . ."; SL, 545-46: "The necessary is an *actual*; as such it is . . ."; "The contingent, therefore, is necessary. . . ."

21. Cf. WL II, 174: "Dies *absolute Unruhe* des *Werdens* . . ."; SL, 545: "This *absolute unrest* of the *becoming.* . . ."

22. WL II, 175: "Aber eine solche, die, −. . . ."; SL, 546: "But one which . . ."

23. WL II, 175-76: "Die reale Wirklichkeit *als solches* ist . . ."; "Die formelle Möglichkeit ist die . . ."; SL, 546-47: "Real actuality *as such* is . . ."; "Formal possibility is . . ."

24. WL II, 176: "Diese Mannigfaltigkeit des Daseins . . ."; SL, 547: "This existing multiplicity . . ."

25. WL II, 178-79: "Was daher real möglich ist, das kann . . ."; SL, 549: "Therefore what is really possible . . ." The whole of WL II, 178 is relevant (cf. SL, 548-49).

26. WL II, 179: "Reale Möglichkeit und die Notwendigkeit sind daher . . ."; SL, 549: "Real possibility and necessity are therefore . . ."

27. WL II, 179-80: "Die Relativität der realen Notwendigkeit . . ."; SL, 550: "The relativity of real necessity . . ."

28. For the play in the Hegelian dialectic between "positing" and "presupposing", see Di Giovanni, "Reflection and Contradiction", especially pp. 148-51.

29. WL II, 181: "So enthält die reale . . ."; ". . . Sie ist daher es selbst . . ."; SL, 551: "Thus real necessity . . ."; "It is therefore necessity itself . . ."

30. Hegel points out that the notion is absolute precisely because it contains contingency.

WL II, 248: "Er ist die absolute Macht gerade darum . . ."; SL, 608: "The notion is absolute power . . ."

31. WL II, 182; SL, 552.

32. For the purely reflective character of the Logic, cf. WL II, 230 ff.: "Indem es zunächst die *Logik* . . ."; 485: "Die absolute Idee selbst hat näher . . ."; SL, 592ff.: "Since it is primarily logic . . ."; 825: "More exactly the absolute Idea itself . . ." On the nature of the Logic and its relation to Hegel's '*Realsystem*', I find L. Puntel's recent work very helpful: *Darstellung*, . . .; see footnote 4 above.

33. Thus, at the end of its reflection upon itself, thought is back to the immediacy with which it began—except that now the nature of the immediacy has been understood. Cf. WL II, 499: "Dies *Resultat* ist daher die *Wahrheit* . . ."; SL, 837: "This *result* is therefore the *truth* . . ."

34. Cf. WL II, 213 ff.

35. 19a, 23-24.

X

The Necessity of Contingency:

An Analysis of Hegel's Chapter on "Actuality" in the *Science of Logic*

by

JOHN W. BURBIDGE

In an article published in 1958, Dieter Henrich wrote: "According to Hegel's theory, contingency itself is necessary without qualification."[1] Henrich's purpose in that paper did not require an examination in detail of Hegel's justification for this claim. Since, however, the strength of the Hegelian philosophy lies not simply in its comprehensive scope, but also in the detailed execution whereby each link is finely and carefully articulated, this paper will pick up Henrich's point that Hegel establishes the necessity of contingency, and will explore the way it is defended within the pages of the larger *Logic* by reconstructing the argument in the chapter on "Actuality."[2]

Hegel calls his logic "the system of pure reason"[3] and "the science of the pure Idea, that is, the Idea in the abstract element of thought."[4] It proceeds, free from the specific content of sensible intuition and experience. Indeed, its intellectual activity probes beyond the representations and ideas which are but indirect generalizations from experience, either arbitrarily universal, or concretely expressed in metaphor and illustration. The content of the logic is that which is present when pure thought simply thinks concepts and categories apart from their application and use. To become a science, and hence an ordered discipline, however, thought must also articulate the *relations* between concepts with precision and clarity. It cannot, in its turn, proceed by means of arbitrary intuition or insightful analogy. For Hegel it employs the reflective procedures of thought: 1) the careful *understanding* of precise, positive characteristics; 2) reflection on *dialectical* implications of that precision; and 3) explanation which integrates these specific contrary terms into a *speculative,* inclusive unity.[5] These three logical procedures, understanding, dialectical and speculative reason, will provide the schematic structure of our analysis.

A. *"Contingency, or Formal Actuality, Possibility and Necessity"*

As a first step in exploring the necessity of contingency, we must understand clearly what contingency means. "The contingent," writes Hegel, "is an actual which is determined at the same time only as possible—whose other, or opposite is just as [possible]."[6] In this statement are included two words which are themselves highly ambiguous in ordinary usage: actual and possible. To understand precisely what is involved in contingency, then, these concepts must be clarified in turn.

1.[7] When thought first considers the concept, actuality, it is taken to be synonymous with being, or with existence. "What is actual" seems to be similar to the expressions: "what is" and "what exists". But careful reflection leads to more precise discriminations. In the first place, "what is" is more abstract than either of the other two expressions; in the second place, the existence of an entity is distinguished from its essence, whereas actual incorporates the sense of actualizing the essence. That essence, capable of being actualized, is more precisely thought of as the possibility of the actual. That the actual actualizes the possible, specifies its difference from the apparently synonymous terms, being, and existence. Reflective thought, then, must consider the meaning of possibility to complete its understanding of actuality.

2.[8] The possible is the ground of the actual. As ground, however, it is not simply other than the actual, for it is, implicitly, what the actual is explicitly. This identity of the implicit and the explicit defines the positive sense of possibility, while its distinction from the actual provides its negative determination.

[9]There are, then, two distinct sides to the meaning of possibility. On the one hand it is intrinsically related to, but other than, the actual and not positively definable on its own. On the other hand, it has the

positive sense of being the self-identity of the actual. For the actual is possible because it does not contradict itself. Compared to the simple and immediate sense of actuality with which we began, this double sense of possibility is complex and dialectical. Reflection must explore how the two distinct senses are related.

[10]We take the positive sense first. What is possible is self-identical. In other words, everything is possible which does not contradict itself. The universality of that statement, however, poses problems. For the term 'everything' includes within its range all distinct possibilities, some of which will contradict others. Therefore there is a sense in which *every*thing — stressing the potential universality of *every* — is not possible.

[11]This paradox becomes explicit when thought does not think about possibility in general, but about a specific possible. If something, let us say A, is possible, then according to the positive meaning of the term, A is self-identical, or $A = A$. But according to that same definition, the opposite, or contrary, of A is also possible, since what is not A is what is not A ($-A = -A$).

While *each* of A and -A is thus possible, it is not possible for *both* to be possible, since (A & -A) is a contradiction, and not self-identical. At this point the second aspect of possibility appears, since it is not possible for both possibles to become actual.

[12]Reflection finds that it is faced with an intriguing dialectic. It began thinking of possibility as the ground of the actual — what the actual actualizes. In its positive sense, however, the possible is what is self-identical. Reflection on the latter has shown that it is no longer possible to claim that the actual is simply the possible actualized. For a distinction has been introduced between possibles which have been actualized and those which have not. Thought must now explain speculatively the significance of this new sense of actuality.

3.[13] The actual still is intrinsically possible. The immediate identity remains. But the possible *per se* is only possible and is not inevitably actualized. Therefore the actual, as now thought, is not simply the possible, but only one possible of many. This complex reflection, which includes possibility as only possible, transcends and cancels the original sense of the actual. Indeed, since that original immediate sense did not distinguish between possibles, it is now evident that it did not do justice to the more inclusive sense of actuality now developed. As the simple identity of actuality and possibility, it was only a possibility itself.

[14]But this implies in turn that possibilities are actual. To be sure, they are not *really* actual, or absolutely and completely actual. The sense is rather that original one where actuality can barely be distinguished from the vague generality of being, or the universality of simple existence. Possibilities are immediately present to thought. *In this sense*, all possibilities are, have existence, and are actual.

[15]On the other hand, the more developed sense of actual, as that which actualizes one of several possibilities, brings us to the definition of contingent with which we began. For, you will recall, "the contingent is an actual which is determined at the same time only as possible — whose other, or opposite, is just as possible." From our review we can now see that by actual we mean an existing actual which has actualized one possibility out of many. The other term, possible, means simply that which is self-identical, and which can be thought without contradiction. That one particular possibility become actual is not the inevitable result of its possibility, but is itself contingent.

[16]What are the implications of this definition of contingent? In the first place, there is no reason or ground why the contingent actual, rather than its opposite, was actualized. Whatever ground it has is simply its own actuality. To this extent it is groundless. Similarly, the range of self-identical possibilities is indifferent to its multiplicity and implicit contradictions. There is nothing within any particular possible which can explain the actuals which do result. They, too, lack any inherent ground or justification. Therefore, within the meaning of contingency, both the actual and the possible are groundless.

[17]But this is not the total picture. For that which specifically defines the actual is that which actualizes the possible. The two terms are used in the definition of contingency because the actual is, in some sense, grounded in the possible. Similarly the possible is thought of as self-identical because it is implicitly what the actual is explicitly. Its meaning is grounded in the actual. Thus the term, contingency, also includes within its meaning the mutual grounding of the actual in the possible and the possible in the actual.

[18]In other words, analysis of the meaning of contingency gives the paradoxical conclusion that, as contingent, it lacks a ground, and, as contingent, it is grounded.

[19]In thinking through this contradiction implicit in the term, contingency, thought finds itself moving from moment to moment with a restless somersaulting of meanings. Four stages can be distinguished:[20] (1) The contingent *actual* is thought of as immediately one with its possibility—with what it is in itself. It is simple existence without a ground. Yet, lacking a ground which it actualizes it loses the distinctive sense of actual. It is simply *possible*. (2) The *actual* is thought of as distinct from the possible which is its ground. But the possible is not sufficient to ground its actuality as contingent, since as actual it is only one of a number of *possibles*. (3) The *possible* is thought in its simple, positive sense of self-identity. But as such it does have actuality in the universal sense of "that which is". It is immediately *actual*. (4) The *possible*, thought of as distinct from, and reflectively derived from, the actual, lacks actuality. But even so it has a bare existence which is not reflectively constituted. Again it is immediately *actual*.

[21]In the concept of contingency, actuality and possibility are each taken, first in their immediate positive sense, and secondly as distinct from its contrary. But none of these four senses remains where it began; it converts into its opposite. This total conversion of senses is the result when thought endeavours to render clear the concept, contingency.

Yet that concept incorporates all of these aspects. Reflection on this complex identity leads to a strange implication. For an actuality which is the same as its possibility, and a possibility which is nothing other than actual is necessary. When the process of transition from one meaning into another is collapsed into a simple unity, contingency is no longer the appropriate term.

[22]This curious consequence needs to be justified. What is necessary is an actual which both is immediately present and needs no further justification. Since the actualization of one possibility excludes its opposite from being actualized, the latter is thereby rendered impossible. But that whose opposite is not possible is necessary. As actual, then, the necessary is immediate and not grounded in something else, yet it *is* grounded in its own intrinsic possibility, since its opposite is impossible. In this sense, the necessary is an actual which is intrinsically its own possibility, and thus lacks a ground while being yet grounded in that possibility. And its possibility is simply its own actuality, even though it is thought as possible through reflection on that actuality.

The complex of meanings which resulted from careful analysis of the meaning of contingency turns out to be identical with this formal sense of necessity as that whose opposite is not possible. In the meaning of contingency, the various moments are left distinct and are not thought together. In the meaning of necessity they are explicitly united, and the distinctions are left implicit. In this sense, then, the contingent is the same as the necessary.

We would seem to have reached the goal of our quest. For the meaning of contingency, when thoroughly explored, is shown to be identical with the meaning of necessity. Therefore what is contingent is necessary. But the subject of that sentence ("what is contingent") refers to the meaning as relationship of moments; the predicate ("necessary") refers to the meaning as unity.

A moment's reflection will lead to dissatisfaction with that result. We have defined necessity in a purely formal sense as the reflective impossibility of the opposite of any given actuality. It is the unity of possibility as ground and of actuality as groundless. But these two terms have been equally formal and independent of content. The actual is simply what is, and the possible is simply self-identity. These are not the only senses of these terms, and therefore the result is a somewhat specious victory. For the necessity of contingency as yet established would lead to no more than the concession that whatever is actual is necessary, since what is actual cannot be otherwise. Although this sense of necessity was used in the argument for fatalism developed by the Megarans, it does not cover the sense of necessity which is more common in the contemporary world. However, Hegel himself recognizes this consequence. And by recognizing it, he takes us further in exploring what the necessity of contingency means.

B. "Relative Necessity, or Real Actuality, Possibility and Necessity"

1.[23] In fact, we have already begun the further development of his argument. As we have seen, the formally necessary is a contingent actual. But it is not an actual as simple being, or bare existence. It is an actual determined to be *one* self-identical possible and which thereby *excludes* others. In contrast to the earlier, pre-reflective sense of actual, this includes those precise determinations which have resulted from reflection. As determinate, it is thought of as real. Understanding must now render precise this more developed sense of actual.

[24]The real actual is a thing with many determinate properties. But the term, actual, is not simply equivalent to the thing as distinct from its properties, nor to existence as distinct from appearance. It has, in addition, the sense of *act*ivity, of actualizing through its own inherent dynamic what it is in itself.

2.[25] As we have seen in the previous section, that which is actualized is the possible. When, however, we look for that which makes possible real actuals we are not satisfied with the formal definition of self-identity. Instead, the possibility of an actual is the dynamic ground, "pregnant with content", out of which the specific characteristics are actualized. In other words, it is real possibility in both senses of the phrase: it is real *possibility* as that which has the likelihood of becoming actual; and it is *real* possibility as the full range of actual conditions which are sufficient to generate that which they condition. Reflective thought once again becomes dialectical as it explores the tension between these two senses.

[26]Real possibilities are *actual* conditions. Each one is an actuality as well as a possibility. But the identity is an identity of content — of the particular determination which is thus characterized. After all, it is not the possibility of its own actuality. It is a possible only through its relation, as ground, to *another* actuality. Reflection has exposed this relation to the actuality towards which it is directed. On the other hand, for reflection to determine the real possibility of some actuality, it must discover not simply one, but the totality of actual conditions on the basis of which all the determinations of that real actuality are actualized. For if all the conditions are not present, the actual is not possible. A diverse multitude of actualities are put together under real possibility. That specific integration is thought as one only because of an actuality which is distinct from any one of those integrated conditions.

[27]The concept of real possibility is a highly complex concept, requiring a more thorough dialectical analysis. On the one hand, since the content is an actual in one respect, and a possible in another, the sense of possible is purely formal — it is that which does not contradict

itself. On the other hand, as the totality of conditions for one actuality, it must be such that these conditions can be integrated without contradiction. Both formally and with respect to specific determinations it is that which does not contradict itself.

Further considerations, however, complicate the picture. For reflection on the multiplicity which is inherent in real possibility distinguishes formally the different conditions. Each condition, as self-identical and immediately actual, is distinct from the others. As such it stands over against the others. But this means that it is contradictory to say that together they are *the* one possibility. Using the purely formal sense of possibility as self-identical, it is not possible for a variety of different conditions to be one. This strange conclusion follows not only from formal considerations, but also from material considerations of real possibility as totality of conditions. A set of conditions is called the real possibility of an actual because, when brought together, the multiplicity will be cancelled, and indeed collapse, as possibility. It *cannot* maintain itself as many. In other words, it is *not possible* for all the conditions to be integrated as a totality and still be simply possible. For when all the conditions of something are present, it becomes actual. Indeed, the actuality as a thing with many properties is itself nothing else but this integration of the conditions.

On the one hand, a set of conditions are not the real possibility of a thing unless all the conditions are present. On the other hand, when all the conditions are present, the thing is no longer simply possible, but actual.

Indeed, the paradox is even stronger than this. Real possibility is that which, to be possible, contradicts itself neither formally nor materially. Yet real possibility can be a simple self-identity neither formally nor materially.

Reflection on real possibility shows that it is not possible to be both a *real* possibility of an actuality, and yet be distinct from that actuality as possibility.

[28]When we recall all the steps through which we have moved in explicating real possibility, we discover a double process of cancelling. In the first place, the immediate actuality of the possible is cancelled as significant, and it is seen primarily as the possibility of another—as what that other is in itself. But in the second place we have now seen that its character as possible cannot be maintained. At the very point

where it is really possible as the condition for another, it ceases to be possibility and becomes the resultant actuality. Its possibility is cancelled in turn. And the resultant actuality *is* the immediate being of real possibility.

The result of our dialectical reflection is that it has become impossible to distinguish possibility and actuality. In the earlier discussion, where possibility was simple self-identity, the opposite of what was actual was also possible. Here, however, once all the conditions which make a thing possible are present, nothing else is possible. The actuality of these conditions is simply their actuality *as* conditions. But that actuality *of* the possible cannot now be distinguished from what is actualized *by* the possible.

When reflective thought turned to that possibility which is the ground of real actuality, it began by distinguishing the one from the other. But in the last analysis, having worked through all the dialectical implications, it can no longer draw any clear distinctions at all. Simply as one condition among many, something cannot be a *real* possibility at all. As the totality of conditions, it can only arbitrarily be distinguished from what was to be grounded. Thought reaches the conclusion that the distinctions between real possibility and real actuality can no longer be maintained. They have become integrated into a complex unity which must now have its positive, speculative sense explained.

3.[29] What is really possible in any complete sense *must* be actual. As that possibility which can do nothing else but become actual, it is necessity. This sense of necessity is different from the earlier, formal, one. For there we saw that the contingent actuality which is both grounded and groundless is other than formal possibility *per se*. Here, however, real possibility is itself the necessity. "Under these conditions and circumstances," we say, "nothing else can follow." [WL II, 179] The distinction between real possibility and necessity is only apparent. When we say that something is really necessary, we include in that necessity all the content which constitutes and characterizes that something — that content which was originally included in the determinate sense of real possibility.

[30] Real necessity is relative. It is based upon a presupposition which is itself contingent. By this Hegel is not simply making the obvious

point that our reflection on the implication of the meaning of contingency has led us to this sense of real necessity, so that the former is the premise for the reflective procedure. Rather it is implicit in the content of the discussion itself. We began by reflecting on the meaning of real actuality—immediate, but determinate, reality. Real necessity concerns the relation between real possibility as condition, and this real actuality as conditioned. It presupposes, but is indifferent to, the specific determinations of whatever is so related. On the one hand, such content is the condition of the reflective analysis; on the other, what that content is specifically is irrelevant. Whatever it is, it could have been otherwise. All that is required is that it be a possible content in the simple formal sense of self-identity. As actual, it could have been other than itself. Indeed, it is a contingent matter what content real actuality is given. Given that content, however, reflection will show that it *had to* be actual because of the total set of conditions.

[31]One cannot think of real necessity, then, without presupposing contingency. The relation is necessary but the content is contingent. Because of real possibility A, B must become actual. But the nature of the necessity is contingent on the specific determinations of B.

Not only is the content of the necessary relation contingent, but also the relation itself. For the distinction between real possibility and the resultant actual is the result of reflection on that actual. But that reflective distinction is itself contingent and not inevitable. What thought distinguishes as the real possibility of an actual is not itself determined with necessity. Both in terms of content and form, real necessity presupposes contingency.

What we have, then, is a unity of necessity and contingency, since contingency is implicit in real necessity insofar as it is determinate, and insofar as it requires, as a necessary condition, the reflective distinction between possibility and actuality.

[32]The speculative explanation of real necessity requires the distinction between real possibility and its actualization, even though this distinction cannot be maintained as absolute. Just as, however, thought moved from contingency to formal necessity by shifting the stress from the implicit relation of explicitly distinct terms to the explicit integration of implicit distinctions, so here reflection can collapse into a unity the moments which constitute real necessity. When thought no longer makes explicit distinctions between real possibility

and real actuality, it takes the actual in its totality. Whatever is actual is simply actual, for the reference to a distinct possibility which grounds it is no longer appropriate. What thought now thinks is an actuality which has no external possibility in terms of which it is conditioned. Since there is no other, relative to which it becomes actual, it is absolute actuality.

C. *"Absolute Necessity"*

(1)[33] The logical demand to understand precisely drives us further. To advance, however, we must recall our earlier conclusions. In the first section, the contingent, as both grounded and groundless, could not be distinguished from the formally necessary. In the second section, real necessity, both in content and form, is contingently determined. These two moments come together in thought into a contingency which is necessary, and a necessity which is contingent. When these distinctions, however, are integrated into one thought, what results is the total complex of actuality. When we endeavour to understand precisely the ground of this actuality, there is no distinct possibility to which we can turn. This means that it is intrinsically necessary. It is absolutely actual.

(2)[34] Absolute actuality, then, has no possibility which is other than, or distinct from, its actuality. Its ground is its necessity. Yet reflective thought can still ask the question: why? Since it can now not simply talk of formal self-identity, nor can it distinguish some actual from those others which render it possible, it can only enquire why there is anything at all. The ground which is sought in this question is empty of all content, for all determinate possibilities have collapsed into the absolutely actual. Therefore there is no answer to this reflective question. It is completely contingent that there be anything at all. It could have been absolutely otherwise.

When reflection entertains this possibility, no longer does it think the formal possibility of simple self-identity, nor, indeed, the real possibility of conditions. It is the possibility which reason entertains when it confronts the actual as necessary and absolute. But such possibilities can either remain a pure possibility with no actualization at all, or become the possibility of what is, in fact, actual. There is no reason why it should be the one rather than the other.

We are again faced with a dialectical tension. What is absolutely actual is intrinsically necessary, yet it is completely contingent. On the one hand it is grounded in necessity because there is no distinct possibility to which we can turn. On the other hand it is grounded in absolute possibility which is independent of any reference to the actual.

(3)[35] This dialectical contradiction requires resolution and explanation. Since there is no further external point of reference to provide such an explanation, thought must reconsider the earlier argument in light of this new development. The concept of absolute actuality was the result of collapsing the distinctions in the concept of real necessity. The latter distinguished between real possibilities and the resultant actualities. Only on the basis of this distinction does real necessity become possible. Since this distinction was collapsed into the concept of absolute actuality, it is implicit within it. What is thus implicit, but overlooked, in the concept of absolute actuality needs now to be reconsidered. The distinction between possible and actual is reintroduced, not as a relation of contradictory opposites where both cannot be present at the same time, but as a relation of sub-contraries whose meanings are distinct and opposite, but which are yet explicitly related within a larger universe of discourse. In place of the earlier moves of thought which first treated the distinctions as explicit, and the relations as only implicit, and then shifted to collapsing the distinctions into an explicit unity, we now are in a position where it is necessary that we take both the distinctions and the relation as explicit component parts of the meaning of the concept. On the one hand, the two moments of possibility and actuality are explicitly distinguished as the negation of each other; on the other, this negative relation is explicitly negated to reaffirm the unity.

[36]This new content of thought is what is actual, period. No longer do we contrast immediate or formal actuality with reflective considerations on its logical possibility. Nor do we distinguish determinate actuality from its real conditions. Nor indeed do we think of absolute actuality as simply necessary in itself. We are, instead, thinking of the actual as it is actually. We distinguish actuals which are real pos-

sibilities from that which they actualize. Indeed, the determinations which are actually present result from the internal relations by which the distinctions between actual and possible are both constituted as distinct and then related as part to whole. In other words, possibility is established as the opposite of the actual through the reflective determination of distinctions within the actual itself.

This process by which reflection distinguishes the possible from the actual mediates and grounds the actual. It renders the actual possible. The distinction and its resolution actualize and render determinate what the actual is implicitly. It is its *possibility* in a final and pre-eminent sense. Instead of thinking about absolute possibilities, explanatory thought considers the mediating process by which the actual determines itself.

[37]Careful consideration shows that the actual, as we are now thinking the term, constitutes itself as determinate by means of the relation in which possibility grounds actuality, and actuality is grounded by possibility. At the same time it generates that relation as the explicit form of its implicit character. As that which constitutes its own ground—as self-constituting—it is absolute necessity. This means, however, that absolute necessity gives rise to contingency as the ground of its own necessity. For it is contingent which moments are distinguished, separated and repelled from its actuality as its own conditions. Whatever moments are thus rendered determinate, however, it is necessary that they thereby become the means to its absolute self-determination. Without these contingent, determinate moments, it could not be established as necessary. This play of countervailing forces determines the actual to be necessary by annulling, even as it establishes, contingency. It generates, even as it transcends, the repelling moment of contrast and counterthrust. This necessity is necessity absolute. For it alone establishes the absolute necessity of contingency.[38]

With that, our assigned task has been accomplished. Contingency itself has been shown to be necessary without qualification.

Necessity as thus defined, however, is blind. There is no reason or purpose for the way in which it determines itself. Only where the meaning of necessity is taken up into the explicitly rational perspective where it is given conceptual meaning will it become the basis of freedom as intentional self-determination. But that is beyond the terms of reference for this paper.

Conclusion

A few comments may be in order about the necessity of Hegel's method. You will recall that, at the beginning of the paper, it was suggested that Hegel's logic develops through the process of reflective thought: "the careful understanding of precise, positive characteristics; reflection on the dialectical implications of that precision; and explanation, which integrates these specific contrary terms into a speculative, inclusive unity." These procedures took us from the most primitive sense of actuality, through a dialectical reflection on the possible, to the integrating concepts of contingency and necessity. These again became the object of understanding's precision, dialectical reflection, and speculative explanation until the meaning of relative, or real, necessity was reached. Further speculation showed how the previous moments were integrated into the complete sense of necessity absolute.

Wherein lies the necessity of the movement? The answer can be suggested in three stages. In the first place, the concept with which we began, actuality, is a universal concept. It is used to characterize all that is. But as first present in thought it is immediate and indeterminate. In the second place, to render it more determinate without introducing inappropriate considerations, understanding must draw careful and clear distinctions. Such distinctions, however, are partial. When they are considered in themselves, apart from their context, their inherent limitations clash with the universality of that which they were to define. Dialectical reflection explores the various aspects of this clash until the intrinsic relation between defining characteristic and defined concept is reconstituted. This process of reconstitution is rendered necessary by the partiality which results from understanding's precision. Yet the latter was what made the original concept possible. In the third place, then, thought must explore how the various moments interact within the integrated unity: how the original characterization of actuality is rendered possible, and how the possibility in turn constitutes its necessity. Each stage of the process is a necessary moment of its full, determinate development.

This paper is a contingent effort to understand Hegel, which began arbitrarily with the concept, contingency. It cannot pretend to have completed a thorough dialectical reflection on the text. Nor indeed does it explain speculatively the integration between this process of thought and the actual world in which we live—an explanation which would justify the logic as metaphysics. It ends, therefore, with an invitation to reflective dialogue—to explore whether it is, even partially, an adequate understanding of Hegel's text.

NOTES

1. "Hegels Theorie über den Zufall," *Kantstudien*, 50 (1958-9), p. 135, reprinted in *Hegel in der Sicht der neueren Forschung,* ed. I. Fetscher, (Wissenschaftliche Buchgesellschaft, Darmstadt, 1973), p. 168n8. Also reprinted in *Hegel im Kontext* by D. Henrich, (Suhrkamp, Frankfurt am Main), 1971.

2. Because of the close exegesis of the principal text,—the chapter on Actuality (*Wirklichkeit*) in Section Three, Book Two, Volume One of the *Logic*,—references to that part of the text will be given with the *incipit* of the passage in the German edition of G. Lasson, *Wissenschaft der Logik*, (Felix Meiner, Hamburg, 1966), 2 Bde., reprinted from the edition of 1934; and designated WL with appropriate volume and page number. Following this, reference will be given with *incipit* to the English translation by A. V. Miller, *Hegel's Science of Logic*, (Humanities Press, New York, 1969); and designated SL with appropriate page number. Finally, reference will be given to the older translation of the same title by W. H. Johnston and L. G. Struthers, published by George Allen and Unwin, London, 1929, 2 vols.; and designated JS with appropriate volume and page number but no *incipit*. The capital letters A,B,C and the arabic numbers at the beginning of some paragraphs repeat Hegel's own divisions; the bracketed numbers in C, however, are not in Hegel's text.

3. WL I, 31.

4. *Enzyklopädie der Philosophischen Wissenschaften im Grundrisse (1830)*, ed. F. Nicolin and O. Pöggeler, (Felix Meiner, Hamburg, 1959⁶), No. 19.

5. *Ibid.*, §79.

6. WL II, 173, my own translation, in which I assume the parallelism of the two subordinate clauses, so that *ebensosehr* repeats *als möglich bestimmt*.

7. WL II, 171: "Die Wirklichkeit ist formell, . . ."; SL, 542: "Actuality is formal . . ."; JS II, 174-5.

8. WL II, 171: "2. Diese Möglichkeit ist . . ."; SL, 542: "This possibility is . . ."; JS II, 175.

9. WL II, 171: "Weil aber die Bestimmung . . ."; SL, 543: "But because the determination . . ."; JS II, 175.

10. WL II, 171: "Nach der ersten, . . ."; SL, 543: "According to the first, . . ."; JS II, 175.

11. WL II, 171-2: "Die bloss formelle . . . ," "Das mögliche enthält . . . ," "Zunächst

drückt sich . . ."; SL, 543-4: "This merely formal . . . ," "The possible, however, contains . . . ," "This is expressed first . . ."; JS II, 175-6.

12. WL II, 173: "Als diese Beziehung . . ."; SL, 544: "But this relation . . ."; JS II, 176.

13. WL II, 173: "3. Diese Wirklichkeit ist nicht . . ."; SL, 544: "3. This actuality is not . . ."; JS II, 176-7.

14. WL II, 173: "Hiermit ist zugleich . . ."; SL, 544: "Here at the same time . . ."; JS II, 177.

15. WL II, 173: "Diese Einheit der Möglichkeit . . .": SL, 545: "This unity of possibility . . ."; JS II, 177.

16. WL II, 173-4: "Das Zufällige bietet daher . . ."; SL, 545: "The contingent therefore presents . . ."; JS II, 177.

17. WL II, 174: "Das Zufällige ist aber *zweitens* . . ."; SL, 545: "But secondly, the contingent . . ."; JS II, 177.

18. WL II, 174: "Das Zufällige hat also . . ."; SL, 545: "The contingent, then, has . . ."; JS II, 177.

19. WL II, 174: "Es ist das *gesetzte* . . ."; SL, 545: "It is the *posited* . . ."; JS II, 177-8.

20. The four stages are actuality and possibility, each considered as grounded and as groundless.

21. WL II, 174: "Diese *absolute Unruhe* . . ."; SL, 545: "This *absolute unrest* . . ."; JS II, 178.

22. WL II, 174-5: "Das Notwendige ist ein . . ."; SL, 545-6: "The necessary is an . . ."; JS II, 178.

23. WL II, 175: "1. Die Notwendigkeit, die . . ."; SL, 546: "1. The necessity which . . ."; JS II, 178-9.

24. WL II, 175-6: "Die reale Wirklichkeit *als solche* . . .", "Die reale Wirklichkeit hat nun . . ."; SL, 546-7: "Real actuality *as such* . . .", "Now real actuality likewise has possibility . . ."; JS II, 179.

25. WL II, 176: "2. Diese Möglichkeit als das . . .", "Diese reale Möglichkeit ist selbst . . ."; SL, 547: "2. This possibility as the . . .", "This real possibility is itself . . ."; JS II, 179.

26. WL II, 176-7: "Diese Mannigfaltigkeit des Daseins . . ."; SL, 547: "This existing multiplicity . . ."; JS II, 179-80.

27. WL II, 177: "Was real möglich ist . . ."; SL, 547-8: "What is really possible . . ."; JS II, 180-81.

28. WL II, 178: "In der sich aufhebenden . . ."; SL, 548-9: "Now in self-sublating . . ."; JS II, 181.

29. WL II, 178-9: "3. Die *Negation* der realen . . .", "Was notwendig ist . . ."; SL, 549: "The *negation* of real . . .", "What is necessary . . ."; JS II, 181-2.

30. WL II, 179-80: "Diese Notwendigkeit aber . . .", "Die Relativität der realen . . ."; SL, 549-50: "But this necessity . . .", "The relativity of real . . ."; JS II, 182.

31. WL II, 180: "In der Tat ist somit . . ."; SL, 550: "Thus in point of fact . . ."; JS II, 182-3.

32. WL II, 180: "An sich ist also . . ."; SL, 550: "Here, therefore, the unity . . ."; JS II, 183.

33. WL II, 180: "Die reale Notwendigkeit . . .", "Diese Bestimmtheit aber . . ."; SL, 550: "Real necessity is . . .", "But this determinateness . . ."; JS II, 183.

34. WL II, 180-81: "Aber damit ist diese . . ."; SL; 550-51: "But because this . . ."; JS II, 183.

35. WL II, 181: "So enthält die reale . . ."; SL, 551: "Thus real necessity not only . . ."; JS II, 183-4.

36. WL II, 181: "Eben darin aber ist . . ."; SL, 551: "But it is in this very act . . ."; JS II, 184.

37. WL II, 181-2: "So hat die Form . . ."; SL, 551-52: "Thus form in its realization . . ."; JS II, 184.

38. WL II, 183: "Die absolute Notwendigkeit ist daher *blind* . . .", "Aber diese *Zufälligkeit* . . ."; SL, 552-3: "Absolute necessity is therefore *blind* . . .", "But this *contingency* is . . ."; JS II, 185.

Hegel's Dialectic of the Organic Whole as a Particular Application of Formal Logic

by
CLARK BUTLER

It is notorious that a good part of the difficulty of Hegel stems from the fact that he is inexplicit but suggestive where seventy years of analytic philosophy have taught us at least to aim at explicitness. My purpose here is to formalize what is best called Hegel's "dialectic of the organic whole." It is the classical Hegelian dialectic which I wish to analyze here. Some may think that my purpose risks running Hegel's suggestiveness into an un-Hegelian definiteness. Hegel, like Dewey (his one-time follower), seems to have used vague, impressionistic style as a means of conveying a certain philosophical belief as to the continuity and fluidity of all being, the untenability of fixed distinctions. However, this stylistic method of communication seems to have no advantage over the method of explicit assertion, and in fact to have the singular disadvantage that we sometimes do not know whether to assent to what Hegel says because we do not know what he is saying. Further, the unity of form and content is no true Hegelian ground for objecting to the isolation of the formal pattern of dialectical logic. This pattern is indeed an abstract moment incapable of subsisting by itself, but Hegel would be the first to admit that abstraction has its use as an aid to the understanding. And let us not be too quick to belittle the understanding. For not only does it have the intrinsic value of providing "clear and distinct" ideas; reason has only the forceful pressing of the claims of the understanding to thank for the stimulus of its own counterclaims. Finally, reason in transcending the understanding needs not so much to abolish the clarity of its distinctions as to clearly assert their non-absoluteness.

Hegel's inexplicitness has apparently given rise to two contrary and rather extreme interpretations of the dialectic. First there is the "minimalist" interpretation of J. N. Findlay and Walter Kaufmann. Partly no doubt to avoid the thesis-antithesis-synthesis caricature, both concur in denying any formal rigor to Hegel's dialectic. "I am not so much rejecting the dialectic," Kaufmann writes, "as I say: there is none. . . . See what Hegel says about it and observe what in fact he does. You will find some suggestive remarks, not all of them in the same vein, as well as all kinds of affectations; but you will not find any plain method that you could adopt even if you wanted to."[1] Findlay is less outspoken. Yet even he invites us to ignore Hegel's claims regarding the "necessity" of dialectical transitions, urging us instead to construe them as merely "natural".[2]

At the other extreme is the "maximalist" interpretation of, among others, Michael Kosok. Kosok counters the tendency to construe Hegel's pronouncements on dialectic very loosely by proposing a full-fledged "formalization" of "dialectical logic."[3] The suggestion is clear that there is a rigorous dialectical logic implicit in Hegel, a logic which, however, differs fundamentally from what Kosok calls "ordinary logic."

The position which I shall defend is opposed to both extreme interpretations. In contrast to Findlay and Kaufmann, I hold that the progress of Hegelian dialectic is inferentially necessary. And, over against Kosok, I hold that the dialectic can be formalized by means of ordinary symbolic logic of the deductive type. I hope to re-instate the dialectic in its central position in Hegel's philosophy, but I also want to lay to rest the misconception, traceable to statements by Hegel understandable only in the light of the limited formal logic of Hegel's own day, that there is a kind of dialectical logic basically different from ordinary formal logic. If I am not mistaken, so-called dialectical logic differs from formal logic merely in being a very particular application of the latter. Central to this application, I shall argue, is indirect proof. Hegel, like Kant, identified formal logic with the classical school logic dating from Aristotle. Although the method of indirect proof had been used at least since Zeno, Aristotle did not incorporate it into his formal logic. Holding that science must proceed from true premises, and failing to distinguish contra-factual conditional assumptions from false premises, Aristotle dismissed indirect proof as unscientific "dialectic." Hegel's innovation on Aristotle, I suggest, consists in seeing indirect proof as "scientific", indeed as essential to science conceived as the intellectual internalization of experience in its course of development. Since modern symbolic logic did not exist in Hegel's time, since the only formal logic was Aristotelian, Hegel held that dialectical thought could not be adequately analyzed by formal logic. Modern formal logic, however, has caught up with Hegel. The notational recognition of I.P. and the distinction between a premise and conditional assumption allow us to do what Hegel could not do, to formalize dialectical logic. If successful, the interpretation here proposed may serve the purpose, for some, of making Hegel's dialectic more respectable. (For others, it may even serve the purpose of making symbolic logic more respectable.)

Here is the plan I intend to follow. I shall first enumerate and discuss six essential inferential rules implicit in the practice of Hegelian dialectic. Secondly, it will be shown how these rules can be translated into the rules of deductive logic. A formal pattern of deductive inference will be proposed as the tacit model to which dialectical inference conforms itself. An attempt will be made to justify this pattern by proposing an actual formalization of a section of the Hegelian opus.

The following rules of dialectical logic may now be distinguished. All are rules of inference in the strict sense except the first. The first, the rule of abstraction, is not strictly a rule of inference; rather, through its application the ultimate starting point for inference is established.

1. *Rule of Abstraction.* Any entity falling within immediate experience may be referred to, i.e., conceptually abstracted. Such an act of abstraction presupposes unconditionally the "being"[4] of what is abstracted. To exist is to exemplify determinate or distinguishing properties,[5] and it is only by the notice of such properties that any entity can be conceptually abstracted. Linguistically, the operation of abstraction is indicated explicitly by the use of a term mentioning the entity abstracted. All thought begins in abstraction. To think is to think about something to which thought must, whether implicitly or explicitly, refer.

2. *Rule of Absolutization.* This rule states that any entity which has been abstracted may be judged conditionally to exist as an absolute subject, essentially unrelated to anything else; that is, it may be absolutized. "Absolutization" has a more definite meaning than "reification" or "hypostatization". To be absolute is not merely to be non-

relative; it is also to be comprehensive or all-encompassing, since if there existed something apart from what is taken to be absolute, what is absolute would self-contradictorily be relative to it. Hegel adopts from Spinoza the principle that the existence of two absolutes would be self-contradictory.

Although any object abstracted from experience may be absolutized, absolutization is inevitable in the case of the very first abstraction of an entity. By "first abstraction" I mean the abstraction of an entity which occurs before the organic whole which is its context has been abstracted. The product of first abstraction cannot be conceived in relation to anything else, since nothing else has yet been conceived at this stage of thought. But to conceive something without internal relationship to anything else is to conceive it as essentially absolute. Hegel gives recognition to the concomitance of first abstraction and absolutization by including both operations within the province of a single mental faculty, which he designates the "understanding".

3. *Rule of Internal Relation.* This is the rule that whatever the object abstracted is internally related to may also be abstracted and judged to exist unconditionally. One entity is said to be internally related to another if and only if the statement that the first entity exists may be so analyzed as to logically entail the statement that the second also exists. The rule of internal relation may also be described as the rule of abstraction of the other. If two entities are internally related to each other, they exist distinguishably but inseparably. They are distinguishable in that they are non-identical as judged by the identity of indiscernables. And they are inseparable in that they are identical in the Hegelian sense of identity in difference: each exists one with the other.

The rule of internal relation is a rule of discovery. Application of the rule is motivated by the disquietude of explicitly absolutizing an entity which is implicitly experienced to be relative. It is clear that the course of dialectic must be psychologically motivated. In this sense, Findlay is right in saying that the progress of the dialectic is "natural", although this does not prevent it from also being necessary.

4. *Rule of Negation of the Other.* Any abstracted entity other than what has been absolutized[6] may be conditionally negated, its existence

conditionally denied. If abstraction of the other is, motivationally, an act of protest, the motive behind conditional negation of the other is self-defense. The maintenance of the absolutization of one entity requires negation of another entity. If what has been abstracted is only an aspect of the whole, if abstraction is understood in the sense of abstraction *from* the whole, the abstract aspect will be internally related to something else which, if the absolutization is to be maintained, will be abstracted only to be negated.

5. *Rule of Self-Negation.* When the existence of an entity is asserted unconditionally, a contradictory conditional assertion of the entity's non-existence may be unconditionally denied, and this will in turn lead to the negation of the conditional absolutization which resulted in the assertion of the entity's non-existence. The application of rule four establishes a contradiction. But thought cannot rest with a recognized contradiction. The conditional assumption leading to the contradiction must therefore be rejected.

6. *Rule of Negation of the Negation.* This is the final rule of dialectical logic. It is the rule that any entity whose absolutization has been negated by the application of rule five may be judged to exist unconditionally only in relation to its necessary other which has also been judged to exist unconditionally. The previously absolutized entity is now conceived to be what it is only through its other. By means of negation of the negation, a non-negative or non-exclusive judgment of the once absolutized entity's existence replaces the previous exclusive judgment of its existence. Negation of the negation is for Hegel the principle operation of "reason" as opposed to the "understanding".

Following a notation suggested in part by Kosok, we may introduce symbols to abbreviate the results of applying the rules. The operation of abstraction may be indicated by the use of "e" to represent any entity abstracted. The absolutization of an entity may be represented by placing the letter designating the entity in parentheses: "(e)". We will then represent the other to which the entity is internally related by the letter "o". The negation of the other will be indicated by placing between "e" and "o" a slash line falling down upon "o": "(e)/o". The self-negation of the original entity designated by "e" will be represented by the addition of a slash line this time falling down on "(e)":

"(e)Xo". Self-negation may also be called "negation of the self by the other."[7] Negation of the negation will be represented by elimination of the parentheses and slash lines in favor of a simple bar linking "e" and "o": "e-o". We thus have the following pattern of dialectical inference:

1. e	Abstraction
2. (e)	1, Absolutization
3. (e)o	2, Internal Relation
4. (e)/o	3, Negation of Other
5. (e)Xo	4, Self-Negation
6. e-o	5, Negation of Negation

Once the complex designated "e-o" has been conceived, it can serve as a new starting point for absolutization and a repetition of the cycle. If the "e-o" dyad is relative to something else, the cycle will repeat itself, and it will continue to do so until an absolutization is reached which is stable, which is not subject to negation by something not included within it. At each repetition of the cycle, different, more concrete aspects of the whole are articulated. The conclusion of the dialectic is a fully concrete, internally articulated whole of internally related aspects.

The three main spheres of the *Logic*, being, essence and the concept, may be distinguished in relation to the above simple pattern as follows. The distinction pertains to the attitude of thought characteristic of each sphere rather than to the basic pattern of inference. In the sphere of being thought is fixated at the level of absolutized finitude. Thought here relinquishes only with reluctance one absolutization, only to fall into another. Hegel characterizes this type of thought as dogmatic, and it is an expression of the understanding. In the sphere of essence, thought is arrested in its development at the level of self-negation. This is the sphere of skeptical thought, of negative reason. Finally, at the level of the concept, thought reaches fulfillment in concrete thinking. No longer arrested in its development, it passes effortlessly to negation of the negation. This totally mobile form of thought is the distinctive mark of speculative reason.

It may be objected here that I let the stage of absolutization drop out in subsequent stages of the dialectic, while Hegel insists that past stages are preserved even in being transcended. But I take Hegel to mean that every aspect of the organic whole is, once abstracted or conceived, preserved as conceived within subsequent, more inclusive absolutizations. Certainly he does not mean that every aspect absolutized is preserved as absolutized, since then the dialectic would be a mere accumulation of contradictions and could make no progress at all. However, although past absolutizations may and indeed must be surrendered, they may be repeated. Speculative comprehension of the whole does not simply exclude either absolutization of the abstract or the resulting recognition of contradiction; on the contrary, this absolutization and recognition recur indefinitely, but are cancelled no sooner than they recur. If the comprehension with which the dialectic concludes is not an inert or lifeless terminus, it is because abstraction and absolutization here recur, but such abstraction is no longer "first abstraction," and such absolutization is no longer taken dead seriously. No longer does thought stop dead in its tracks before absolutized finitude. Nor does it stop with confessions of contradiction. For thought has artfully re-enacted these transcended moments simply to exert itself anew, to re-assert itself by applying itself against the obstacle which has been contrived for the purpose. Philosophy, for Hegel, is a kind of eternal return; it is this tranquil activity of continual re-enactment.

We pass now to the question of translating dialectical inference into ordinary formal logic. The view that it is impossible to reduce dialectical logic to formal logic has been supported by the view that Hegel rejected the law of non-contradiction. Hegel, it must be said, contributed to the confusion with statements such as that the law of non-contradiction is valid only for "finite situations." However, in affirming identity in difference, Hegel does not really mean that A is both identical and non-identical to non-A in the same sense of "identical". He means that A is "identical" to non-A in that it is internally related to it, but that A is not "identical" to non-A in that it is a different determination or aspect of the organic whole. Thus the notion of identity-in-difference, despite Hegel's effort to shock us, implies no violation of ordinary formal logic. If it is true that for Hegel an appearance sets itself apart from reality through being self-contradictory, falsely presenting itself as absolute, within the dialectical process of reality it loses its self-contradictory appearance. The appearance is unreal insofar as it is self-contradictory. It is a "vanishing moment." The whole progress of the dialectic depends on the law of non-

contradiction, on the fact that thought cannot rest with an acknowledged contradiction.

Self-negation, negation by the other, consists in rejection of a
judgment precisely because the judgment issues in contradiction.
Given that nothing real is self-contradictory, thought is bound to deny
the judgment that something is both absolute and relative, that entity
"o" both does not and does exist. Either the absolutized but essentially
relative aspect "e" does not exist, because it is conceived to be self-
contradictory; or it is real, but has somehow been misconceived as
self-contradictory. Its existence cannot be denied, for it is manifest or
present to mind as an object of immediate experience. Therefore, it
must have been misconceived. It can be reconceived to avoid contradiction by withdrawing one of the contradictory assertions. The
newly discovered relativity of the initially abstracted aspect to something else is an essential truth which cannot be denied. Therefore, it is
the assertion of its absolute status which must be withdrawn.

It may now be noted how the pattern of dialectical inference which
we have just sketched can be formalized by means of symbolic logic.
Central to this formalization is the rule of indirect proof: the thesis
that something abstracted from experience exists absolutely is provisionally assumed, in order to see if a contradiction results from the
assumption. So long as contradiction does not result, the assumption is
maintained. But once contradiction is discovered, the assumption is
rejected, and the aspect which had been absolutized is reconceived to
be relative.

A basic pattern of Hegel's dialectical argumentation may be formalized as follows:

Abstraction	1. Fa	Immediate Premise
Absolutization	2. $(x)(f)(fx \supset f = F)$	Assumption
Abstraction of Other	3. $(x)(Fx \equiv (\exists y)(Gxy \cdot -Fy))$	Mediately Discovered
	$\cdot$	Premise
	$\cdot$	
	$\cdot$	
	$k_1.\ (\exists y)-Fy$	
Negation of Other	$k_2.\ -(\exists y)-Fy$	
Self-negation	$k_3.(\exists y)-Fy \cdot -(\exists y)-Fy$	k_1, k_2, Conjunction
	$k_4.-(x)(f)(fx \supset f = F)$	2-k_3, Indirect Proof
	$k_5.(x)(Fx \equiv (\exists y)(Gxy \cdot -Fy))$	Mediately Discovered
		Premise
	$k_6. Fa \equiv (\exists y)(Gay \cdot -Fy)$	k_5, Univ. Instantiation
	$k_7.(\exists y)(Gay \cdot -Fy)$	$1, k_6$, Equiv. & Modus Ponens
Negation of Negation	$k_8. Fa \cdot (\exists y)(Gay \cdot -Fy)$	$1, k_7$, Conjunction

It should be noted that variations on the above pattern are possible. The assumption "$(x)(f)(fx \supset f = F)$" represents absolutization of a class: the class of entities having the property "F" is said to be the only class there is. Also possible is absolutization of an instance: $(x)(Fx \supset x = a)$, i.e., only the entity "a" has the property "F". Another possibility is absolutization of a property: $(f)(fa \supset f = F)$, i.e., the property "F" is the only property of the entity "a".

If dialectic is more than mere formal logic, it is because it is a psychologically compelling application of it. Indirect proof is a powerful pedagogical and heuristic tool. Learning and discovery are largely polemical processes of trial and error, conjecture and refutation. Most importantly, indirect proof meets several requirements which Hegel places on the dialectical method. First, it is a principle of internal criticism.[9] The dialectician places himself provisionally in the standpoint of the position to be refuted. Secondly, it is a means of learning by means of error and contradiction. The very first error, Hegel says, is the fear of error itself.[10] Thirdly, the pattern of indirect proof which we have outlined does not result in the total rejection of any position criticized.[11] The premise of entity "e's" existence is retained even though the absolutization of "e" is rejected. And, finally, it should be remarked that Hegel concurs with Aristotle in calling Zeno the originator of dialectic,[12] and that Zeno earned this title because he originated what is now called indirect proof. Hegel goes beyond Zeno in conceiving dialectic to be enacted spontaneously and unconsciously in the process of individual and collective experience, and not merely self-consciously in the polemic of a philosopher.

In order to illustrate the application of the formal pattern let us consider the famous dialectic of being, nothing and becoming at the beginning of the *Logic*. I think it may be said that formalization is not a sterile or merely academic exercise, and in fact that it is the best method of focusing the question as to just what Hegel is saying. The *Logic* starts out with the abstraction and absolutization of "pure being." Mere being is the most all-encompassing of categories. The initial premise in the dialectic may be expressed as the judgment that an entity, which we may call "a", exists:

1. Ea   Immediate Premise

But since no category other than being has yet been abstracted, being is absolutized, thus becoming "pure being." The absolutization of being amounts to the judgment not only that something has being, but also that whatever exists *merely* exists. 13 This last judgment is introduced as a conditional assumption:

2. $(x)(f)(fx \supset f = E)$ Assumption

In other words, what has any property has only the property of being. This absolutization of being, or more precisely of the class of entities which share in being, has the function of calling attention to the essential relativity of pure or indeterminate being to the particular, determinate types of being which serve to distinguish one entity from others. Being is a totally indeterminate property, but it is the indeterminate property of having or exemplifying determinate properties. Thus it is analytic that whatever exists has some determinate property other than mere being:

3. $(x)(Ex \equiv (\exists x)(fx \cdot f \neq E))$ Mediately Discovered Premise

It can be shown to follow from the assumption, together with the stated premises, that what merely exists does *not* exist. If to be is to be determinate, if to be is to be something in particular, then to merely be without being anything in particular is not to be at all. From line three, we conclude that there is some property of "a" other than mere existence:

4. $Ea \supset (\exists f)(fa \cdot f \neq E)$ 3, Univ. Instantiation
5. $(\exists f)(fa \cdot f \neq E)$ 1,4, Modus Ponens

Line five represents what we have called "abstraction of the other." But it also is possible to derive from the stated premises and assumption the negation of line five, the statement that there is no property of "a" other than mere existence:

6. $(f)(fa \supset f = E)$ 2, Univ. Instantiation
7. $Fa \cdot F \neq E$ 5, Existential Instantiation
8. $Fa \supset F = E$ 6, Universal Instantiation
9. Fa 7, Simplification
10. $F = E$ 8,9, Modus Ponens
11. $F \neq E \cdot Fa$ 7, Commutation
12. $F \neq E$ 11, Simplification
13. $F = E \; v \text{-}(\exists f)(fa \cdot f \neq E)$ 10, Addition
14. $\text{-}(\exists f)(fa \cdot f \neq E)$ 12,13, Disjunctive Syllogism

Line fourteen represents negation of the other. Self-negation, negation of the initial absolutization of the class of existing things, is now derived by indirect proof:

15. $(\exists x)(fa \cdot f \neq E) - (\exists x)(fa \cdot f \neq E)$ 5, 14, Conjunction
16. $-(x)(f) \cdot (fa \cdot f \neq E)$ 2-15, Indirect Proof.

Finally, negation of the negation emerges as the judgment that the entity "a" has existence in conjunction with properties other than mere existence:

17. $(x)(Ex \equiv (\exists f)(fx \cdot f \neq E))$ Mediately Discovered Premise
18. $Ea \equiv (\exists f)(fx \cdot f \neq E)$ 17, Univ. Instantiation
19. $[Ea \supset (\exists f)(fa - f \neq E)] - [(\exists f)(fa - fa - \neq E) \supset \exists a]$ 18, Equivalence
20. $Ea \supset (\exists f)(fx \cdot f \neq E)$ 19, Simplification
21. $(\exists f) \cdot (fa \cdot f \neq E)$ 1, 20 Modus Ponens
22. $Ea \cdot (\exists f)(fa \cdot f \neq E)$ 1, 21, Conjunction

The last line asserts that the entity "a" has determinate being. Since the denial that "a" has any other properties than being is, in view of the analysis of being given in line three, a denial of "a's" being, line fourteen is the derivation of the non-being of "a" from the assumption of "a's" *mere* being. We have here the famous passage from being to non-being. It will be noticed that becoming is not represented in our formalization by any single line. Becoming for Hegel is the passage from being to non-being conjoined with the reverse passage from non-being to being. This reverse passage is obtainable as a return to line two. Becoming is not logically essential to the dialectic at all, but is due to a merely possible return to the absolutization of indeterminate being and repetition of the derivation of non-being. But this return, we shall see, is required psychologically if not logically.

To this interpretation of becoming it may be objected that no past stage of the dialectic is ever exactly repeated. But Hegel explicitly says that becoming is a repetitive process.[14] Moreover, insofar as it is correctly maintained that no stage is repeated, this can only mean that no stage can be repeated within a single complete cycle of the dialectic. For Hegel describes philosophy as a circle; when the dialectic as a whole reaches completion, it *is* repeated. The principle that no stage of the dialectic is repeated short of the dialectic's completion is not violated by my interpretation of becoming so long as the process of being, including both going in and going out of being, is taken as a single

stage or "category" and not as a succession of stages. Becoming as here
interpreted illustrates the point that the sphere of being is distinguished from those of essence and the concept by fixation at the level
of absolutized finitude. (We might even speak here of "the absolutization of (abstract) absolutization.") The absolutization of what is relative, in this case of indeterminate being, is self-negated in the dialectic. The repetition of this absolutization, which we have seen entailed
by becoming, may be explained by this fixation. When thought runs
up against self-negation, it is both repelled by the self-negation and as
yet unfamiliar with negation of the negation. It thus returns to the se-
curity of dogmatic definiteness, to absolutized finitude, only to be
forced once more to experience the necessary negation of its position.

    The complexity of Hegel's exposition cannot be fully understood
unless it is recognized that the terms "being" and "nothing" change
meaning in its course. Hegel explicitly admits this.[15] "Being" starts
out meaning the same as indeterminateness", "nothing" (or "non-
being") accordingly meaning "determinateness". But when it transpires that in itself (as contrasted with what may be the case for
thought) being is identical with nothing, "nothing" has suddenly acquired the sense of "indeterminateness" and, by implication, "being"
has accordingly acquired the sense of "determinateness." (The statement that being is identical with nothing thus employs "being" in two
different senses, once explicitly and secondly by implication.) How are
we to account for these semantic shifts? From the initial Parmenidean
standpoint of pure being, non-being is identifiable with the sphere of
determinateness; what is, e.g., green as opposed to blue is, as such,
not being, i.e., non-being. But from the standpoint of the *disillusioned*
Parmenidean who recognizes pure indeterminate being's self-
contradictory inseparability from determinateness, it is Parmenidean
being itself which now presents itself as non-being. There is a shift in
subjective attitude towards what is wholly empty or indeterminate.
We move from an initial pro-attitude, which leads us to speak of "being", to a negative attitude, which makes us speak of "nothing". Thus
"being" and "nothing" may be so used that they are cognitively (or
conceptually) synonymous, but emotively non-synonymous. There
transpires in the dialectic an emotive shift against emptiness and indeterminateness. But with the transition to determinate being, still
another semantic shift occurs. Determinate being is, for Hegel, a

synthesis of being and non-being,[16] of indeterminate being and determinateness; this is the "rest" into which the repetitive process of becoming collapses. It is clear that "nothing" or "non-being" has here its original sense of determinateness or particularization once more. However, the emotive preference for determinateness is preserved as a permanent ingredient of the Hegelian position.

The statement "Being is identical with nothing" is based on an implicit absolutization of determinateness as exclusive "being". Thus the opening dialectic of the *Logic* must in its full complexity be represented by the following pattern, rather than the simpler one (page 224) considered thus far:

1. e	Abstraction
2. (e)	1, Absolutization
3. (e)o	2, Abstraction of Other
4. (e)/o	3, Negation of Other
5. (e)/(o)	4, Absolutization
6. (e)X(o)	5, Negation of Other
7. e-\(o)	6, Negation of the Negation
8. e—o	7, Negation of the Negation

In conclusion, I hope that what has been said serves to interest others in the task of examining further the translatability of dialectical logic into symbolic logic, both with reference to the dialectic of being and to other sections of the Hegelian opus. Finally, I would like to suggest that the really interesting questions have not been broached in this paper. The real interest of the dialectic of the organic whole, one could argue, is its spontaneous enactment in the course of much practical experience, both individual and collective.[17] If the thesis of this paper is correct, this may also constitute part of the real interest of symbolic logic.[18]

NOTES

1. *Hegel: A Re-interpretation* (New York: Doubleday, 1965), p. 160.

2. J. N. Findlay, *Hegel: A Re-Examination* (New York: Collier, 1962), p. 71.

3. Michael Kosok, "The Formalization of Hegel's Dialectical Logic," in *Hegel: A Collection of Critical Essays*, ed. A. MacIntyre (New York: Doubleday, 1972). See also the following ef-

forts at formalization: L. Apostel, "Logique et Dialectique," *Logique et Connaissance scientifique* (Paris: Gallimard, 1967); D. Dubarle and André Doz, *Logique et Dialectique* (Paris: Larousse, 1971); Y. Gauthier, "Logique hegelienne et formalisation," *Dialogue*, vol. VI, no. 2, 1967; G. Günther, "Das Problem einer Formalisierung der transzendental-dialektischen Logik, unter besonderer Berücksichtigung der Logik Hegels," *Heidelberger Hegel-Tage*, ed. H.-G. Gadamer (Bonn: Bouvier, 1964). These efforts all appeal to some formalism, whether appropriated from an existing branch of mathematics or contrived for the purpose, other than the standard formalism of quantification logic. I do not so much suggest that these formalizations fail as I raise the question as to whether they go beyond an external representation of dialectical logic to offer a form of comprehension in which dialectical thought is able to recognize itself. A liar, we know, may be truthfully represented to have misspoken; but he has not been comprehended until he has been represented as a liar.

4. That is, "existence" in the broadest sense of the term, as distinguished from the technical Hegelian sense.

5. I have defended such an analysis of the concept of existence, while attempting to show that it is in essential agreement with Quine's linguistic analysis in a paper entitled "On the Impossibility of Metaphysics without Ontology," (*Metaphilosophy*, Vol. 7 (1976) pp. 116-32. If the argument is successful, a certain common ground is established between Quine and the Hegelians.

6. That is, other than any given absolute. The negated other may be itself another alleged absolute. (See p. 329.)

7. But only so long as it is understood that it is the self (i.e., the original absolutization) which, by negating the other, calls forth upon itself the negation of itself by the other.

8. That is, the parentheses in the above schema (p. 320).

9. G. W. F. Hegel, *Phenomenology of Mind,* trans. J. B. Baillie (London: Allen and Unwin, 1931), p. 85.

10. *Ibid.,* p. 132.

11. *Ibid.,* p. 85.

12. G. W. F. Hegel, *Lectures on the History of Philosophy,* trans. E. S. Haldane and F. H. Simson (London: Routledge and Kegan Paul, 1955, 3 vols.), vol. I, pp. 261-78.

13. Note that by the identity of indiscernibles this absolutization implies the Parmenidean view that only one entity exists: "2."

14. G. W. F. Hegel, *The Logic of Hegel,* trans. W. Wallace (London: Oxford, 1873), p. 170.

15. G. W. F. Hegel, *The Science of Logic,* trans. A. V. Miller (London: Oxford, 1968), pp. 107-08.

16. *Ibid.,* pp. 109-10.

17. Some spontaneous enactments of the dialectic of the organic whole in the course of human experience are examined in two articles of mine: "On 'Hegelo-Freudianism,' " *Philosophy and Phenomenological Research*, Vol. 36 (1976), pp. 506-523 and "Technocratic Society and Its Counterculture: A Hegelian Analysis," *Inquiry*, Vol. 18 (1975), pp. 195-212.

18. For a longer version of this paper incorporating some replies to the commentary by Professor Findlay which follows, see "On the Reducibility of Dialectical to Standard Logic," *The Personalist*, Vol. 56 (1975), pp. 414-31.

COMMENT

J. N. FINDLAY

Mr. Butler has made a praiseworthy attempt to show that Hegel's dialectical proceedings do not really violate the canons of formal logic, and can even be expressed with such formalism. I think that Mr. Butler has in part succeeded. For obviously a negation that can be joined with its contradictory affirmation in a rational reconciliation is not a negation in the formal-logical sense, but some other sort of negation altogether, and so does not really violate but by-passes the ordinary formal logical laws. And obviously too the moves of the dialectic which lead to this sort of novel combination of affirmation and negation involve no negation and contradiction in the ordinary senses of these terms. A certain way of affirming a certain content breaks down because it involves its own negation, which in its turn breaks down because it involves the contradictory affirmation, and we are then forced to seek a way out of this whole imbroglio by having recourse to the new type of reconcilable contradiction. This "breaking down" process obviously is a case of indirect proof and involves the rejection of an assertion because it involves a contradiction in the ordinary sense of the word. Mr. Butler revives the view of Edward Caird in his manual on Hegel that Hegel does not violate but builds on the law of non-contradiction, and that his reconcilable contradictions merely mean to assert the necessary *relations* of certain propositions which are distinct and opposed, but not exclusive and contradictory. I do not think, however, that Mr. Butler has done justice to the profound difference between Hegel's extraordinary sense of reconcilable negation and the ordinary exclusive sense which he also uses, and the formal strangeness of seeing a formal contradiction in the isolated, exclusive assertion of either p or not-p, and yet no formal contradiction in the compound statement of both. And I also do not think he has thought out the extraordinary character of the Hegelian conception of an Identity which is reconcilable with Difference as opposed to the ordinary formal conception which is not. It seems plain that, even if the queerness of the Hegelian negation and identity is acknowledged, Mr. Butler's formalization fails to generate perfectly the content of each stage of the dialectic. He may be able to provide a pattern which it fits, but this pattern will not be able to arrive at the content which fits it, or develop it out of a given beginning. New propositions have to be dragged in *ab extra*, and the whole proceeding does not amount to what I should call a formalization in which axioms, definitions and rules determine the whole course and content of derivations.

I may say at the start that I should not be bracketed with Walter Kaufmann as a minimalist in my interpretation of the dialectic. Though I said in the first edition of my book that I regarded the triadic pattern of the dialectic as no more a method than the *terza rima* of Dante's *Divine Comedy,* I wrote a long note in the second edition explaining that Hegel *did* throughout follow a method of higher-order comment, which at each new step's onset asserts what was true of the content one had had before and so was implied by it, but was not explicitly part of its content. Thus the assertion of the Absolute, as simply being being, really asserts what is asserted by saying that it is simply Nothing, though it does not *mean* to do so. (I am in the position of seeming to disagree with Mr. Butler in his analysis of the dialectic with propositions or assertions while Hegel treats *Begriffe* or Notions; one can, however, propositionalize these by making them assertions about the Absolute.) Mr. Butler goes on to say that he differs from myself in making the progress of the dialectic inferentially necessary. But whether I deny the progress of the dialectic to be inferential depends on the sense given to "inferential". If seeing what is undoubtedly true of assertions is inferential, (i.e., seeing that it is a case of its opposite, that it requires a certain completion), then I undoubtedly believe that the progress of the dialectic is inferential; it certainly develops what a notion implies in virtue of being the notion that it is. But if "inferential" means that each higher-order comment is the *only* higher-level comment that can be made on that notion at a given stage, and that other implications of its content cannot be explored, then I do not believe that the progress of the dialectic is inferential, since I do think it could have taken a different course, and that there is an element of choice or arbitrariness in making it take a certain course. I believe the dialectic to resemble in some ways a Chinese jig-saw puzzle in which one could piece element with element in very different ways ending up always with the same picture or color-pattern. But as the ordinary sense of "inference" allows one to prove the same theorem in different ways, I fail to see that I am denying the inferential character of the dialectic. Plainly, however, it is not inferential in the sense of being perfectly determined by inferential rules. For it is a matter of direct insight that makes us see what a notion implies for its complete viability, and this insight is specific and differs from case to case. It also always goes beyond the content of its premises. I do not, however, think that Mr. Butler disagrees with me on this point, as it is by a necessary, direct discovery that he makes progress at certain crucial points. He does not uniformly proceed by inference in the rule-governed sense of the word.

I turn to Mr. Butler's set of rules of dialectical logic. The first rule is the rule of Abstraction, which he tells us is not a rule of inference since it provides us with an underived beginning for inference; it is what Carnap would call a rule for deriving something from the null class or total absence of premises. But Mr. Butler's statement of this rule is not formal: the rule says that we may affirm that any thought-referent abstracted from experience exists through the possession or instantiation of the property by the instance from which it was abstracted. This account is unsatisfactory since plainly thought-referents may be simple thought-contents, e.g. beauty, which *are* properties rather than *have* them, and the existence involved is plainly the

Aussersein of Meinong, since being a round square is plainly a definite thought-content and also a referent. From the rule of Abstraction Mr. Butler proceeds to the rule of Absolutization, again stated metalogically. Any thought-content may be held as conditionally being all there is, and as being without relation to anything other than itself. It seems to me that Mr. Butler is here doing a strange thing formally: explicitly allowing me to make a conditional assertion which may afterwards be rejected. In ordinary formal logic one can assert a contradiction (e.g.,p.~p)conditionally and then show, e.g., that it would entail anything and everything, including its own falsehood, but there is no rule explicitly *permitting* one to assert a contradiction. How can one be explicitly permitted to assert what afterwards turns out to be disallowed? I also think that the absolutization required is merely a *capacity* for being all there is, i.e., Hegel supposes that some content *can* be conceived without context in order to show that it cannot. A content could be absolute if there were other contents, provided it could exist in their absence: it need not be all-encompassing. Mr. Butler goes on to say that every thought-content is discovered on reflection to be internally related to some other thought-content: it is not the same as this second thought-content, but it cannot *be* if the other content is not there to supplement it. This need of supplementation by another content is taken by Mr. Butler to be what Hegel means by Identity in Difference. Mr. Butler says the rule of Internal Relation is a Rule of Discovery—it does not tell us *what* supplement a content will require, but it tells us that *some* supplement is needed, and leads us to look for one and to find it, such a supplement being seen as necessary to the first content. Rule Four now tells us that the absolutized first content, having been credited with absolute independence, must necessarily reject the internally related supplement which is offered to satisfy Rule Three, and this leads (Rule Five) to its own self-rejection, since if it rejects what is its necessary supplement it rejects itself. (Mr. Butler's argument is more complex; this covers its essentials.) We have now simply (Rule Six) to replace the Absolutized content which needs its supplement, and whose supplement needs it, by a relativized content which encompasses its supplement. This new relativized content may then be absolutized, but may also require a further supplement, and the conflict is resolved by again de-absolutizing the content, and repeating the same process indefinitely.

I have several comments to make on this account. First, that it in no sense resembles an ordinary set of formal rules of inference. It explicitly permits conditional assertions which are afterwards rejected, it tells us to look for supplements without telling us how to find them, and it makes indirect proof obligatory whereas in other systems it is optional. My second comment is that Hegel does not conceive of dialectical development as a new addition of supplements which are distinct but inseparable. He holds that we cannot successfully hold apart the inseparable items he distinguishes, that they lose themselves in one another or pass into one another, that they are genuinely the same though different. Hegel is not content to think in terms of inseparability: he wishes to *deny* difference as it is ordinarily conceived. He again and again repudiates the *insofar* way of having it: X insofar as it is A is M; insofar as it is B is not M, etc. He asserts that this is an illegitimate subterfuge. It is the undivided X which is at once M and not-M. I think it plain that Hegel is not simply conforming to the ordinary notions of identity and negation, he is both trying to use them and then abandoning them as unusable, while still retaining something which is their ghost. We are to believe in an otherness which is only an attempted alienation, and a negation which only tries to negate: the attempt necessarily fails, but it remains a failed attempt, and so preserves the sense that it has been unable to fulfill. These procedures of radical conceptual revision are alien to formal logic: its diversities do not change into identities, nor its negations into their negations. One might take the later view of Stace that Hegelian reason is not really reasonable, but is a mystically motivated abandonment of reason. I do not take this view since I think that our thought perpetually oscillates from hard-and-fastness to fluidity, the first fluid element becoming a new element of hard-and-fastness and so on. Identity and difference are, I think, systematically ambiguous, and the one kind of them is perpetually turning into the other. This is rational thought, but it is not formal logic, though it does not conflict with it. My third comment is that Mr. Butler has ignored the *übergreifende*, overreaching character of the dialectic. Aspects are not merely integrated into a neutral whole, but one of them *absorbs* the other. Thus subjectivity overreaches objectivity. One of the aspects of the whole is both itself and its other, which does not return the compliment. For example, Hegel speaks of the identity of identity and difference, not the difference of identity and difference. Somehow, however, this overreaching character is paradoxically shared by many aspects: thus the various elements in a necessitating causal nexus are not merely elements in the whole. Each *is* the whole, and contains all the other aspects within itself. This is what Hegel means by totality, which is more a Leibnizian than a Spinozistic concept. But deep and true as it is, it cannot be assimilated to formal logic. I think Mr. Butler recognizes this on page 230 where he acknowledges that he is not preserving the absoluteness of his distinguished aspects in their final reconciliation, and that their sense is therefore being altered. I should say that, as in modalized statements, the original sense is after a sense preserved, but preserved with brackets which modify it. If this is confusing, then it is truth which thus confuses.

I shall now comment very briefly on Mr. Butler's attempt to expound all his principles in the symbolic dialect. I cannot regard the formulations of Absolutization as satisfactory. Hegel does not believe in three categories of classes, instances and properties, and an instance is not absolutized if it is the only instance of a property F, nor is a property absolutized if it is the only property of an instance a. As regards the possibility of there being a unique class with a unique member determined by a unique property, I do not know what to think of it, and it presupposes concepts of formal identity and diversity I find obscure. What would it mean for there to be only one class? This is plainly only possible if nothing at all exists. What would it mean for a unique class to have only one member? If it were the null-class it could have no members. And what would it mean for a unique member to have only one property? On one sense of property there necessarily are other equivalent properties, e.g., ϕ and not-not ϕ, etc. And if properties are identical if they have coincident extensions, then all properties are identical. I think all this requires clarification. The symbolization does not illuminate it, but only gives one a headache. The mediately discovered premises are simply new axioms. Symbolization is worthwhile only if it also mechanizes, if it works automatically once one starts it going. Mr. Butler's symbolization does not.

Mr. Butler goes on finally to consider the first famous triad in the *Logic*: Being, Nothing and Becoming. Here we start by saying of everything that it merely is. We then drag in the analytically necessary premise that whatever is also is something more than merely being, which entails that what merely is, really is not. We then infer by a long series of steps, some of which excite scepticism, that if anything is, it is not merely, and that it therefore is something other than and more than simply being. It seems to me that Mr. Butler has walked in a valid but not very interesting circle; he has assumed that to be one must do more than be, and has then shown that this refutes the assumption of possible mere being which conflicts with it. But why not prove the reality of mere being by refuting the more than being that conflicts with it? Plainly, it seems to me it is not formalization but insight which shows us that the belief in mere being is empty and that the belief in more than mere being is to be accepted.

In his interpretation Mr. Butler has ignored Becoming and I agree with him that it is not necessary to the dialectical progress. He also mentions that the notions of Being and Non-Being alter their sense in the course of the argument. I agree that they do, but I think that this shows that the argument cannot be successfully formalized.

In conclusion may I say that Mr. Butler's paper is interesting because it grapples with the real essentials of Hegel's method and tries to understand them instead of merely describing them. He has used formalization to assist understanding. I believe, however, that Hegel's concepts, if they are concepts, are essentially iridescent: they change color as one considers them, and vanish if one fixes them. This means I think that one cannot formalize them except externally and superficially. But it is worth trying to do so. Mr. Butler has tried hard and well.

Bibliography
by
JOSEPH C. FLAY

The following bibliography is devoted to works in the secondary literature which are devoted entirely or for the most part either to Hegel's aesthetics or to his logic. In the case of the former category, I have considered not only studies of his *Lectures on the Philosophy of Art* but as well works which deal with his aesthetics in the *Phenomenology of Spirit* or the *Lectures on the Philosophy of Religion* or the *Encyclopedia of the Philosophical Sciences*. In the case of studies of his logic, I have limited myself to the logical works themselves, i.e., either of the *Science of Logic*, the *Logic* of the *Encyclopedia,* or the early attempts at a *Logic*. I have not included general studies of the dialectic or of the logic of his thought in general. In the case of both aesthetics and logic I have eliminated for the most part general introductions or studies of his thought which deal in passing with these two topics.

The works are arranged alphabetically by author and then by title, and again are largely limited to the languages of English, German, French, Spanish, Italian, and Dutch. I have tried to list works appearing in major journals and from major publishing houses. The entries in Spanish, Italian, and Dutch are markedly less complete than those in the other languages. This should be remedied when the larger bibliography is published.

I wish to thank the Department of Philosophy and the College of the Liberal Arts Fund for Research of the Pennsylvania State University for the released time and monies which have made my bibliographical research possible. I also especially acknowledge the contributions of Mr. Michael DeArmey to the general bibliography early in my search of the literature. Finally, I wish to express my thanks to the graduate research assistants who over the years have helped me in the search of the literature.

STUDIES OF HEGEL'S AESTHETICS

1. Antoni, Carlo. "L'estetica di Hegel," *Giornale Critica della Filosofia Italiana,* 1960 (14), 1-22.

2. Aslanow, A. M. "Das Künstlerische Schaffen Orientvölker in der Ästhetik von Hegel," *Hegel-Jahrbuch,* 1971, 249-59.

3. Assunto, Rosario. "Le relazioni fra arte e filosofia nella *Philosophie der Kunst* di Schelling e nelle *Vorlesungen über die Ästhetik* di Hegel," *Hegel-Jahrbuch,* 1965, 84-121.

4. Axelos, Christos. "Zu Hegels Interpretation der Tragödie," *Zeitschrift für Philosophische Forschung,* 1965 (19), 655-67.

5. Bartling, D. "Het Schoone en de Kunst in het Stelsel van Hegel en in de Gedachtengangen van Bierens de Hann;" *Algemeen Nederlands Tijdschrift voor Wijsbegeerte en Psychologie,* 1944 (37), n. 2, 26-43.

6. Bartsch, Heinrich. *Register zu Hegels Vorlesungen über die Ästhetik.* Mainz, Fabersche Buchhandlung, 1844.

7. Basch, Victor. "Des origines et des fondements de l'*Esthétique* de Hegel," *Revue de Métaphysique et de Morale,* 1931 (38), 341-66.

8. Bassenge, Friedrich. "Hegels Aesthetik und das Allgemeinmenschliche," *Deutsche Zeitschrift für Philosophie,* 1956 (4), 540-58.

9. Bauer, Bruno. *Hegels Lehre von der Religion und Kunst von dem Standpunkt des Glaubens aus beurteilt.* Leipzig, O. Wigand, 1842.

10. Bénard, Charles. "Analytical and Critical Essay upon the Aesthetics of Hegel," *Journal of Speculative Philosophy,* 1867 (1), 36-52, 91-114, 169-76, 220-24; 1868-1869 (2), 39-46, 157-64; 1869 (3), 31-46, 147-66, 281-88, 317-36.

11. Bense, M. "Die Aktualität der hegelschen Ästhetik, anlässlich der Ausgabe von G. Lukacs," *Texte und Zeichen,* 1957 (11), 76-84.

12. Bertrand, Pierre. "Le sens du tragique et du destin dans la dialectique hégélienne," *Revue de Métaphysique et de Morale,* 1940 (47), 165-86.

13. Biemel, Walter. "La estética de Hegel," *Convivium,* 1962, n. 13-14, 147-62.

14. Blocker, Gene. "Hegel on Aesthetic Internationalization," *British Journal of Aesthetics,* 1971 (11), 341-53.

15. Boatright, Mody Coggin. "Whitman and Hegel," in *Studies in English* (University of Texas Bulletin), 1929 (9), 134-50.

16. Bodei, R. "Il primo romanticismo come fenomeno storico e la filosofia di Solger nell'analisi di Hegel," *Aut Aut,* 1967 (101), 68-80.

17. Bohler, M. J. "Die Bedeutung Schillers für Hegels Ästhetik," *Publications of the Modern Language Association of America,* 1972 (87), 182-91.

18. Bosanquet, Bernard. "On Croce's Conception of the 'Death of Art' in Hegel," *Proceedings of the British Academy,* 1919-1920 (9), 280-88.

19. Bradley, A. C. "Hegel's Theory of Tragedy," *Hibbert Journal,* 1903-04 (2), 662-80.

20. Brelet, Gisèle. "Hegel et la musique moderne," *Hegel-Jahrbuch,* 1965, 10-26.

21. _____ . "Temps historique et temps musical chez Hegel," *Hegel-Jahrbuch,* 1968-1969, 444-51.

22. Brissoni, Armando. *Richerche sull'estética di Hegel.* Padova, Liviana, 1968.

23. Brocker, Walter. "Hegels Philosophie der Kunstgeschichte," in *Auseinandersetzungen mit Hegel* (Wissenchaft und Gegenwart, 30), 33-57. Frankfurt am Main, 1965.

24. Bryant, W. M. "Hegel's Aesthetics," *Journal of Speculative Philosophy,* 1879 (13), 399-403.

25. Bukofzer, Manfred. "Hegels Musikästhetik," in *Deuxième Congrès International d'Esthétique et de Science de l'Art,* II, 1937, 32-35.

26. Cantillo, Giuseppe. "L'Arte nella filosofia dello spirito della *Jenaer Realphilosophie,*" *Il Pensiero,* 1970 (15), 153-97.

27. Carritt, Edgar Frederick. "Intellectualist Theories: Hegel," in *The Theory of Beauty,* 149-78. London, Methuen & Co., Ltd., 1928.

28. Chalybaeus, Heinrich Moritz. *Historical Development of Speculative Philosophy from Kant to Hegel,* trans. Alfred Edersheim. Edinburgh, 1854.

29. Cordua, Carla. "El Arte y la prosa del mundo," *Dialogos* (Puerto Rico), 1973 (9), n. 25, 7-32.

30. Croce, Benedetto. "La 'fine dell' arte' nel sistema hegeliano," *La Critica,* 1934 (32), 425-34.

31. D'Hondt, Jacques. "Meurtre dans la cathédrale. La significa-tion de l'art chrétien selon Forster et Hegel," *Revue d'Esthétique,* 1963 (16), 261-89.

32. _____. "Problèmes de la religion esthétique," *Hegel-Jahrbuch,* 1964, 34-48.

33. Danzel, Theodor Wilhelm. "Über den gegenwärtigen Zustand der Philosophie der Kunst und ihre nächste Aufgabe," *Zeitschrift für Philosophie und Spekulative Theologie,* 1844 (12), 201-42; 1845 (14), 161-207; 1845 (15), 192-248.

34. _____. *Ueber die Ästhetik der Hegelschen Philosophie.* Hamburg, J. A. Meissner, 1844.

35. De Sanctis, Francesco. "Critica del principio dell' esthetica hegeliana," in *Pagine sparse.* Bari, G. Laterza & Figli, 1934.

36. Döderlein, Johann Ludwig. "Hegel und die Aufgabe der Musikphilosophie," *Hegel-Jahrbuch,* 1965, 65-69.

37. Domke, Helmut Georg. *Grundfragen der Hegelschen Kunstphilosophie.* Lengerich, W. Lengericher Handelsdruckerei, 1939.

38. Dulckeit-von Arnim, Christa. "Hegels Kunstphilosophie," *Philosophisches Jahrbuch,* 1958 (67), 285-304.

39. Fehr, Bernhard. "Walter Pater und Hegel," *Englische Studien* (Leipzig), 1916-1917 (50), 300-08.

40. Fischer, Ernst. "Die Zukunft der Kunst," *Hegel-Jahrbuch,* 1965, 154-64.

41. Flam, Leopold. "Poetische existentie en prozaische werkelij-kheid bij Hegel," *Dialoog,* 1970-1971 (11), 1-65.

42. Formigari, Lia. "Hegel e l'estetica dell' Illuminismo," *De Homine,* 1963 (5-6), 473-81.

43. Frömbgen-Essen, Hanns. "Hegel und die musikalische Romantik. Die Erhellung der Musik durch die Philosophie," *Die Musik,* 1928-1929 (21), 650-57.

44. Frost, Walter. *Hegels Aesthetik.* Die bedeutendste Kunstphilosophie der neueren Zeit in ihrer Beziehung zum modernen Menschen. München, E. Reinhardt, 1928.

45. Girardot, Rafael Gutierrez. "Hegel y lo tragico," *Sur,* 1964, n. 287, 73-86.

46. Girnus, Wilhelm. "Volksgeist und Kunst (Herder, Goethe, Hegel)," *Hegel-Jahrbuch,* 1965, 70-83.

47. Glockner, Hermann. "Die Ästhetik in Hegels System," in

Verhandlungen des zweiten Hegelkongresses (1932), 149-67.

48. Grubich, Hans. *Die Stellung der Ästhetik im Hegelschen System und ihre Verhältnis zur Religionsphilosophie.* Hohensalza, Kujawischer Bote, 1913.

49. Guzzo, Augusto. "Hegel e la musica," in *Idealisti ed empiristi.* Firenze, Vallecchi, 1935.

50. _____. "Hegel e la pittura," *La Cultura,* 1924-1925 (4), 345-48.

51. _____. "Hegel e la poesia," *La Cultura,* 1921-1922 (1), 439-47.

52. _____. "Hegel e la scultura," *La Cultura,* 1922-1923 (2), 541-51.

53. _____. *Studi su l'estetica di Giorgio Hegel.* Napoli, Detken e Roeholl, 1919.

54. _____. "La triade dialettica 'arte, religione, filosofia'," *Rivista di estetica,* 1960 (5), 5-14.

55. Hahn, Peter. "Kunst zwischen Ideologie und Utopie; Studien über die theoretischen Möglichkeiten eines gesellschaftsbezogenen Kunstbegriffs," in *Literaturwissenschaft und Sozialwissenschaften,* 151-234. Stuttgart, 1971.

56. Harries, Karsten. "Hegel on the Future of Art," *Review of Metaphysics,* 1973-1974 (27), 677-96.

57. Hartmann, Jürgen. "Der Humor, dargestellt nach kunstphilosophischen Erwägungen Hegels. Ein Vortrag," *Jahrbuch für Ästhetik und allgemeine Kunstwissenschaft* (Köln), 1963 (8), 215-25.

58. Hegenberg, Leonidas. "A poesia e a prosa na *Estética* de Hegel," *Kriterion,* 1959 (12), 327-36.

59. Heimann, Betty. *Hegels ästhetische Anschauungen.* Strassburg, DuMont Schauberg, 1916.

60. Heimsoeth, Heinz. "Zum Begriff des 'Romantischen' in Hegels Ästhetik," *Studia estetzczne* (Warszawa), 1967 (4), 87-98.

61. _____. "Hegels Philosophie der Musik," *Hegel-Studien,* 1963 (2), 161-201.

62. Heise, Wolfgang. "Gedanken zu Hegels Konzeption des Komischen und der Komödie," *Hegel-Jahrbuch,* 1966, 8-31.

63. Henrich, Dieter. "Kunst und Kunstphilosophie der Gegenwart (Überlegungen mit Rücksicht auf Hegel)," in *Immanente Ästhetik— ästhetische Reflexion. Lyrik als Paradigma der Moderne,* hrsg. W. Iser, 11-32. München, 1966.

64. Hettner, Hermann. "Gegen die spekulative Ästhetik," in *Kleine Schriften,* 164-208. Braunschweig, F. Vieweg und Sohn, 1884.

65. Hirt, E. "Hegels Geschichtsphilosophie und der Geist der Poesie," in *Dichtung und Forschung.* Festschrift für Emil Ermatinger, hrsg. W. Muschg und R. Hunziker, 138-61. Frauenfeld/Leipzig, Huber & Co. Aktiengesellschaft, 1933.

66. Hoffmeister, J. "Hegel und Creuzer," *Deutsche Vierteljahrsschrift für Literaturwissenschaft und Geistesgeschichte,* 1930 (8), 260-82.

67. Hofstadter, Albert. "Art: Death and Transfiguration. A Study in Hegel's Theory of Romanticism," *Review of National Literatures,* 1970 (1), 149-64.

68. Honegger, Rudolf. "Goethe und Hegel. Eine literar-historische Untersuchung," *Jahrbuch der Goethe-Gesellschaft,* 1925 (11), 38-111.

69. Horn, András. *Kunst und Freiheit.* Eine kritische Interpretation der Hegelschen Ästhetik. Den Haag, Martinus Nijhoff, 1969.

70. Jones, Rhys S. "Hegel and French Symbolism. Some Observations on the 'Hegelianism' of Paul Valéry," *French Studies* (Oxford), 1950 (4), 142-50.

71. Kainz, Howard P. "Hegel's Theory of Aesthetics in the *Phenomenology,*" *Idealistic Studies,* 1972 (2), 81-94.

72. Kaminsky, Jack. *Hegel On Art.* An Interpretation of Hegel's Aesthetics. Albany, N.Y., State University of New York, 1962.

73. Kaufmann, Walter. "Hegel's Ideas about Tragedy," in *New Studies in Hegel's Philosophy,* ed. Warren E. Steinkraus, 201-20. New York, Holt, Rinehart, & Winston, 1971.

74. Kedney, John Steinfort. *Hegel's Aesthetics.* A Critical Exposition. Chicago, Griggs and Co., 1892.

75. Kerkoff, M. "Hegel sobre arte simbólico e imaginación simbolizante," *Dialogos,* 1970 (7), n. 20, 101-23.

76. Knox, Israel. *The Aesthetic Theories of Kant, Hegel, and Schopenhauer.* New York, Columbia University Press, 1936.

77. Kogan, Jacobo. "Filosofía y poesia en Heidegger y en Hegel," *Cuadernos Americanos,* 1967 (26), n. 2, 106-32.

78. Kohn, J. "Hegels Aesthetik," *Zeitschrift für Philosophie und Philosophische Kritik,* 1902 (120), 160-86.

79. Kouzel, Daisy Fornacca. "The Hegelian Influence in the Literary Criticism of Francesco De Sanctis," *Review of National Literatures,*

1970 (1), 214-31.

80. Krenzlin, Norbert. "Bürgerliche Ideologieentwicklung und ästhetische Theorie. Untersucht an der phänomenologischen Konzeption der Ästhetik," *Deutsche Zeitschrift für Philosophie,* 1969 (17), 1285-1309.

81. Kuhn, Helmut. "Hegels Ästhetik als System des Klassizismus," *Archiv für Geschichte der Philosophie,* 1931 (40), 90-105.

82. _____. *Die Vollendung der klassischen deutschen Ästhetik durch Hegel* (Die Kulturfunktion der Kunst, 1). Berlin, Junker, 1931.

83. Lauener, Henri. *Die Sprache in der Philosophie Hegels mit besonderer Berücksichtigung der Ästhetik.* Bern, Haupt, 1962.

84. Levèque, Charles. *La science du beau, étudiée dans ses principes, dans ses applications et dans son histoire.* Paris, A. Durand, 1861.

85. Lewkowitz, Albert. *Hegels Aesthetik im Verhältnis zu Schiller.* Leipzig, Dürr, 1910.

86. Linden, Walter. *Solger und Hegel.* Hamburg, 1938.

87. Lissa, Zofia. "Die Prozessualität der Musik," *Hegel-Jahrbuch,* 1965, 27-38.

88. Lucas, R. S. "Hegel und die Abstraktion. Ein Beitrag zur Problematik der modernen Kunst," *Deutsche Vierteljahrschrift für Literaturwissenschaft und Geistesgeschichte,* 1964 (38), 361-87.

89. _____. "A Problem in Hegel's Aesthetics," *Renaissance and Modern Studies* (Nottingham), 1960 (4), 82-118.

90. Lukacs, Georg. "Hegels Ästhetik," *Sinn und Form,* 1953 (5), n. 6, 17-58.

91. Mann, Michael. "H. Heine and G. W. F. Hegel zur Musik," *Monatshefte für Deutschen Unterricht,* 1962 (54), 343-53.

92. Maslin, A. N. "Die Ästhetik Hegels und die Gedanken der russischen revolutionären Demokraten des XIX Jahrhunderts," *Hegel-Jahrbuch,* 1964, 82-89.

93. Massolo, Arturo. "Hegel e la tragedia greca," *Studi Urbinati,* 1971 (45), 1272-75.

94. Mitchells, Kurt. "Zukunftsfragen der Kunst im Lichte von Hegels Ästhetik," *Hegel-Jahrbuch,* 1965, 142-53.

95. Mitin, M. B. "Hegel's Aesthetics in the Perspective of Our Day," *Soviet Studies in Philosophy,* 1965 (3), n. 4, 21-31.

96. Moos, Paul. *Die Philosophie der Musik von Kant bis Eduard von Hartmann. Ein Jahrhundert deutscher Geistesarbeit.* Berlin, 1901.

97. Morawski, Stefan. "Hegels Ästhetik und das 'Ende der Kunstperiode'," *Hegel-Jahrbuch,* 1964, 60-71.

98. Morpurgo-Tagliabue, Guido. "Attualita dell' estetica hegeliana," *Il Pensiero,* 1962 (7), 82-106.

99. _____. "L'estetica di Hegel, oggi," *De Homine,* 1963 (5-6), 463-72.

100. Moss, Leonard. "The Unrecognized Influence of Hegel's Theory of Tragedy," *The Journal of Aesthetics and Art Criticism,* 1969-1970 (28), 91-97.

101. Mouloud, N. "Forme, sens et dialectique dans l'esthétique de Hegel," *Revue d'Esthétique,* 1963 (16), 33-63.

102. Müller, Gustav E. "The Function of Aesthetics in Hegel's Philosophy," *The Journal of Aesthetics and Art Criticism,* 1946 (5), 49-53.

103. _____. "Solger's Aesthetics. A Key to Hegel (Irony and Dialectic)," in *Corona.* Commemorative Essays for Samuel Singer, 212-27. Durham, North Carolina, 1941.

104. Müller, Joachim. "Hegel und die Theorie des Romans," *Wissenschaftliche Zeitschrift der Friedrich-Schiller-Universität Jena,* (Gesellschaft- und Sprachwissenschaftliche Reihe), 1970 (19), 637-44.

105. Mundt, Theodor. *Ästhetik.* Die Idee der Schönheit und des Kunstwerkes im Lichte unserer Zeit. Berlin, 1845.

106. Nadler, Käte. "Die Idee des Tragischen bei Hegel," *Deutsche Vierteljahrschrift für Literaturwissenschaft und Geistesgeschichte,* 1941 (19), 354-68.

107. Negri, Antimo. "Estetica e dialettica in Hegel," *Logos* (Napoli), 1969 (1), 510-59.

108. _____. "Hegel ed il barocco della borghesia protestante," *Rivista di Estetica,* 1970 (15), 23-48.

109. _____. "La similitudine nella poesia drammatica secondo Hegel," *Rivista di Estetica,* 1960 (5), 105-12.

110. Nowak, Adolf. *Hegels Musikästhetik.* Regensburg, Gustav-Bosse-Verlag, 1971.

111. Oelmüller, Willi. "Hegels Satz vom Ende der Kunst und das Problem der Philosophie der Kunst nach Hegel," *Philosophisches Jahrbuch,* 1965-1966 (73), 75-94.

112. Orsini, Napoleone. "De Sanctis, Hegel e la 'situazione poetica'," *Civilta Moderna,* 1942 (14), 138-40.

113. Orsiannikov, M. F. and Srednii, D. D. "Hegel's Esthetics and the Contemporary Struggle of Ideas," *Soviet Studies in Philosophy*, 1970-1971 (9), n. 4, 374-93.

114. Paolucci, Anne. "Bradley and Hegel on Shakespeare," *Comparative Literature*, 1964 (16), 211-25.

115. Paolucci, Henry. "The Poetics of Aristotle and Hegel," *Review of National Literatures*, 1970 (1), 165-213.

116. Patočka, Jan. "Die Lehre von der Vergangenheit der Kunst," in *Beispiele*. Festschrift für Eugen Fink zum 60. Geburtstag, hrsg. L. Landgrebe, 46-61. Den Haag, Martinus Nijhof, 1965.

117. _____. "Zur Entwicklung der ästhetischen Auffassung Hegels," *Hegel-Jahrbuch*, 1964, 49-59.

118. Patri, Aimé. "En relisant l'*Esthétique* de Hegel," *Monde Nouveau Paru*, 1954 (10), n. 80-81, 132-36.

119. Petruzzellis, Nicola. "L'estetica hegeliana," in *L'estetica dell' idealismo*. Padova, CEDAM, 1942.

120. Pierola, Rául Alberto. "El destino del arte en el sistema de Hegel," in *Actas ex Facultad de Ciencias Culturales y Artes* (Tucuman), 1949 (1), 93-100.

121. _____. *Hegel y la estética* (Cuadernos de filosofia, 1956 (10)). Universidad Nacional de Tucuman, Instituto de Filosofia, 1956.

122. _____. "La subordinación del arte a la filosofia en la estética de Hegel," *Congresso Internacional de Filosofia*, 1954, III, 1035-38.

123. Pöggeler, Otto. "Hegel und die griechische Tragödie," Hegel-Studien, Beiheft 1, 285-305.

124. Puglisi, Filippo. *L'estetica di Hegel e i suoi presupposti teoretici*. Padova, CEDAM, 1953.

125. Reese, H. "Hegel über die Darstellung Christi in der Malerei," *Jahrbuch für die Evangelisch-Lutherische Landeskirche Bayerns*, 1892, 22-32.

126. Rehder, Helmut. "Of Structure and Symbol: The Significance of Hegel's *Phenomenology* for Literary Criticism," in *A Hegel Symposium*, ed. D. C. Travers, 115-37. Austin, Texas, The Department of Germanic Languages, The University of Texas, 1962.

127. Ripalda, Jose María. "Poesie und Politik beim frühen Hegel," *Hegel-Studien*, 1973 (8), 91-118.

128. Robert, Bernard-Paul. "Breton, Hegel et le surréel," *Revue de l'Université d'Ottawa*, 1974 (44), 44-48.

129. Rohrmoser, Günter. "Schiller et Hegel. La réconciliation esthétique," *Archives de Philosophie,* 1960 (23), 186-206.

130. ———. "Zum Problem der ästhetischen Versöhnung. Schiller und Hegel," *Euphorion,* 1959 (53), 351-66.

131. Rosenstein, Leon. "Metaphysical Foundations of the Theories of Tragedy in Hegel and Nietzsche," *The Journal of Aesthetics and Art Criticism,* 1970 (28), 521-33.

132. Rüsen, Jorn. "Die Vernunft der Kunst. Hegels geschichtsphilosophische Analyse der Selbsttranszendierung des Ästhetischen in der modernen Welt," *Philosophisches Jahrbuch,* 1973 (80), 292-319.

133. Russo, Salvatore. "Hegel's Theory of Tragedy," *Open Court,* 1936 (50), 133-44.

134. Sabatini, Angelo. "La 'morte dell' arte' in Hegel e la critica come momento costitutivo della poesia contemporanea," *De Homine,* 1963 (5-6), 482-500.

135. Salditt, Maria. *Hegels Shakespeare-Interpretation.* Berlin, J. Springer, 1927.

136. Schultheis, Bernd. "Zur Voraussetzungsproblematik der Ästhetik Hegels," *Wiener Jahrbuch für Philosophie,* 1970 (3), 223-34.

137. Schultz, Werner. "Die Bedeutung des Tragischen fur das Verstehen der Geschichte bei Hegel und Goethe," *Archiv für Kulturgeschichte,* 1956 (38), 92-115.

138. Schwarz, Balduin. "Die Zukunft der Kunst—Hegel und Newman," *Hegel-Jahrbuch,* 1965, 122-41.

139. Seidman, Isidor. *Hebbels Beziehungen zu Hegels Ästhetik.* Breslau, Druck der Breslauer Genossenschafts-Buchdruckerei, 1927.

139a. Steinkraus, Warren. "The Place of Art in Hegel's System," *Pakistan Philosophical Journal,* 1972 (10), 41-51.

140. Steinkrueger, W. A. *Die Asthetik der Musik bei Schelling und Hegel.* Ein Beitrag zur Musikästhetik der Romantik. Bonn, 1927.

141. Stoikov, Athanas. "Hegel et le destin de l'art," *Hegel-Jahrbuch,* 1971, 268-72.

142. Sutcliffe, F. E. "Hegel et Valéry," *French Studies* (Oxford), 1952 (6), 53-57.

143. Szondi, P. "Zu Hegels Bestimmung des Tragischen," *Archiv für das Studium der Neueren Sprachen,* 1961-1962 (198), 22-29.

144. ———. *Poetik und Geschichtsphilosophie.* Bd. I: *Antike und*

Moderne in der Ästhetik der Goethezeit. Hegels Lehre von der Dichtung. Hrsg. S. Metz und H.-H. Hildebrandt. Frankfurt am Main, Suhrkamp, 1974.

145. Talgeri, Pramod. *Otto Ludwig und Hegels Philosophie.* Die Widerspiegelung der *Ästhetik* Hegels im "poetischen Realismus" Otto Ludwigs. Tübingen, Niemeyer, 1972.

146. Taminiaux, Jacques. "La pensée esthétique du jeune Hegel," *Revue Philosophique de Louvain,* 1958 (56), 222-50.

147. Teyssèdre, Bernard. *L'esthétique de Hegel.* Paris, Presses Universitaires de France, 1958.

148. _____. "Hegel à Stuttgart (Essai sur la formation esthétique de Hegel d'après des documents inédits en français, réunis en collaboration avec Armin Raith)," *Revue Philosophique de la France et de l'Etranger,* 1960 (150), 197-227.

149. _____. "Les soirées parisiennes de Hegel (d'après une documentation traduite avec l'aide de M. Armin Raith)," *Revue d'Esthétique,* 1958 (11), 40-74.

150. Ujfalussy, Josef. "Abstrakte Musik—konkrete Musik," *Hegel-Jahrbuch,* 1965, 53-64.

151. Vaross, Marian. "Das Problem der Vergegenständlichung und die moderne Kunst," *Hegel-Jahrbuch,* 1966, 32-39.

152. Vecchi, Giovanni. *L'estetica di Hegel: saggio di interpretazione filosofica.* Milan, Università catholica del Sacro Cuore, 1956.

153. Vischer, Friedrich Theodor. *Über das Erhabene und Komische.* Ein Beitrag zu der Philosophie des Schönen. Stuttgart, 1837.

154. Wagner, Frank Dietrich. *Hegels Philosophie der Dichtung.* (Abhandlungen zur Philosophie, Psychologie, und Pädagogik, 88). Bonn, Bouvier Verlag, 1974.

155. Waldemar, Georges. *Présence de l'esthétique de Hegel.* Paris, Editions d'Art, 1967.

156. Wellek, René. "Critica e teoria letteraria di Hegel," *Inventario,* 1954 (6), 118-32.

157. Wiese, Benno von. *Die deutsche Tragödie von Lessing bis Hebbel.* Hamburg, Hoffman und Campe, 1948.

158. _____. "Das Problem der ästhetischen Versöhnung bei Schiller und Hegel," *Jahrbuch der Deutschen Schillergesellschaft* (Stuttgart), 1965 (9), 167-88.

159. Weisse, C. H. *System der Ästhetik als Wissenschaft von der Idee der Schönheit.* Leipzig, 1830.

160. Wiehl, Reiner. "Über den Handlungsbegriff als Kategorie der Hegelschen Ästhetik," *Hegel-Studien,* 1971 (6), 135-70.

161. Wolandt, Gerd. "Zur Aktualität der Hegelschen Ästhetik," *Hegel-Studien,* 1967 (4), 219-34.

162. Wolff, Emil. "Hegel und Shakespeare," in *Vom Geist der Dichtung.* Gedächtnisschrift für Robert Petsch, hrsg. F. Martini, 120-79. Hamburg, Hoffmann und Campe Verlag, 1949.

163. Zander, Hartwig. *Hegels Kunstphilosophie.* Eine Analyse ihrer Grundlagen und ihrer Aktualität. Wuppertal, Henn, 1970.

164. Zappa, Giorgio. "L'estetica di Hegel nel pensiero del Giovane De Sanctis," *Svizzera Italiana,* 1957 (17), n. 124, 9-13; n. 125, 30-36.

165. Zoltai, D. "Die Problematik der bürgerlichen Gesellschaft in der hegelschen Ästhetik und bei den Romantikern," *Hegel-Jahrbuch,* 1971, 148-52.

STUDIES OF HEGEL'S LOGIC

1. Adoratski, W. "Lenin über die Hegelsche Logik und Dialektik," *Unter dem Banner des Marxismus,* 1929 (3), 633-59.

2. Albrecht, Wolfgang. "Hegels Gottesbeweis," *Zeitschrift für Philosophische Forschung,* 1957 (11), 593-601.

3. _____. *Hegels Gottesbeweis.* Eine Studie zur *Wissenschaft der Logik.* Berlin, Duncker & Humblot, 1958.

4. _____. "Hegels Leitfaden der Entdeckung des Kategorien," *Zeitschrift für Philosophische Forschung,* 1960 (14), 102-06.

5. Alexander, Dietrich und Barth, Helmut. "Hegels *Wissenschaft der Logik* und einige konzeptionelle Fragen der marxistisch-leninistischen Erkenntnistheorie", in *Hegel und wir,* hrsg. Erhard Lange, 51-100. Berlin, Deutsche Verlag der Wissenschaften VEB, 1970.

6. Allievo, Giuseppe. "La logica hegeliano e la logica della scuole," in *Saggi filosofici,* 119-44. Milan, G. Francesco, 1866.

7. Althusser, Louis. "Lénine devant Hegel," *Hegel-Jahrbuch,* 1968-1969, 45-58.

8. Antoni, Carlo. "Sulla dialettica di Hegel," *Poesia e Verità,* 1945 (1), 3-16.

9. Apostol, P. *Probleme de logicà dialecticà in filosofia lui G. W. F. Hegel.* Bucaresti, Ed. Acad. R. P. R., 1957.

10. Aquila, Richard E. "Predication and Hegel's Metaphysics," *Kant-Studien,* 1973 (64), 231-45.

11. Asmus, V. F. "Hegel's View of the Rights and Limits of Formal Thinking," *Soviet Studies in Philosophy,* 1970-71 (9), 336-56.

12. Bachman, Karl Friedrich. *Ueber Hegels System und die Notwendigkeit einer nochmaligen Umgestalten der Philosophie.* Leipzig, Vogel, 1833.

13. Baillie, James B. *The Origin and Significance of Hegel's Logic.* A General Introduction to Hegel's System. London, MacMillan and Co., Ltd., 1901.

14. Balbino, Giuliano. "Il torto di Hegel," *Coenobium,* 1911 (Anno V, Fasc. V), 24-33.

15. Bankov, Angel. "Hegels Theorie der Beziehung zwischen Denken und Sprache," *Hegel-Jahrbuch,* 1971, 204-18.

16. _____. "Logische Grundlagen der Geschichte," *Hegel-Jahrbuch,* 1968-1969, 304-17.

17. Barion, Jakob. "Zur Dialektik Hegels," in *Ideologie, Wissenschaft, Philosophie,* 188-201. Bonn, Bouvier, 1966.

18. Becker, Werner. *Hegels Begriff der Dialektik und das Prinzip des Idealismus.* Stuttgart, Berlin, Kohlhammer, 1969.

19. Belaval, Yvon. "La doctrine de l'essence chez Hegel et chez Leibniz," *Archives de Philosophie,* 1970 (33), 547-78.

20. Biedermann, Gustav. *Kants Kritik der reinen Vernunft und die Hegelsche Logik in ihrer Bedeutung für die Begriffswissenschaft.* Prag, F. Tempsky, 1869.

21. Biemel, Walter. "Das Wesen der Dialektik bei Hegel und Sartre," *Tijdschrift voor Filosofie,* 1958 (2), 269-300.

22. Bole, Thomas J., III. "The Dialectic of Hegel's Logic as the Logic of Ontology," *Hegel-Jahrbuch,* 1974, 144-51.

23. Bolland, G. J. P. J. *Alte Vernunft und neuer Verstand, oder der Unterschied im Princip zwischen Hegel und Eduard von Hartmann.* Leiden, A. H. Adriani, 1902.

24. Bröcker, Walter. *Formale, transzendentale und spekulative Logik* (Wissenschaft und Gegenwart, 23). Frankfurt am Main, Klostermann, 1962.

25. Bruaire, Claude. *Logique et religion chrétienne dans la philosophie de Hegel.* Paris, Éditions du Seuil, 1964.

26. Brunet, Christian. "L'ontologie dans l'*Encyclopédie* de Hegel," *Revue de Métaphysique et de Morale,* 1960 (65), 449-62.

27. Bubner, Rüdiger. "Zur Struktur dialektischer Logik," *Hegel-Jahrbuch,* 1974, 137-43.

28. Bullinger, Anton. "Hegel's Doctrine of Contradiction," *Journal of Speculative Philosophy,* 1888 (22), 118-38.

29. _____. *Hegels Lehre vom Widerspruch Missverständnissen gegenüber verteidigt.* Dillingen, Kolb, 1884.

30. _____. *Hegelsche Logik und gegenwärtig herrschender antihegelscher Unverstand.* München, T. Ackermann, 1900.

31. Calkins, Mary W. "The Order of the Hegelian Categories in the Hegelian Argument," *Mind,* 1903 (12), 317-40.

32. Calogero, G. "Logica antica e dialettica hegeliana," in *La con-*

clusione della filosofia del conoscere, 163-72. Firenze, Le Monnier, 1938.

33. Caramella, Santino. "Le tre logiche di Hegel," *Hegel-Studien,* Beiheft 4 (1969), 103-14.

34. Casares, A. J. "La doctrina del juicio en la Ciencia de la Lógica," *Diálogos,* 1970 (7), n. 20, 75-99. Also in *Cuadernos de Filosofia* (Buenos Aires), 1969 (9), n. 12, 221-44.

35. Ceriani, Grazioso. "La logica di Hegel," *Rivista di Filosofia Neo-Scolastica,* 1939 (31), 299-306.

36. Chaix-Ruy, Jules. "Hegel et saint Thomas: dialectique et logique," in *Sapientia Aquinatis* (Communicationes IV Congressus Thomistici Internationalis, Romae, 13-17 Septembris, 1955), I, 212-20.

37. Chandler, Hugh S. "Excluded Middle," *Journal of Philosophy,* 1967 (64), 807-14.

38. Clark, Malcolm. *Logic and System.* A Study of the Transition from "Vorstellung" to Thought in the Philosophy of Hegel. Löwen, Universitaire Werkgemeenschap, 1960.

39. Conche, Marcel. "Essai d'explication des §§135-141 de *l'Encyclopédie des sciences philosophiques* de Hegel," *Revue de Métaphysique* et de Morale, 1970 (75), 50-78.

40. Contri, Siro. "L'interna dialettica della sostanza nel sistema tomistico e nel sistema hegeliano," in *Sapientia Aquinatis* (Communicationes IV Congressus Thomistici Internationalis, Romae, 13-17 Septembris, (1955), I, 221-30.

41. Coreth, Emerich. *Das dialektische Sein in Hegels Logik* (Glaube und Forschung. Beitrag I). Wien, Verlag Herder, 1952.

42. Costa, Filippo. "Il problema della posizione prima del pensiero e la logica hegeliana," *Atti della Accademia di Scienze, Lettere, e Arti di Palermo,* 1947-48, Parte Secundo, 277-326.

43. Cottier, Georges Marie-Martin. "Signification de la dialectique chez Hegel," *Revue Thomiste,* 1969 (69), 378-411.

44. Croce, Benedetto. *Ciò che è vivo e ciò che è morto della filosofia di Hegel?* Bari, G. Laterza e Figli, 1907.

45. _____. "Intorno a Hegel e alla dialettica," *Quaderni della Critica,* 1951 (7), 2-13.

46. Crudeli, Paolo. "Note su Hegel dialettico e teorico della dialettica," *Rivista di Studi Crociani,* 1973 (10), 307-14, 421-29.

47. D'Ercole, Pasquale. "Kant quale immediato antecessore di

Hegel nella logica ontologica," *Rivista di Filosofia Neo-Scolastica,* 1911 (3), 437-39.

48. _____. *La logica aristotelica, la logica kantiana ed hegeliana e la logica matematica, con accenno alla logica indiana.* Torino, V. Bona, 1912.

49. D'Hondt, Jacques. "Téléologie et praxis dans la *Logique* de Hegel," in *Hegel et la pensée moderne,* ed. Jacques d'Hondt, 1-26. Paris, Presses Universitaires de France, 1970.

50. De Giovanni, Biagio. "La critica al tempo della conscienza nella Grande Logica," in *Incidenza de Hegel,* a cura di Fulvio Tessitore, 167-213. Napoli, Morano Ed., 1970.

51. _____. "Tempo e storia nella Grande Logica," in *Annali della Facoltà di Lettere e Filosofia (Bari),* 1969 (14), 123-39.

52. De Ruvo, Vincenzo. *I massimi logici e la logica della possibilità.* Napoli, Libreria Scientifica Editrice, 1953.

53. _____. "Riflessioni intorno alla logica hegeliana," *Sophia,* 1953 (21), 52-77.

54. Deckers, Hermannus. "La notion d'être chez Hegel et saint Thomas," in *Sapientia Aquinatis* (Relationes, Communicationes et Acta IV Congressus Thomistici Internationalis, Romae, 13-17 Septembris, 1955), II, 142-48.

55. Devizzi, Aldo. "Il significato del principio di contradizione nella logica hegeliana," *Rivista di Filosofia Neo-Scolastica,* 1939 (31), 463-73.

56. Di Giovanni, George. "Reflection and Contradiction. A Commentary on Some Passages of Hegel's *Science of Logic,*" *Hegel-Studien,* 1973 (8), 131-61.

57. Doniela, William V. "Movement, Continuity, Contradiction," *Hegel-Jahrbuch,* 1974, 46-50.

58. Doumit, E. "Hegel et l'infinitésimal," in *Les signes et leur interprétation,* ed. Noel Mouloud, 75-93. Paris, Éditions Universitaires, 1972.

59. Doz, André. "Hegel et l'idée de système," *Hegel-Jahrbuch,* 1973, 81-84.

60. _____. "Sur le passage du concept à l'être chez Descartes et Hegel," *Revue de Métaphysique et de Morale,* 1967 (72), 216-30.

61. Dresser, Horatio W. "The *Logic* of Hegel," in *The Philosophy of Spirit,* 387-537. New York, London, G. P. Putnam's Sons, 1908.

62. Dubarle, Dominique. "La logique de la réflexion et la transition de la logique de l'être à celle de l'essence," *Revue des Sciences Philosophiques et Théologiques,* 1972 (56), 193-222.

63. _____. et Doz, André. *Logique et dialectique.* Paris, Librairie Larousse, 1972.

64. Dubarle, Dominique. "Logique formalisante et logique hégélienne," in *Hegel et la pensée moderne,* ed. Jacques d'Hondt, 113-59. Paris, Presses Universitaires de France, 1970.

65. _____. "Sur la Réflexion dans la *Science de la logique* (IIe Partie, Section I, Chapitre 1)," *Hegel-Jahrbuch,* 1968-1969, 346-54.

66. Dubarle, Pierre-Louis. "L'absolu et le système chez Hegel," in *Akten des XIV. Internationalen Kongresses für Philosophie* (1968), II, 28-33.

67. Dürr, Agnes. *Zum Problem der Hegelschen Dialektik und ihrer Formen* (Philosophische Untersuchungen, 1938 (4)). Berlin, Verlag für Staatswissenschaften und Geschichte G.m.b.H., 1938.

68. Dürr, Karl. "Die Entwicklung der Dialektik von Plato bis Hegel," *Dialectica* (Neuchatel), 1947 (1), 45-62.

69. Dulckeit-von Arnim, Christa. "Die Dialektik der drei endlichen Seinsbereiche als Grundlage der Hegelschen Logik," *Philosophisches Jahrbuch,* 1957 (66), 72-93.

70. Ehrenberg, Hans. *Die Parteiung der Philosophie.* Studien wider Hegel und die Kantianer. Leipzig, Felix Meiner, 1911.

71. Eley, Lothar. *Metakritik der formalen Logik* (Phaenomenologica, 31). Den Haag, Martinus Nijhoff, 1969.

72. Emge, Carl August. *Hegels Logik und die Gegenwart.* Karlsruhe, Braun, 1927.

73. Enriques, Federigo. "La metafisica di Hegel considerata da un punto di vista scientifico," *Rivista di Filosofia,* 1910 (2), 56-75.

74. Erdei, Laszló. *Der Anfang der Erkenntnis.* Kritische Analyse des ersten Kapitels der Hegelschen Logik. (Studia Philosophia Academiae Scientiarum Hungaricae. 4). Budapest, Akademiai Kladó, 1964.

75. _____. "Der Gegensatz und der Widerspruch in der Hegelschen Logik," *Hegel-Jahrbuch,* 1973, 18-23.

76. Erdmann, Johann Eduard. *Grundriss der Logik und Metaphysik.* Eine Einführung in Hegels *Wissenschaft der Logik.* Leyden, Adriani, 1901.

77. Esslen, Julius. *Der Inhalt und die Bedeutung des Begriffs der Idee in*

Hegels System. Jena, Grevenmacher, Obermozelzeitung, Esslensche Druckerei, 1911.

78. Fabro, Cornelio. "L' "esse" tomistico e il "Sein" hegeliano," in *Sapientia Aquinatis* (Communicationes IV Congressus Thomistici Internationalis, Romae, 13-17 Septembris, 1955), I, 263-70.

79. Fazio Allmayer, Vito. "La riforma della dialettica hegeliana," *Giornale Critico della Filosofia Italiano,* 1947 (26), 103-16.

80. Ferrara, Vincent J. "Some Reflections on the Being-Thought Relationship in Parmenides, Anselm, and Hegel," *Analecta Anselmiana,* 1972 (3), 95-111.

81. Fichera, Giuseppe. "Il problema del cominciamento logico e la categoria del divenire in Hegel e nei suoi critici," in *Catania,* ed. Instituto universitario di magistero (Tip. La nuografica), 1956.

82. Findlay, J. N. *Hegel. A Re-examination.* London, G. Allen & Unwin, 1958.

83. Fischer, Julius. "Die Hegelsche Logik und der Goethesche Faust, eine vergleichende Studie," *Archiv für Geschichte der Philosophie,* 1909 (22) (N.F. 15), 319-41.

84. Flach, Werner. "Hegels dialektische Methode," *Hegel-Studien,* Beiheft 1, 55-64.

85. Flam, L. "Hegel 1770-1970. De taak en het bedrijf van de dialectische logica," *Dialoog,* 1969-70 (10), 157-95.

86. Fleischmann, Eugene. "Hegels Umgestaltung der Kantischen Logik," *Hegel-Studien,* 1965 (3), 181-207.

87. ———. *La science universelle ou la logique de Hegel.* (Recherches en sciences humaines, 25). Paris, Plon, 1968.

88. ———. "Die Wirklichkeit in Hegels Logik. Ideengeschichtliche Beziehungen zu Spinoza," *Zeitschrift für Philosophische Forschung,* 1964 (18), 3-29.

89. Fleischmann, Jakob. "Objektive und subjektive Logik bei Hegel," *Hegel-Studien,* Beiheft 1, 45-54.

90. Franchini, Raffaello. "Hegel e la logica della filosofia," *Rivista di Studi Crociani,* 1966 (3), 38-55.

91. Fulda, Hans Friedrich. *Das Problem einer Einleitung in Hegels Wissenschaft der Logik.* Frankfurt am Main, Klostermann, 1965.

92. Gabler, George Andreas. *Kritik des Bewusstseins.* Eine Vorschule zu Hegels *Wissenschaft der Logik.* Leiden, A. H. Adriani, 1901.

93. Gadamer, Hans-Georg. *Hegels Dialektik.* Tübingen, Mohr, 1971.

94. _____. "Signification de la *Logique* de Hegel," *Archives de Philosophie,* 1970 (33), 675-700.

95. Gaos, José. "Seminario sobre la *Lógica* de Hegel," *Diánoia* (México), 1957 (3), 169-87.

96. Garaudy, Roger. "Contradiction et totalité dans la logique de Hegel," *Revue Philosophique de la France et de l'Étranger,* 1964 (154), 67-78.

97. Gauthier, Yvon. "Logique Hégélienne et Formalisation," *Dialogue,* 1967 (6), 151-65.

98. Glockner, Hermann. *Der Begriff in Hegels Philosophie.* Versuch einer logische Einleitung in das metalogische Grundproblem des Hegelianismus. Tübingen, Mohr, 1924.

99. _____. *Beiträge zum Verständnis und zur Kritik Hegels Sowie zur Umgestaltung seiner Geisteswelt.* (*Hegel-Studien,* Beiheft 2). Bonn, Bouvier, 1965.

100. Gordon, W. M. "Zur Frage der Kategorie Werden," *Hegel-Jahrbuch,* 1971, 335-40.

101. Grazia, Wincenzo de. *Su la logica di Hegel e su la filosofia speculative, discorsi.* Napoli, tip. de Gemelli, 1850.

102. Grégoire, Franz. "La dialectique hégélienne de l'être, du néant et du devenir," *Revue de Métaphysique et de Morale*, 1957 (62), 88-95.

103. Griffiss, James E. "The Kantian Background of Hegel's Logic," *New Scholasticism,* 1969 (43), 509-29.

104. Günther, Gotthard. *Grundzüge einer neuen Theorie des Denkens in Hegels Logik.* Leipzig, Felix Meiner, 1933.

105. _____. "Das Janusgesicht der Dialektik," *Hegel-Jahrbuch,* 1974, 89-117.

106. _____. *Die logisch-methodischen Voraussetzungen zu Hegels Theorie des Denkens.* Potsdam, 1933.

107. _____. "Das Problem einer Formalisierung der transzendentaldialektischen Logik. Unter besonderer Berücksichtigung der Logik Hegels," *Hegel-Studien,* Beiheft 1, 65-123.

108. Haag, Karl Heinz. *Philosophischen Idealismus.* Untersuchungen zur Hegelschen Dialektik mit Beispielen aus *Wissenschaft der Logik.* Frankfurt am Main, Europäische Verlagsanstalt, 1967.

109. Harris, William Torrey. *Hegel's Doctrine of Reflection.* New York, D. Appleton and Co., 1881.

110. _____. "Hegel's Four Paradoxes," *Journal of Speculative Phil-*

osophy, 1882 (16), 113-22.

111. _____. *Hegel's Logic.* A Book on the Genesis of the Categories of Mind and a Critical Exposition. Chicago, Griggs, 1890.

112. _____. "Hegel's Philosophic Method," *Journal of Speculative Philosophy,* 1874 (8), 35-48, 91-92.

113. _____. "What is Meant by 'Determined'?", *Journal of Speculative Philosophy,* 1868-1869 (2), 190-91.

114. Hartmann, Klaus. *Grundzüge der Ontologie Sartres in ihrem Verhältnis zu Hegels Logik.* Berlin, Walter De Gruyter & Co., 1963.

115. Havas, Katalin G. "Die Hegelsche Dialektik und die moderne Logik," *Hegel-Jahrbuch,* 1974, 362-65.

116. Hedwig, Klaus. "German Idealism in the Context of Light Metaphysics," *Idealistic Studies,* 1972 (2), 16-38.

117. Heintel, Erich. "Einige Gedanken zur Logik der Dialektik," *Studium Generale,* 1968 (21), 203-17.

118. Henrich, Dieter. "Anfang und Methode der Logik," *Hegel-Studien,* Beiheft 1, 19-35.

119. _____. "Formen der Negation in Hegels Logik," *Hegel-Jahrbuch,* 1974, 245-56.

120. _____. "Hegels Theorie über den Zufall," *Kantstudien,* 1958-1959 (5), 131-48.

121. Hermann, Conrad. *Hegel und die logische Frage der Philosophie in der Gegenwart.* Leipzig, Moritz Schäfer, 1878.

122. Hibben, John Grier. *Hegel's Logic.* New York, Charles Scribner's Sons, 1902.

123. Hipelä, Jyrki. "The Concept of Methodology and the Possibility of Dialectical Methodology," *Hegel-Jahrbuch,* 1974, 400-03.

124. Holz, Harard. "Anfang, Identität und Widerspruch. Strukturen von Hegels *Wissenschaft der Logik,* gezeigt an dem Abschnitt 'Womit der Anfang der Wissenschaft gemacht werden muss' sowie der 'Logik des Seins'," *Tijdschrift voor Filosofie,* 1974 (36), 707-61.

125. Hyppolite, Jean. "Essai sur la logique de Hegel," *Revue Internationale de Philosophie,* 1952 (6), n. 19, 35-49.

126. _____. *Logique et existence.* Paris, Presses Universitaires de France, 1962.

127. Jünger, Friedrich Georg. "Vermittlung und Grenze. Zur Geschichte der hegelschen Dialektik," *Merkur* (Stuttgart), 1960 (14), 201-25.

128. Kemp, Peter. "Le nom de Sartre à la logique de Hegel," *Revue de Théologie et de Philosophie*, 1970 (20), 289-300.

129. Klaus, Georg. "Hegel und die Dialektik in der formalen Logik," *Deutsche Zeitschrift für Philosophie*, 1963 (11), 1489-1503.

130. Klein, Ansgar. "Hegel y la razón dialéctica," *Cuadernos de Filosofía* (Buenos Aires), 1968 (8), n. 12, 269-87.

131. Klein, Augusta. "Negation Considered as a Statement of Difference in Identity," *Mind*, 1911 (20), 521-29.

132. Koch, Traugott. *Differenz und Versöhnung*. Eine Interpretation G. W. F. Hegels nach seiner *Wissenschaft der Logik*. Gütersloh, Gütersloher Verlagshaus, 1967.

133. Koncz, Ilona. "Die Entwicklung der Hegelschen Urteilstheorie," in *Aufsätze über Logik*, 111-51. Budapest, 1971.

134. Kopnin, Pawel W. "Die Einheit von Logik, Dialektik und Erkenntnistheorie und ihre Bedeutung für die Auffassung des philosophischen Wissens," *Hegel-Jahrbuch*, 1970, 22-33.

135. _____. "Hegel und Lenin. Dialektik, Logik und Erkenntnistheorie," *Wissenschaft und Weltbild*, 1971 (24), 3-12.

136. Kopper, Joachim. "Reflexion und Identität in der Hegelschen Philosophie," *Kantstudien*, 1967 (58), 33-53.

137. Kosok, Michael. "The Formalization of Hegel's Dialectical Logic. Its Formal Structure, Logical Interpretation, and Intuitive Foundation," *International Philosophical Quarterly (IPQ)*, 1966 (6), 596-631.

138. Krahl, Hans-Jürgen. "Bemerkungen zum Verhältnis von *Kapital* und Hegelschen Wesenslogik," in *Aktualität und Folgen der Philosophie Hegels*, hrsg. Oskar Negt, 137-50. Frankfurt am Main, Suhrkamp, 1970.

139. Kröber, Günter. "Negation und Wissenschaftsentwicklung," *Hegel-Jahrbuch*, 1974, 236-44.

140. Krohn, Wolfgang. *Die formale Logik in Hegels* Wissenschaft der Logik. Untersuchungen zur Schlusslehre. München, Carl Hauser Verlag, 1972.

141. Kruithof, Jaap. "De zijnsproblematiek bij Hegel," *Algemeen Nederlands Tijdschrift woor Wijsbegeerte en Psychologie*, 1957-1958 (50), 240-50.

142. Kryger, Edna. "Identität und Unterschied," *Hegel-Jahrbuch*, 1974, 173-89.

143. Kuspit, Donald. "Hegel and Husserl on the Problem of the Difficulty of Beginning Philosophy," *The Journal of the British Society for Phenomenology,* 1971 (2), n. 1, 52-57.

144. Labarriere, Pierre-Jean. "Le concept hégélien, identité de la mort et de la vie," *Archives de Philosophie,* 1970 (33), 579-604.

145. _____. "Histoire et liberté: les structures intemporelles du procès de l'essence," *Archives de Philosophie,* 1970 (33), 701-18.

146. Lakebrink, Bernhard. "Anselm von Canterbury und die Hegelsche Metaphysik," in *Parusia. Studien zur Philosophie Platons und zur Problemgeschichte des Platonismus.* (Festgabe für Johannes Hirschberger.), 455-70. Frankfurt am Main, Minerva G.m.b.H., 1965.

147. _____. "Der Begriff des Einzelnen und die Hegelsche Metaphysik," *Studium Generale,* 1968 (21), 515-37.

148. _____. "Causalität und Finalität bei Hegel," *Freiburger Dies Universitatis,* 1963-1964 (11), 103-15.

149. _____. "Freiheit und Notwendigkeit in Hegels Philosophie," *Hegel-Studien,* Beiheft 1, 181-92.

150. _____. *Hegels dialektische Ontologie und die Thomistische Analektik.* Köln, Bachem, 1955.

151. _____. *Die Europaische Idee der Freiheit.* Teil I: Hegels Logik und die Tradition der Selbstbestimmung. Leiden, Köln, E. J. Brill, 1968.

152. _____. "Der Platonismus und die Hegelsche Metaphysik," in *Dialektik und Dynamik der Person* (Festschrift für Robert Heiss zum 60. Geburtstag), 239-51. Köln und Berlin, Kiepenheuer und Witsch, 1963.

153. _____. *Studien zur Metaphysik Hegels.* Freiburg im Breisgau, Rombach, 1969.

154. Lasalle, Ferdinand. "Die Hegelsche und die Rosenkranzische Logik und die Grundlage der Hegelschen Geschichtsphilosophie im Hegelschen Systeme," *Der Gedanke* (Berlin), 1861 (2), 123-50. Reprinted as a monograph, Leipzig, W. Heims, 1927.

155. Lemaigre, B.-M. "Hegel et la dialectique des idées transcendantales dans la Métaphysique d'Iéna (1801-1802)," *Revue des Sciences Philosophiques et Théologiques,* 1966 (50), 3-50.

156. _____. "Hegel et le problème de l'infini d'après la Logique d'Iéna (1801-1802)," *Revue des Sciences Philosophiques et Théologiques,* 1965 (49), 3-37.

157. Lenin, W. I. *Hefte zu Hegels Dialektik.* München, Rogner & Bernhard, 1969.

158. Léonard, André. *Commentaire littéral de la Logique de Hegel.* Paris, J. Vrin; Louvain, Éditions de l'Institut Supérieur de Philosophie, 1974.

159. Leopoldsberger, Jürgen. "Anfang und Methode als Grundproblem der systematischen Philosophie: Reinhold, Fichte, Hegel," *Salzburger Jahrbuch für Philosophie,* 1968-1969 (12-13), 7-48.

160. Lewes, G. L. "Lagrange and Hegel: The Speculative Method," *The Contemporary Review* (London), 1874 (24), 682-95.

161. Ley, Hermann. "Fliessende Kategorien," *Hegel-Jahrbuch,* 1974, 429-37.

162. Liebrucks, Bruno. "Idee und ontologische Differenz," *Kantstudien,* 1956-1957 (48), Heft 2, 268-301.

163. _____. "Reflexionen über den Satz Hegels 'Das Wahre ist das Ganze'," in *Zeugnisse.* Theodor W. Adorno zum sechzigsten Geburtstag, hrsg. Max Horkheimer, 74-114. Frankfurt am Main, 1963.

164. _____. "Zum Verhältnis von Transzendenz und Immanenz bei Hegel," *Wiener Jahrbuch für Philosophie,* 1970 (3), 108-29.

165. Lorenzen, Paul. "Das Problem einer Formalisierung der Hegelschen Logik," *Hegel-Studien,* Beiheft 1, 125-30.

166. Lowy, M. "De la grande logique de Hegel à la gare finlandaise de Petrograd," *L'Homme et la Société,* 1970, n. 15, 255-67.

167. Lugarini, Leo. "Logica hegeliana e problema dell' intero," *Il Pensiero,* 1971 (16), 154-70.

168. Lunati, Giancarlo. "Studi hegeliani: logica e metafisica di Jena," *Rivista di Filosofia Neo-Scolastica,* 1951 (43), 197-212.

169. _____. "Studi hegeliani: osservazioni sul principio logico e sul disegno del sistema," *Rivista di Filosofia Neo-Scolastica,* 1952 (44), 229-42.

170. _____. "Studi hegeliani. Le preoccupazioni sistematice prima del 1812," *Rivista di Filosofia Neo-Scolastica,* 1951 (43), 512-32.

171. Mackenzie, J. S. "Time and the Absolute," *Mind,* 1927 (36), 34-53.

172. Maluschke, Günther. *Kritik und absolute Methode in Hegels Dialektik.* (*Hegel-Studien,* Beiheft 13.) Bonn, Bouvier, 1974.

173. Marcuse, Herbert. *Hegels Ontologie und die Grundlegung einer*

Theorie der Geschichtlichkeit. Frankfurt, Klostermann, 1932.

174. Margiotta, Umberto. "Il tema della ragione in Hegel," *Aquinas,* 1970 (13), 425-35.

175. Marx, Wolfgang. "Speculative Wissenschaft und geschichtliche Kontinuität. Uberlegungen zum Anfang der Hegelschen Logik," *Kantstudien,* 1967 (58), 63-74.

176. Maschner, Horst. *Dialectic, Money and Commodity*. Hegel's *Science of Logic* and the *Capital* of Marx. Selbstverlag des Autors, 1971.

177. Masci, Filippo. "Le categorie del finito e dell' infinito. Studio sulla scienze della logica di G. W. F. Hegel," *Rivista Bolognese,* 1869 (3), 559-76.

178. Massolo, Arturo. "La hegeliana dialettica della quantità," *Società* (Firenze), 1945 (1), n. 4, 148-70.

179. _____. *Logica hegeliana e filosofia contemporanea*. Firenze, Giunti, 1967.

180. _____. *Richerche sulla logica hegeliana ed altri saggi*. Firenze, Marzocco, 1950.

181. McGilvary, Evander Bradley. "The Dialectical Method," *Mind,* 1898 (7), 55-70, 233-42, 388-403.

182. _____. "The Presupposition Question in Hegel's Logics," *Philosophical Review,* 1897 (6), 497-520.

183. _____. *The Principle and the Method of the Hegelian Dialectic*. A Defence of the Dialectic Against Its Critics. Berkeley, University of California, 1897.

184. McTaggart, J. Ellis. "The Changes of Method in Hegel's Dialectic," *Mind,* 1892 (1), 56-71, 188-205.

185. _____. *A Commentary on Hegel's Logic*. Cambridge, Cambridge University Press, 1910.

186. _____. "Hegel's Treatment of the Categories of the Idea," *Mind,* 1900 (9), 145-83.

187. _____. "Hegel's Treatment of the Categories of the Objective Notion," *Mind,* 1899 (8), 35-62.

188. _____. "Hegel's Treatment of the Categories of Quality," *Mind,* 1902 (11), 503-26.

189. _____. "Hegel's Treatment of the Categories of Quantity," *Mind,* 1904 (13), 180-203.

190. _____. "Hegel's Treatment of the Categories of the Subjective Notion," *Mind,* 1897 (6), 164-81, 342-58.

191. _____. "Time and the Hegelian Dialectic," *Mind,* 1893 (2), 490-504; 1894 (3), 190-207.

192. Merker, Nicolao. *La origini della logica hegeliana.* Hegel a Jena. Milano, Feltrinelli, 1961.

193. Merlan, Philip. "Ist die 'These-Antithese-Synthese' Formel unhegelisch?", *Archiv für Geschichte der Philosophie,* 1971 (53), 35-40.

194. Meyer, Rudolf. "Ist Dialektik definierbar?", *Hegel-Jahrbuch,* 1974, 118-27.

195. Moore, Jared S. "A Reconsideration of the Hegelian Forms," *Monist,* 1934 (44), 1-58.

196. Mouloud, Noel. "Logique de l'essence et logique de l'entendement chez Hegel," *Revue de Métaphysique et de Morale,* 1961 (66), 159-83.

197. Mueller, Gustav E. "The Hegel Legend of 'Thesis-Antithesis-Synthesis'," *Journal of the History of Ideas,* 1958 (19), 411-14.

198. _____. "The Interdependence of the *Phenomenology, Logic,* and *Encyclopedia,*" in *New Studies in Hegel's Philosophy,* ed. W. E. Steinkraus, 18-33. New York, Holt, Rinehart, Winston, 1971.

199. Mulligan, R. W. "Note on Negativity," *New Scholasticism,* 1959 (33), 162-83.

200. Mure, G. R. G. "Some Elements in Hegel's Logic," *Proceedings of the British Academy* (1958), 21-34.

201. _____. *A Study of Hegel's Logic.* Oxford, Clarendon Press, 1950.

202. Muscio, Bernard. "The Hegelian Dialectic," *Mind,* 1914 (23), 522-41.

203. Narski, I. S. "Hegel and Contemporary Logic," *Soviet Studies in Philosophy,* 1970-1971 (9), 354-73.

204. _____. "Hegel und die Logik unserer Zeit," *Deutsche Zeitschrift für Philosophie,* 1971 (19), 66-81.

205. _____. "Hegel und die Logik des 20. Jahrhunderts," *Hegel-Jahrbuch,* 1970, 255-65.

206. Navickas, Joseph L. "The Hegelian Notion of Subjectivity," *Darshana International,* 1967 (7), n. 2, 57-76.

207. Nedeljković, Dušan. "La logique de Hegel et la dialectique matérialiste comme système," *Hegel-Jahrbuch,* 1974, 211-17.

208. Noël, Georges. *La logique de Hegel.* Paris, 1897.

209. _____. "La logique de Hegel: Hegel et la pensée contemporaine," *Revue de Métaphysique et de Morale,* 1896 (4), 585-614.

210. _____. "La logique de Hegel: L'idéalisme absolu et la logique spéculative," *Revue de Métaphysique et de Morale,* 1894 (2), 36-57.

211. _____. "La logique de Hegel: La logique dans le système," *Revue de Métaphysique et de Morale,* 1895 (3), 503-26.

212. _____. "La logique de Hegel: La science de l'essence," *Revue de Métaphysique et de Morale,* 1894 (2), 644-75.

213. _____. "La logique de Hegel: La science de l'être," *Revue de Métaphysique et de Morale,* 1894 (2), 270-98.

214. _____. "La logique de Hegel: La science de la notion," *Revue de Métaphysique et de Morale,* 1895 (3), 184-210.

215. _____. "La logique de Hegel: Le dogmatisme de Hegel," *Revue de Métaphysique et de Morale,* 1896 (4), 62-85.

216. O'Farrell, Francis. "Aristotle's, Kant's and Hegel's Logic," *Gregorianum,* 1973 (54), 477-515, 655-76.

217. Oiserman, T. I. "Lenin und die Hegelsche Konzeption der Einheit von Dialektik, Logik, und Erkenntnistheorie," *Hegel-Jahrbuch,* 1974, 81-88.

218. _____. "W. I. Lenin über die Dialektik Hegels," *Deutsche Zeitschrift für Philosophie,* 1958 (6), 273-86.

219. O'Sullivan, John M. *Vergleich der Methoden Kants und Hegels auf Grund ihrer Behandlung der Kategorie der Quantität.* Berlin, Reuther und Reichard, 1908.

220. Olivier, H. "Commencement et rationalité chez Leibnitz et Hegel," *Recherches hégéliennes* (Bulletin d'information du Centre de Recherche et de Documentation sur Hegel et Marx de l'Université de Poitiers), 1971, n. 4, 23-39.

221. Overstreet, H. A. "The Process of 'Reinterpretation' in the Hegelian Dialectic," *Journal of Philosophy, Psychology and Scientific Method,* 1904 (1), 512-19.

222. Palma, Norman. *Moment et processus.* Essai de compréhension de la dimension psycho-socio-historico-existentielle de la "Logique" de l'*Encyclopédie* de Hegel. Paris, Ed. Hispano-americanas, 1970.

223. Panowa, Elena. "Über die Identität von Logik, Gnoseologie und Metaphysik und der dialektische Materialismus," *Hegel-Jahrbuch,* 1971, 245-48.

224. Papa, Franca. *Logica e stato in Hegel.* Bari, De Donato, 1973.

225. Pastore, Annibale. "Ripensamento logico sui principio della dialettica Hegeliana," *Archivio de Filosofia* (Roma), 1938 (8), 103-15.

226. Pelloux, Luigi. *La logica di Hegel.* Milano, Società Editrice "Vita e Pensiero", 1938.

227. _____. "Lo sviluppo delle categorie nella logica di Hegel," *Rivista di Filosofia Neo-Scolastica* (Milano), 1938 (30), 357-61.

228. Pensa, M. "Le logos hégélien," *Dialectica* (Neuchâtel), 1947 (1), 277-87, 347-53; 1948 (2), 47-62.

229. Pöggeler, Otto. "Hegels Jenaer Systemkonzeption," *Philosophisches Jahrbuch,* 1963-1964 (71), 286-318.

230. Prantl, Carl von. *Die Bedeutung der Logik für den jetztigen Standpunkt der Philosophie.* München, Christian Kaiser, 1849.

231. Pró, Diego F. "Concepción de la lógica en Aristóteles, Santo Tomás y Hegel," *Philosophia* (Mendoza), 1945 (2), 229-63; 1946 (3), 71-78, 275-90.

232. Pucciarelli, Eugenio. "Hegel y el enigma del tiempo," *Cuadernos de Filosofia* (Buenos Aires), 1970 (10), n. 14, 257-90.

233. Puntel, L. Bruno. "Sinn und Aktualität von G. W. F. Hegels *Wissenschaft der Logik,*" *Theologie und Philosophie,* 1972 (47), 481-507.

234. _____. "Die Seinsmetaphysik Tomas von Aquins und die dialektisch-spekulative Logik Hegels," *Theologie und Philosophie,* 1974 (49), 343-74.

235. Purpus, W. *Eduard von Hartmanns Kritik der dialektischen Methode Hegels.* Ansbach, Brügel, 1911.

236. Rademaker, Hans. *Hegels objektive Logik.* Eine Einführung. (Abhandlungen zur Philosophie, Psychologie, und Pädagogik, 58.) Bonn, Bouvier, 1969.

237. Radermacher, Hans, "Zum Problem des Begriffs 'Vorausset-zung' in Hegels *Logik,*" *Hegel-Studien*, Beiheft 4, 115-28.

238. Reale, Miguel. "Logica e Ontognoseologia," *Revista Brasileira de filosofia,* 1970 (20), 363-72.

239. Redlich, Annelise. *Die Hegelsche Logik als Selbsterfassung der Persönlichkeit.* Meisenheim am Glan, A. Hain, 1971.

240. Rehm, Margarete. *Hegels spekulative Deutung der Infinitesimal-rechnung.* Köln, 1963.

241. Reiff, Jacob Friedrich. *Der Anfang der Philosophie, mit einer Grundlegung der Enzyclopädie der philosophischen Wissenschaften.*

Stuttgart, 1840.

242. _____. *Ueber die Hegelsche Dialektik*. Tübingen, Heinrich Laupp, 1866.

243. Richli, Urs. "Das Problem det Selbstkonstitution des Denkens in Hegels *Wissenschaft der Logik*," *Philosophisches Jahrbuch*, 1974 (81), 284-97.

244. _____. "Wesen und Existenz in Hegels *Wissenschaft der Logik*," *Zeitschrift für Philosophische Forschung*, 1974 (28), 214-27.

245. Bitschl, Dietrich. "Kierkegaards Kritik an Hegels *Logik*," *Theologische Zeitschrift* (Basel), 1955 (11), 437-65.

246. Roeder von Diersburg, Egenolf. "Hegels Methode gemessen an der Methode des Aristotcles," *Archiv für Philosophie*, 1960 (10), 3-23.

247. Rohs, Peter. *Form und Grund*. Interpretation eines Kapitels der Hegelschen *Wissenschaft der Logik*. (*Hegel-Studien*, Beiheft 6.) Bonn, Bouvier, 1969.

248. _____. "Das Problem der vermittelten Unmittelbarkeit in der Hegelschen Logik," *Philosophisches Jahrbuch*, 1974 (81), 371-80.

249. Rosenkranz, Karl. *Kritische Erläuterung des Hegelschen Systems*. Königsberg, Gebrüden Bornträger, 1840.

250. _____. *Erläuterungen zu Hegels* Enzyklopädie der philosophischen Wissenschaften. Leipzig, 1874.

251. _____. *Die Modifikationen der Logik, abgeleitet aus dem Begriff des Denkens*. Leipzig, 1840.

252. _____. "The Science of Logic," *Journal of Speculative Philosophy*, 1872 (6), 97-120.

253. Rosmini-Serbati, Antonio. *Saggio storico-critico sulle categorie e la dialettica*, 1846-1847. Turin, 1883.

254. Rossi, Alejandro. "Razón y fundamento en Hegel," *Diánoia* (Mexico), 1959 (5), 117-32.

255. Rossi, Mario. "L'incondizionato e la dialettica," in *Actes du XI ème Congrès International de Philosophie*, XIII, 131-37.

256. Rossi, Pietro. "La dialettica hegeliana," *Rivista di Filosofia*, 1958 (49), 284-333.

257. Rotenstreich, Nathan. "Some Remarks on the Formal Structure of Hegel's Dialectic," *Philosophy and Phenomenological Research*, 1945 (5), 242-54.

258. Rotta, Paolo. "Intorno alla logica di Hegel," *Rivista di Filosofia Neo-Scolastica*, 1910 (2), 679-82.

259. _____. "Kant quale immediato antecessore di Hegel nella logica ontologica," *Rivista di Filosofia Neo-Scolastica*, 1911 (3), 439-41.

260. Ruben, Peter. "Von der *Wissenschaft der Logik* und dem Verhältnis der Dialektik zur Logik," in *Zum Hegelverständnis unserer Zeit*, hrsg. H. Ley, 58-99. Berlin, 1972.

261. Ruehle von Lilienstern, O. A. J. J. *Über Sein, Werden und Nichts*. Eine Excursion über vier Paragraphen in Hegels *Enzyklopädie*. Berlin, 1833.

262. Sampaio Ferraz, Tercio. "O papel da dialetica en Aristóteles, Kant e Hegel," *Revista Brasileira de Filosofia*, 1970 (20), 474-86.

263. Santucci, Antonio. "Peirce, Hegel e la dottrina della categorie," in *Incidenza di Hegel*, a cura di Fulvio Tessitore, 965-84. Napoli, Morano Ed., 1970.

264. Sarlemijn, Andries. "Dialektik, moderne Logik, moderne Systemideologie," *Hegel-Jahrbuch*, 1973, 127-61.

265. _____. *Hegelsche Dialektik*. Berlin, New York, De Gruyter, 1971.

266. Schaefer, Alfred. "Begriff der Grenze und Grenzbegriff in Hegels Logik," *Zeitschrift für Philosophische Forschung*, 1973 (27), 77-86.

267. Scheptulin, A. P. "Hegels Lösung des Problems vom Zusammenhang der Kategorien," *Hegel-Jahrbuch*, 1971, 326-31.

268. Schinkaruk, W. I. "Der hegelsche Begriff des spekulativen Denkens und das Prinzip der Identität der Gegansätze," *Hegel-Jahrbuch*, 1970, 236-47.

269. Schlawin, Hermann. *Die Dialektik im System Hegels*. Bern, Buchdruckerei Eicher & Co., 1953.

270. Schmid, Aloys. *Entwicklungsgeschichte der Hegelschen Logik*. Ein Hilfsbuch zu einem geschichtlichen Studium derselben mit Berücksichtigung der neuesten Schriften von R. Haym und K. Rosenkranz. Regensburg, Manz, 1858.

271. Schmidt, Franz. "Hegels formale Logik," *Deutsche Zeitschrift für Philosophie*, 1963 (11), 415-21.

272. Schmitz, Hermann. "Die Vorbereitung von Hegels *Phänomenologie des Geistes* in seiner *Jenenser Logik*," *Zeitschrift für Philosophische Forschung*, 1960 (14), 16-39.

273. Schnädelbach, Herbert. "Zum Verhältnis von Logik und Gesellschaftstheorie bei Hegel," in *Aktualität und Folgen der Philosophie*

Hegels, hrsg. Oskar Negt, 58-80. Frankfurt am Main, Suhrkamp, 1970.

274. Schneider, Helmut. "Zur zweiten Auflage von Hegels *Logik,*" *Hegel-Studien,* 1971 (6), 9-38.

275. Schrader-Klebert, Karin. *Das Problem des Anfangs in Hegels Philosophie.* (Überlieferung und Aufgabe, 7.) Wien, München, Verlag R. Oldenbourg, 1969.

276. Schwarz, Justus. "Die Denkform der hegelschen *Logik,*" *Kant-studien,* 1958-1959 (50), 37-76.

277. Seidel, George J. "Hegel on Ground," *Idealistic Studies,* 1971 (1), 219-26.

278. Sfard, David. *Du rôle de l'idée de contradiction chez Hegel.* Nancy, 1931.

279. Shebbeare, C. J. "Hegel's Logic and Modern Religion," in *Actes du huitième Congrès International de Philosophie,* 1934, 414-19.

280. Simon, Josef. "Die Kategorien im 'gewöhnlichen' und im 'spekulativen' Satz. Bemerkungen zu Hegels Wissenschaftsbegriff," *Wiener Jahrbuch für Philosophie,* 1970 (3), 9-37.

281. Slawow, Slawi. "Hegels Prinzipien von der Identität von Sein und Denken, von Ontologie und Logik im Lichte des Leninismus," *Hegel-Jahrbuch,* 1971, 332-40.

282. Smith, John E. "The Relation of Thought and Being: Some Lessons from Hegel's *Encyclopedia,*" *New Scholasticism,* 1964 (38), 22-43.

283. Soll, Ivan. *An Introduction to Hegel's Metaphysics.* Chicago, Chicago University Press, 1969.

284. _____. "Sätze gegen Sätze: ein Aspekt der Hegelschen Dialektik," *Hegel-Jahrbuch,* 1974, 39-45.

285. Spaventa, Bertrando. "Le prime categorie della logica di Hegel," in *Atti della Reale Accademia di Scienze, Morali et Politiche di Napoli,* 1864 (1), 123-85.

286. Spisani, Franco. "Fondamenti di Logica produttiva," *International Logic Review,* 1972 (3), 4-20.

287. Steiner, Rudolf. *Das Ewige in der Hegelschen Logik und ihr Gegenbild im Marxismus.* Dornach, R. Steiner-Nachlassverwaltung, 1958.

288. Stiehler, Gottfried. "Hegel und die Grundgesetze der Dialektik," in *Forschen und Wirken.* Festschrift zur 150-Jahr-Feier der

Humboldt-Universität zu Berlin 1810-1960, I, 117-31. Berlin, 1960.

289. _____. "Die Methode des Aufsteigens vom Abstrakten zum Konkreten bei Hegel und Marx," *Hegel-Jahrbuch,* 1961, 39-51.

290. Stirling, J. Hutchinson. *The Secret of Hegel.* The Hegelian System in Origin, Principle, Form and Matter. London, Longman, Roberts & Green, 1865.

291. Stuhrmann, Johannes. *Die Wurzeln der Hegelschen Logik bei Kant.* Neustadt, 1887.

292. Synowiecki, Adam. "Hegel's Logic in the Light of Graph Theory," *Dialectics and Humanism* (Warszawa), 1973, 87-96.

293. Tanabe, Hajime. "Zu Hegels Lehre vom Urteil," *Hegel-Studien,* 1971 (6), 211-29.

294. Theunissen, Michael. "Krise der Macht. Thesen zur Theorie des dialektischen Widerspruchs," *Hegel-Jahrbuch,* 1974, 318-29.

295. Trede, Johann Heinrich. "Hegels frühe Logik (1801-1803/ 04). Versuch einer systematischen Rekonstruktion," *Hegel-Studien,* 1972 (7), 123-68.

296. Trendelenburg, F. A. *Die logische Frage in Hegels System.* Leipzig, 1843.

297. _____. "The Logical Question in Hegel's System," *Journal of Speculative Philosophy,* 1871 (5), 349-59; 1872 (6), 82-93, 163-75, 350-61.

298. Troilo, Erminio. "Della logica hegeliana," in *Figure e dottrine di pensatori*. Padova, CEDAM, 1941.

299. Tugendhat, Ernst. "Das Sein und das Nichts," in *Durchblicke. Martin Heidegger zum 80. Geburtstag,* 132-61. Frankfurt am Main, 1970.

300. Turner, J. E. "The Essentials of Hegel's Spiritual Monism," *The Monist,* 1934 (44), 59-79.

301. Ulrici, H. "Die falsche und die wahre Dialektik," *Zeitschrift für Philosophie und Philosophische Kritik,* 1848 (19), 238-74.

302. Ushenko, A. "The Logics of Hegel and Russell," *Philosophy and Phenomenological Research,* 1949-1950 (10), 107-14.

303. Van der Meulen, Jan. "Begriff und Realität," *Hegel-Studien,* Beiheft 1, 131-39.

304. _____. *Hegel. Die gebrochene Mitte.* Hamburg, Meiner, 1958.

305. Vanni Rovighi, Sofia. "Il significato metafisico della dialettica hegeliana," in *Sapientia Aquinatis* (Communicationes IV Congressus Thomistici Internationalis, Romae, 13-17 Septembris, 1955), I, 360-66.

306. Vasa, Andrea. "La dialettica della quantità e della misura nella logica di Hegel," *Giornale Critico della Filosofia Italiana,* 1956 (10), 42-78.

307. Vassallo, Angel. "Reflexiones sobre el pensamiento central de Hegel," *Cuadernos de Filosofia* (Buenos Aires), 1970 (10), n. 14, 251-56.

308. Verneaux, R. "La catégorie hégélienne de contradiction," *Sapientia,* 1971 (26), 369-88.

309. Volkmann-Schluck, Karl-Heinz. "Die Entäusserung der Idee zur Natur," *Hegel-Studien,* Beiheft 1, 37-44.

310. _____. "Hegels Begriff der absoluten Negation und ihre Bedeutung fur uns," *Praxis,* 1971 (7), 85-91.

311. Vollrath, Ernst. *Die These der Metaphysik.* Zur Gestalt der Metaphysik bei Aristoteles, Kant und Hegel. Wuppertal-Ratingen, Henn, 1969.

312. Wagner, Hans. "Hegels Lehre vom Anfang der Wissenschaft," *Zeitschrift für Philosophische Forschung,* 1969 (23), 339-48.

313. Wahl, Jean. *Commentaires de la logique de Hegel.* Paris, Centre de Documentation Universitaire, 1959.

314. _____. "Une interprétation de la logique de Hegel," *Critique,* 1953 (9), 1050-71.

315. Wallace, William. *Prolegomena to the Study of Hegel's Philosophy.* Oxford, 1894.

316. Weersma, H. A. "De logische Kern van Hegels dialektische Methode," *Annalen der Critische Philosophie,* 1937 (7), 21-34.

317. _____. "De Ontwikkeling van de Kategorien van het Zijn in Hegels Logica," *Annalen der Critische Philosophie,* 1937 (7), 69-80.

318. Werder, K. *Logik.* Commentar und Ergänzung zu Hegels *Wissenschaft der Logik.* Berlin, Veit und Comp, 1841.

319. Werner, Hans-Joachim. "Spekulative und transzendentale Dialektik. Zur Entwicklung des dialektischen Denkens im deutschen Idealismus," *Philosophisches Jahrbuch,* 1974 (81), 77-87.

320. Wetzel, Manfred. *Reflexion und Bestimmtheit in Hegels* Wissenschaft der Logik. Hamburg, Fundament-Verlag Sasse, 1971.

321. Wiehl, Reiner. "Platos Ontologie in Hegels Logik des Seins," *Hegel-Studien,* 1965 (3), 157-80.

322. Wiplinger, Fridolin. "Grundfragen zur Dialektik Hegels. Gedanken zu Vermittlung, Negation und Nichts in der dialektischen Auslegung der Differenz bei Hegel," *Wissenschaft und Weltbild* (Wien), 1965 (18), 164-78, 257-76.

323. Wisser, R. "Humanismo 'real' y lógica 'especulativa,' o sea, Marx y Hegel," *Folia Humanistica,* 1970 (8), 795-812.

324. Wundt, Max. *Hegels Logik und die moderne Physik.* (Erkenntnis und Bekenntnis, Heft 2). Köln, Westdeutscher Verlag, 1949.

325. Zeleny, H. "Hegels Logik und die Interpretationstendenzen in der gegenwärtigen Grundlagenforschung," *Hegel-Jahrbuch,* 1961, 20-30.

326. Zimmerli, Walther Ch. "Die Beziehung von Dialektik und Realität: zu Hegels früher 'Realdialektik'," *Hegel-Jahrbuch,* 1974, 418-28.

Subject Index

NAME INDEX

Adorno, Theodor 25f, 172, 173, 177n
Anselm 37
Arendt, Hannah 55
Aristophanes 3
Aristotle 3, 10, 47, 68, 111, 124, 126, 129, 139, 140, 150ff, 196f, 220, 228
Ayer, A. J. 55

Bach, J. S. 6, 8
Beardsley, Monroe 37, 54n, 76n
Behler, Ernst 77
Benjamin, Walter 25, 26
Blackmur, J. 56
Bloch, Ernst 23
Bosanquet, Bernard 84
Bowles, William L. 97f
Brahms, J. 8
Brecht, Berthold 23, 26
Buchler, Justus 54
Butler, Clark 233ff

Caird, Edward 233
Carnap, Rudolf 234
Coleridge, S. T. 97f
Croce, Benedetto 8, 13, 67, 73, 77, 84, 86, 89

D'Hondt, Jacques 84
Dante 11, 60, 66, 234
Darring, Walter 55
Darwin, Charles 10, 150, 171
Derrida, J. 29
Descartes, Rene 55, 121, 126f, 139, 151
Dewey, John 219
Donne, John 158
Doré, Gustav 95
Dostoevsky, F. 23

Einstein, Albert 151
Empson, William 37
Fackenheim, E. L. 198n
Fanon, Frantz 174, 177n
Findlay, J. N. 84, 99n, 175, 219f, 222, 231n
Fichte, J. G. 109, 123, 138f, 179f, 184
Fischer, Kuno 19

Gadamer, Hans-Georg 28f, 156f
Galileo 10
Ginsberg, Allen 48
Goethe, J. W. 7, 8, 30, 48
Gombrich, Ernest 6
Gray, J. Glenn 92
Greene, Murray 150f, 155-159

Habermas, Jurgen 156f
Harries, Karsten 84
Heidegger, Martin 28ff, 38, 46, 52, 156
Heisenberg, Werner 155
Heller, Erich 83, 86, 88
Henrich, Dieter 30, 181, 198n, 201
Heraclitus 151
Herrmann, Wilhelm 155
Hesiod 3
Hofstadter, Albert 32n, 61n
Hölderlin, J.C.F. 46
Homer, 1, 3, 7, 21
Horkheimer, Max 26
Hotho, H. 17, 63
Hume, David 47
Hyppolite, Jean 86

Jesus 5, 113
Jonas, Hans 146n, 155, 157n

Kant, Immanuel 12, 15, 29, 31, 47, 60, 104, 121f, 124, 126ff, 132, 139, 142n, 144n, 146n, 151, 164, 166, 184, 220
Kaufmann, Walter 54n, 219f, 233
Kedrov, M. 167
Kierkegaard, S. 52, 55, 61
Kimmerle, Heinz 179
Knox, Israel 84, 86ff
Knox, T. M. 11
Kosik, Karel 174, 177n
Kosok, Michael 220, 223, 231n
Kouzel, Daisy F. 66n

Laplace, P. S. 114, 152
Lask, E. 23
Leibniz, G.W.F. 121, 123, 126, 139, 236
Lenin, V. I. 164, 167f, 174
Loewenberg, J. 54n
Löwith, Karl 176n, 177n
Lukács, Georg 22ff, 33n

MacLeish, Archibald 56
McDonald, Michael 82
McTaggart, J.M.E. 99n
Mallarmé, S. 13
Marcuse, Herbert 20
Marx, Karl 12, 18ff, 27, 150, 154, 166, 172, 174
Maurer, Reinhart 171, 174
Meinong, Alexius 235